DIVORCED – and shit at it.
A no BS programme for men to get over divorce in 21 days

Set by Simon K Williams
Cover artwork and illustrations Simon K Williams

ISBN 978-0-9569250-2-2

The right of Adèle Théron to be identified as the author of this work has been asserted in accordance with sections 77 and 78 of the Copyright Designs and Patents Act 1988.

A CIP catalogue record for this book is available from the British Library.

This book is available online and in all good bookstores.

There really is power
in the breakdown…

Contents

part one

Intro

Why we have no clue about healing

It was a Sunday in November that I sat down in a busy coffee shop in Los Angeles. Most of the people were bustling about but I noticed four women who were sitting together, quietly drinking their coffee. There was nothing momentous or strange about this Sunday except for the fact that I decided to slow my mind down enough to observe these women intensely. I observed their postures, their body language, their facial expressions and noticed the feelings I felt whilst looking at them.

They were barely communicating with one another and I was aware of feeling intense sadness watching them. Just when I felt this sadness, I watched one woman jump up, wipe her eyes and excuse herself and leave the table. I sat like this for some time, observing the remaining three woman who appeared to be drinking their coffee absorbed in a trance of sorts. They paused only long enough for their faces to droop as they became aware of what appeared to be a painful emotion, before another one jumped up and excused herself.

It was the most bizarre experience, almost as if these women had touched a hot plate on a stove and instinctively pulled back. I decided to be bold and introduce myself to the remaining two women, thinking that if there was anywhere in the world where it might be considered 'normal' to approach strangers in a coffee shop, that it had to be Los Angeles. I was brave and told them what I had felt and observed and to my surprise, both of them were incredibly vulnerable and open. We shared a table and had a discussion which became the 'Sliding Doors' moment in my life. They shared that all four of them were going through divorce and that they were in the same divorce support group.

One woman shared how she wasn't sure if the group was working for them because they all felt so depressed and upset all the time. She shared about the pain she experienced when her husband left her and the other choked back tears as she relayed her fears of supporting her two children now that she was all on her own after her divorce.

When I asked them individually what made the other two jump up and excuse themselves, they said 'oh it's just those dark feelings'. They elaborated that they all had these feelings of despair and depression that came and went and almost the moment they tuned into those feelings, they had to get away from them and keep busy. The consensus was clear: "those dark feelings will swallow us whole, we feel so afraid of them", followed by "we cannot fall apart. we just don't have the time."

It's such a tough trauma

Trying hard not to feel anything

That Sunday in the coffee shop changed everything for me. It was in one of those conversations where I began to think about how much human beings don't want to experience their pain. As our lives become more sophisticated and busy, our tolerance for anything painful is low and many professions see painful emotions as a dangerous threat which needs to be neutralised. Consequently we are overwhelmed with the plethora of medications and therapies which are all geared towards removing, blocking or avoiding pain. Societal, social, medical and the psychological care system are all set up to assist in managing the risks of people falling apart and finding emotional avoidance tactics so we need never feel pain. We have learnt to fear our emotions and have become terrified of dipping our toe in anything dark in case we become swallowed whole.

The reality couldn't be further from the truth. Emotions have received a bad rap over the last century and I am here to tell you that they are not to be feared. We have simply forgotten our innate abilities to understand and process emotions as our ancestors once did. The have become mysterious and misunderstood when in fact they are wonderful signals to the condition of the psyche and they stick around below the surface as a nagging reminder that something hasn't been dealt with yet. Ignoring emotions forces them to bubble under the surface and arise whenever we are stressed. What many psychologists don't know because they don't study pharmacology is that emotions cannot be 'dialled down'. You cannot dial down sadness and turn up happiness (not authentically anyway). You can fake it, but the sad emotion remains bubbling under the surface. It's only by working with the emotion that it can truly be released. All this pressure towards fake positivity leads to a suppression of darker emotions which leaves a chemical trail in our body. Our cell receptors can become blocked and from a chemical perspective, if you suppress one emotion, you suppress them all. Numbing yourself so you don't feel them can actually make you suppressed, depressed and sick.

Think for a moment about how much our world is set up to not feel anything, intellectualise emotions and be 'emotionally intelligent'. As a result emotional intelligence is considered by many as the ability to think about emotions VS. actually feel them.

Why was it that those women in the coffee shop could not stand to think about the pain from their divorce? What made those women keep their pain at arm's length? How men process emotions is not much different. Unfortunately all this 'trying to not feel anything' is just one of many misconceptions about healing. Another one is that one should rely on time to heal the wound and that time can somehow influence the healing experience.

There is a misconception that time should heal the wound

I have heard so many therapists say "you just need some time." It is as if these well-meaning people are saying, "Just sit back and in time you'll no longer have the sadness, anguish, yearning, guilt, anger, and fear you're feeling now. Those emotions will fade away, and you'll be fine."

The problem with believing that time heals the wound is that people wind up doing nothing and passively waiting for healing to 'happen to them'. In reality, time doesn't heal anything. Time simply passes by and the strategies people adopt to avoid feeling have simply become more sophisticated over time. Healing is not a function of time. Healing is instead an active process which I discuss in more detail later in this book.

Struggling to take responsibility

Many people tell themselves that the only reason their relationship failed, was because they were with the wrong person.

The focus of their healing journey is all about telling themselves and others how their ex was the reason their relationship failed. It's true that divorce is a very painful trauma but to avoid additional pain, people don't want to confront the failure of their relationship. Many people I have worked with believed that they would die if they felt responsible.

The reality is, wherever a relationship hasn't worked out in your life, you were present in it. You need to put on your big dude pants and face that you had something to do with your relationship not working out. If you don't confront that reality, you will sleepwalk into another failed relationship before you even know it.

Owning your part in the failure of your marriage is very empowering because you will discover the secret formula for a successful relationship and will have more control over your relationships in the future.

A lack in the ability to self soothe

Some people blame themselves for the failure of the relationship. They beat themselves up ferociously and become their own worst enemy. These folks lack the compassion and ability to reflect on their shortcomings with kindness. This is usually because they lack the ability to self-soothe and don't have the ability to confront truths about themselves without self destructing. Learning to self-soothe is a critical component for successful healing.

Frozen in indecision

Sadly many people wait for healing to happen and only do something if they hit the elusive 'rock bottom'. The distinction 'rock bottom' is when human beings become aware of the impact of not taking action and for some, experiencing the negative impact of being at rock bottom can be so traumatic that it's a crushing moment from which they struggle to recover. For others, the experience is just what was required to be jolted into massive decisive action.

The challenge in facilitating healing is to simulate rock bottom whilst teaching compassionate reasoning so that decisive action happens without the experience of being crushed. It is only through an active decisive process, that healing takes place.

Routines go out of the window

For many people, the sudden change makes them want to change absolutely everything so their lives descend into chaos. Bills don't get paid, meals don't get eaten, hair goes unwashed as they find themselves booking a ticket to Bali to go 'find themselves'. All this chaos makes the healing journey even more complex.

A lack in the support required to heal

Honestly, I think it would have been easier for some people if their ex had died. It's a shocking thing to say but for some reason, people are much more supportive during a bereavement than during a divorce. Divorce is akin to catching a disease that no one wants to be associated with. Some people reported feeling ashamed and lonely, almost like they had a scarlet letter D branded on their foreheads. The right kind of support is not readily available: some friends and family will revel in all the drama, some will say inappropriate things, some will say nothing at all and some will simply change the topic. Although friends and family are an important part of life, many are ill equipped to support their loved ones through divorce. This lack of support and loneliness makes divorce one of the toughest traumas to process.

Even therapists don't really want you to heal

So many professionals take advantage of people in a vulnerable space. They operate in a world of exchanging their time for money. Often this means that it is not in their best interest to see people move on and become empowered because then they will lose their client. Many therapists consequently keep their patients a little bit weak and a little bit disempowered to ensure they are still needing them. To me, this is a clear conflict of interest and therapists should not be paid by the hour but by the result they produce or there is no incentive to help their patients truly heal.

I have seen so many psychologists talk their clients into years of therapy where the lack of progress is never blamed on the lack of process being followed, but rather on the inability of the client to have a breakthrough. I discuss the shortcomings of traditional therapy later on in this chapter.

It's no wonder you are Divorced and shit at it!

There are so many misconceptions about healing that it's no wonder you feel like you cannot cope and that you are shit at it. Believe me I have been there and felt everything you are feeling right now.

True healing only takes place when you engage in an active enquiry, feel all the emotions and resolve each loose end. Without this active enquiry, the old emotions become stuck and leave a chemical blueprint in your body. Your future aches and pains will have their source in not healing from this trauma. Breakthroughs only happen inside a specific context of healing. The beginning of the healing journey is supposed to be painful but it does end. The problem is we have been taught that feeling pain is not a good thing so we develop complex safety behaviours designed to not feel this pain.

Try out this analogy...

To not focus on healing is similar to wandering around with a dislocated shoulder. You strap the arm and take painkillers and lead a very small life doing everything you can to avoid bumping the arm which is dangling around dislocated from its socket. Eventually the pain will become 'normal' and the inhibited range of movement is simply something you accept as part of the healing process. You could walk around with a dislocated shoulder for years but this will cause long term damage as scar tissue and frozen shoulder takes its hold, but everyone knows that this is not how to fix a dislocated shoulder. The best treatment involves popping the shoulder back into its socket so it can heal properly. It hurts like hell in the beginning but once back in the socket, the shoulder has a chance to heal. Part of the rehabilitation journey also involves physical therapy and exercises to improve the range of motion until your shoulder has fully healed.

Why is it that we all accept the amount of work involved in healing from a dislocated shoulder but when we have an emotional trauma we sit around waiting for something to happen?

All of these questions, frustrations and thoughts led to the development of my theories about healing from emotional trauma and to the development of all my programmes. In short, I believe that taking time to heal, combined with doing nothing leads to numbness, emotional scars and a feeling of resignation. This quicksand of resignation is a silent killer as it tricks people into believing that they are fine when they are not, so they wind up wandering around a little bit dead and forget that healing was a priority.

All these misconceptions have led to many misunderstandings about healing.

Healing does not need to be a long drawn-out horrendous nightmare. Healing can be a journey of self-discovery. It can also take a shorter period of time than you can even imagine.

How does this book work?

This book and the process I will teach you, will help you become emotionally stable and reclaim yourself after your divorce. Most importantly, you will learn how to limit the amount of power your ex has over you, so that you can move on with your life in a healthy way, with a solid amount of self-awareness.

The goal of this book is to help you move towards acceptance, and strip your ex of the power to make you feel angry or affect you on an emotional level. To break the hold your ex has over you, you will learn to remove her from her pedestal, whilst simultaneously not put her in the dumpster. Doing this will make you more powerful in the process.

Learning the **Naked Divorce** fundamentals, you'll be able to separate your emotional state from the process of healing, let go of the reasons behind the break-up, and move towards the next chapter in your life—the one where you are in control of your own life, in control of your emotions, and ready for whatever excitement lies around the corner.

The programme has been created in a way that virtually guarantees your healing, provided you do everything it says to do in the way it says to do it. If you do that, I guarantee you will heal by applying this programme to your life. That is a bold claim, but hundreds of people have completed this programme now and myself and my amazing team of Divorce Angels have worked with so many people of different ages, backgrounds and break-up and divorce situations that I know the programme works.

I fine-tuned, adjusted and tested all the components until I came up with the Healing Formula. I then distilled the process into 21 days after researching the maximum length of time human beings can remain focused on something to achieve an optimal result. So I have now stopped tweaking. This is it and you are under a month away from beginning your new life.

So here is a summary of what this book is about in its five component parts:

*   PART 1: The introduction and background to the **Naked Divorce** 21 Day Programme, covering the problems surrounding divorce and why proactively taking your healing into your own hands is critical to your future happiness

*   PART 2: How the 21 Day Programme works within the context of the Healing Formula

*   PART 3: Understanding the 7 Foundations of Transformation

*   PART 4: The **Naked Divorce** 21 Day Programme itself

*   PART 5: The future and what comes next including tips on helping your children handle the divorce as well as principles on keeping love alive

After working with many men and women who, until they discovered the **Naked Divorce**, were struggling to heal, move on and live their dream life, there isn't a problem area I haven't seen or a divorce story which shocks me. I am still moved to tears by the desire of the participants in the programme to be happy, heal and feel good about their life.

What moved me the first time somebody sat down and cried in my presence and shared their struggles, still moves me today. The single mom who hadn't dated for three years because she still missed her ex who had moved on with another woman. The hard-working doctor who beat herself up relentlessly after her engagement ended. The mother of two children who was bitter and angry with her ex-husband because she financially supported him during their marriage and now has trust issues with men.

The elderly Chinese man who felt he had wasted his life after his arranged marriage failed after 25 years. The angry divorced woman whose husband cheated on her and left her feeling brittle and prickly. The tormented man who hated his ex-wife so much it impacted his every waking moment. The cab driver who is struggling to move on from a brutal divorce. The single mom who lost everything in her divorce and is struggling to put back the pieces of her life. The gay lecturer crushed by his lover leaving him. The investment banker who lost touch with her femininity when she became a hardened, cold workaholic and now struggles to express herself. The investment banker who was brilliant in her job by day but stuck in a violent relationship at home. The actuary whose twenty-year marriage ended brutally with no explanation or reasoning. I could go on and on. So if you are asking the question if the 21 Day Programme is for you, the answer is yes. The programme works at any stage and in almost any situation. If you are feeling particularly vulnerable, just stay in the *Divorce Cocoon* phase for longer but the steps are always the same: no shortcuts and no changes.

I created this programme because I have been there myself. I know what it feels like to want to make a change but not have the right tools or to be constantly offered solutions that take up a lot of time, energy and money and don't really solve anything.

I created the **Naked Divorce** because it was time for something better.

It was time for passivity to be given a kick and to unveil the courageous steps you can begin to take to heal from your divorce.

So what have you got to lose?

Why not allow yourself to tumble down the rabbit hole with me and discover how many myths about healing from your divorce you have taken on board? Why not allow yourself to discover the person you deserve to be? I wrote this book knowing that although you may be experiencing all kinds of emotions right now, deep within, you have courage that you haven't yet begun to tap into.

There are probably things you have wanted to change about your life. Your divorce can be the catalyst for these life changes.

The only thing standing between you and this new version of yourself is taking some courageous daily steps with the right support in place. This book is therefore an invitation into a world where life is not a struggle and healing doesn't take an indefinite period of time. This might sound like a fantasy. But I promise: no matter what brought you here, or what your personal story is, success is possible.

It won't be easy, but I will walk alongside you every step of the way.

Why I wrote this book

" If you don't know when enough is enough... then you're destined to contribute to your own suffering "

Bruce and I were sitting at the kitchen table when he blurted out that he had slept with two women while he'd been in California. He explained, "I made a conscious choice to experience new pleasures, to see if I was willing to miss out on this in our marriage. I am not."

He swallowed as he sat staring at me, looking slightly terrified.

"I am willing to work on transforming our marriage and have been reading books and working on it. But I feel stuck... I don't know if I can transform my desire for you."

I kept quiet. I felt deep down that my courageous self was willing me on.

I wanted my marriage to be over.

I don't know where the words came from, but I spoke them.

"This is over and you should go."

He nodded his head. I walked out of the kitchen and finally allowed seven years of pent-up frustration to emerge. I sobbed. He came and hugged me.

"Have we just broken up?"

"Yes, Bruce. You should go. You never liked London anyway."

He nodded again.

I wasn't angry. Looking back on the years we'd shared together, this had been inevitable. I had dreaded this day for a long time. As much as I loved Bruce and our time together, I always knew deep down that it would end.

Bruce left soon after and went to stay with his father in South Africa. A few days later he called me. He felt it was time I knew the whole truth.

There were new revelations. There were 18 women that he had been with. Some of them were friends of ours. I screamed down the phone in shock and then hung up and sat in silence. My head was spinning. I had known something was up but I'd ignored my feelings, stepped over them and accepted his years of explanations. I had grown to accept that I was just paranoid.

Now before you start judging Bruce. Don't. I was as much responsible for his affairs as he was. I had known very deep down from the very beginning that something was not quite right in our relationship. I knew I married a man who had declared early on that I was not his fantasy woman and that he did not desire me and I had ignored all the warning signs and my intuition. I had done that. I am therefore responsible for the failure of our marriage. I had chosen to stay and by staying, I had contributed to the inevitable, to him seeking what his heart truly cried out for with someone else. Anger overwhelmed me and left me shaking, my fists clenched ready to strike.

I had been living in a fantasy world and had concocted a dream-like, fake relationship around me. The weeks that followed would turn out to be the most dramatic wake-up call of my life. I had settled for a seemingly contented and happy relationship but with very little passion or intimacy. I had settled with a man who neither loved or desired me. My body was consumed with anger. I had one clear thought; to wreak havoc in my house. I looked around my bedroom, at the familiar and treasured things. I got up with a clear intention to destroy all of it.

How it all started

I first met Bruce in 2002, when I was at a rock concert, I was 24. Bruce was different to the usual type that I went out with; there was something dangerous and edgy about him and that was alluring.

We went out a few times, but I had reservations about being in a relationship with him. Although I was in love, I knew he didn't really love me and we seemed more like friends united by common aims in life, rather than a couple who had just started going out.

Although I resolved to end things, I also found myself caught up in the reverie of what it would be like to date a man like Bruce: the rock star. The guy who was much better looking than me. One day he blurted out, "I think I'm falling in love with you, but it's a different kind of love, a familiar and comfortable one. Maybe this is what real love is supposed to feel like."

Hearing those words from Bruce made me excited, and yet I felt weird. A voice was telling me to stop worrying and enjoy the moment. Here was an amazing man and he said he loved me! Yes, our love did feel familiar and comfortable, and that was wonderful. Yet, I know today that if I had any kind of self-respect that I would never have settled for this lukewarm experience. But, my denial willed me on and so Bruce and I fell into a relationship. We would tell ourselves and others that we'd chosen to be in the relationship but it was never a natural attraction - certainly not for him. I ignored the danger signs, so easily seen in hindsight. At the time I told myself that it could work, that it had to work.

After a year together, I decided to fulfil a lifelong dream of living in London. Part of me longed for an adventure. I told myself that it would be a great opportunity to see if Bruce and I were really meant to be.

After living in London for several months, one day he called me, burdened. He had something to share. That was when he shared that he had fooled around with another woman.

I went into shock, cutting my hand on a plate I dropped as I was washing dishes. As I listened to his profuse apology, the water turned pink. He was so sorry. I could hear the desperation in his voice, begging me not to break-up with him.

I looked for excuses. I told myself that distance had made everything so hard. I blamed myself for not paying him attention, and for flirting with his friend, Gavin, who lived down the road from me. I rallied to the challenge. I resolved that we could overcome this. I told him I forgave him. I told myself that, too.

Two weeks later Bruce proposed and I accepted. I felt something else was willing me on to keep the relationship alive. To be honest, I felt safer being engaged. It was almost as if this invisible thread bound him to me and I could keep him locked away next to me. He was my fiancé. It seemed like a guarantee that he would not stray but it also felt like a noose around my neck. I felt numbed by the relationship. Being with someone who I knew didn't really love me was a dishonour to myself. I longed for him to love me the way I had experienced love before, and his lack of focused love was heartbreaking. I think in truth, I withdrew myself emotionally once I sensed his lack of desire for me but it became my project to turn myself into the woman he wanted. Our relationship became a challenge I would rise to and every suspicion I had that he was cheating was instantly dismissed in my quest to be the perfect couple.

In April 2004 we were married in a registry ceremony surrounded by friends and loved ones in London. It was not the day I had imagined. The night before the wedding, I went for a very long walk and almost didn't return. My gut was gnawing at me but I ignored it. My family were not in attendance so the whole wedding was in slow motion for me. We were hosts at a nice party and although there was love between us, I felt very sad. We moved into an apartment in Battersea and, despite my misgivings, the first years were really happy. We settled into a stable, loving best friendship. Our marriage lacked passion and fire but because we had so much fun getting up to thrilling things together, it seemed not to matter.

I learnt to ride a motorcycle, windsurf, rollerblade, scuba dive and do all the things Bruce was into. We travelled all over the world, visiting exotic and wonderful places. He was a kindred spirit in our quest to learn everything there was to learn about human beings, we attended many psychological courses together, ran seminars together and I learnt so much from him. In a quest for personal development I learnt to be courageous, beyond all the barriers I had erected within myself.

He became my best friend and we were like peas in a pod. Many people said that we were the perfect couple and I believed we were. Being married made me feel safe and invincible. I often told myself that passion was not necessary in a relationship and this lie was the bedrock for my life.

Married life continued much the same, but in April 2006, Bruce started travelling more frequently for business purposes. I spent increasing amounts of time alone. I went to dinners on my own, visited friends on my own, and spent many New Year's Eves, christenings, weddings and birthdays unaccompanied by my husband. In 2007, we were apart for seven months.

I told my friends and family that we had a very cool, hip relationship. We were both extremely independent and very happy together. Inside I was not so sure. I was lonely and felt undesired, unloved and trapped. I often cried myself to sleep but never told anyone about it.

When Bruce did come home in-between business trips he behaved strangely and we argued. Once, I jokingly asked if he'd been with anyone else on his travels. He shouted at me, telling me I was insecure and had issues I needed to resolve. I ignored my suspicions, blaming my insecurity but I knew something was wrong. He kissed me differently and as much as people saw us as a real power couple who looked in love and happy, our relationship never felt quite right. A veneer camouflaged the sadness and deep pain I was hiding.

In 2007 I decided to go to Cuba on a girl's holiday. The tour guide on the trip was completely enamoured by me. We danced till dawn every night and I was swept away by all the Cuban music, rum cocktails and attention I was receiving. I felt beautiful and sexy. One night he told me I was beautiful and the most amazing women he had ever met. I burst into tears. He was the first person I ever told about my experience of my marriage. I confided in him and he kept saying that this was not normal and that I should leave. He told me that I deserved to be loved and treasured and I felt amazing. Secretly I knew my boundaries were wearing away until the last night on the island, I cheated on Bruce. I allowed myself to let go and enjoyed myself completely. At some point, my mind kicked in and I burst into tears. I pushed him away, ran to the bathroom and threw up. I felt horrible. I couldn't continue. I left his room and went back to my hotel.

Even though I backed out before sleeping with him, it was too late, I had betrayed my marriage vows completely and had behaved entirely inappropriately for a married woman. A part of me felt utterly disgusted with myself but a part of me felt alive and wanted. The conflict was overwhelming. My girlfriends confronted me the next day as they knew something was up but I lied to them and said I was hungover. I was too much of a coward to share with them what had really happened.

I rationalised to myself that as I had never shared with my friends what my relationship with Bruce was really like, I didn't think they would truly understand why I did what I did. I was so busy portraying to the world that I had the perfect marriage and perfect life that any kind of honesty would bring my house of cards down. I justified my actions and told myself that lying was okay, "I didn't have sex, so it didn't really count." Yeah right. I was just being a cowardly hypocritical liar. I was more concerned with looking good to my friends than having any integrity.

When I came home I told Bruce what had happened. He was absolutely amazing about it and was so understanding and compassionate. He said that he understood why it had happened, admitted that our lack of passion and intimacy was the source of the cheating and he forgave me. He apologised for not loving me as I deserved to be loved. It was an extraordinary moment and I thought that it would become a turning point in our relationship and that things would all change from then onwards but sadly, from that day onwards, we drifted further and further apart.

After five months apart with a nagging feeling that he was cheating, I knew deep within that we had come to the end of our road together. Needing to deal with that realisation, I signed up for a ten-day silent meditation retreat called Vipassana, to confront things on my own and make the decisions I had to make. It was when I returned from this trip that I made the choice to end our marriage.

Transformation

What would follow would be the most transformational weeks of my life. I could never have predicted that the deepest pain in my life would carve out wells to hold the deepest joy.

Today Bruce and I have forgiven each other and made peace with our marriage. His miraculous story of the power of coming clean is the subject of a very popular Tedx Talk on Secrets which kill our aliveness in life which can be found on www.tedxsincity.com/. I am proud that he had the courage to share his story with the world. He is a good man and we both learnt a great deal from our journey together.

> **❝ The deeper sorrow carves into your being, the more joy you can later contain. ❞**
>
> *Kahlil Gibran from The Prophet*

The reasons we are shit at handling divorce

The problem with divorce is not that a third of all first-time marriages fail, but the fact that there doesn't appear to be any learning happening, which as a consequence, leads to a higher second-time marriage divorce-rate of around 57% and an even higher third-time marriage divorce-rate of 73%. Unless the under-lying critical factors are addressed, there is not much of a chance to stop the cycle of failed relationships into the future.

- On average, approximately 30%-50% of marriages fail globally in first-world countries

- South Africa has the highest average divorce rate of 52%, followed by the USA at 42%, followed closely by the UK, and Russia

- The average marriage lasts 11 years and in half of all divorces there are children involved

Fact-

The majority of people who divorced for a 3rd or 4th time said that they wished they had handled their divorces in a more ethical and graceful way, taking a more active role in their healing.

They also said that they wished they had gotten to the root cause of their divorce so that they didn't ruin their next relationship.

The very worst thing you can do is nothing

As stated at the start of the book, healing doesn't simply happen over time. Healing is an active process, and processing all the feelings and emotions associated with your divorce is essential to getting over it.

The real killer to healing is the complacency and resignation I have seen countless women sink into after their divorce. I have noticed that many people talk about their divorce and announce as quickly as they can ... that ... yes ... it was difficult, but they were, "absolutely fine and glad to be rid of their ex." They say things like, "I feel fine", "I feel perfectly happy with my life", "I am over that bastard", "I never think of my ex" or, "no, I am not dating and I am better off on my own."

All of these statements are a form of resignation. This is a common experience for many women experiencing divorce. They handle the divorce as best they can, often intellectualising and rationalising that they are fine even when they are not. This leads to a false sense of healing, which is on the surface and not really dealing with the healing at the source.

Before we discuss what recovery from divorce is all about, let's ascertain how you've dealt with loss in the past and how the 21-day experience may be different. Here are a few 'warm-up' exercises.

Exercise:

➡

Take some time to think back on your life. How have you dealt with loss in the past? (Whether it was the loss of someone special or a beloved pet)

What steps did you take that were healthy and healing?

What steps did you take, or not take, that hampered your recovery?

Therapy is not geared towards healing quickly

During the very early days of my divorce I took some action and spoke to two therapists. This is what everyone said would be a good idea to do.

Both therapists were extremely experienced and told me that as I had been with my husband for seven years, that it would probably take me at least 18 months to get over the relationship and that with weekly therapy sessions I 'might' heal.

The first therapist commenced the therapy session by taking me back to an incident from my childhood. I was two-years-old and was in hospital for many months due to a congenital hip birth defect. The doctors were spending months building me hip sockets and due to the strict rules of the hospital, my parents were not allowed to visit me very often. Consequently I developed some "abandonment" issues. My therapist looked like she had struck the lottery as I saw the dollar-signs in her eyes. She had just linked my feelings related to the divorce to the fear I'd felt in childhood so rather than focus on helping me tackle the issue at hand, my therapist was going to help me unpack my entire life over several years.

We explored that incident for some time and after two hours of deconstruction (and a hefty bill later), I left feeling thoroughly dis-empowered and confused. Not only had my husband "abandoned me", my parents, doctors and family had abandoned me, and in turn, not only was I now annoyed with my ex, I was now annoyed with the world too.

How on earth was this relevant? Exploring the moment of abandonment in childhood and linking that to my husband leaving, although fascinating, was not helping me get out of bed in the morning and deal with the issues right in front of me. I did not want to spend months dissecting each aspect of my childhood, followed by my teenage years and then adult years in order to make sense of my divorce. I had a career I had to get back to earning money and I wanted to talk about how I felt today and not about my life when I was two-years-old. This process went on for two weeks until I tried another therapist which was a similar tale. I thought the whole experience was a pile of BS.

Now, I know therapy works wonders for many people and not all therapists are like the two I worked with. I also know that therapy works very effectively in many situations and that millions of people all over the world choose therapy above any other process. Personally, it was very nice to have someone to talk to and I won't knock that for a second. I do however think that certain people do not have the need or patience for therapy and I count myself within this category. In the corporate world we would have been murdered if we reported that delivering a project was going to take 18 months. This is part of why I never gelled with psychotherapy or any of those talking therapies as

I just wanted to get on with healing. I wanted to take proactive steps and get to a place of empowerment again. I did not want to indulge in self-pity or gaze longingly at my navel whilst I drifted back into my childhood. It felt disempowering and like a total distraction from the reality and emotions I knew I needed to confront in the here and now. I was seeking an alternative to traditional forms of healing and in most cases, the clients who choose to work with me have similar feelings.

My specific issues with therapy were:

➡ I had no understanding of what I was going through and going to therapy didn't give me any power in taking charge of my own healing. I felt dependent on my therapist

➡ It felt like we were going to do a great deal of analysis during therapy and it was going to take an enormous amount of time. As human beings, we can tend to become fascinated by ourselves and our stories and I believe that taking great time to heal can be very destructive if we allow ourselves to become too self-indulgent. Independent surveys conducted by the Stress Society of the United Kingdom have also shown that those who take a very proactive approach to healing lead happier lives. Additionally a renowned UK psychotherapist Dr Nea Clark in her evaluation of the **Naked Divorce** said:

> "There is no need to indulge your feelings over a long period of time. Time doesn't heal them. Better to do a programme like the Naked Divorce and focus intensively on healing within a defined period of time. It's healthier for your mind but also for your body."

➡ The healing process didn't feel transparent, it felt like the therapists I saw either had no idea how I was going to heal or they had the secret to healing and the only way I was going to find out what the secret was, was to commit to seeing them on a weekly basis for 18 months

➡ I felt that there was no goal or focus to my healing. We would talk and I would say how I felt. This aimless chatting was not my vibe

➡ My therapists were not experts in processing a trauma. They were expert therapists and knew techniques for healing from all kinds of ailments. What I didn't realise then and realise today is that divorce, like most trauma-treatments has a very specific treatment and healing protocol. Working with someone who didn't specialise in trauma treatment and was afraid of any strong emotions I might have was not particularly useful to me

➡️ My healing did not fit into the, "let's meet once a week for one hour" structure. I required around-the-clock support with a phone call here, a text there, an email at 1:00am, or a session with one day's notice. I wanted someone to walk with me through the abyss, which was staring at me and not to interact in a conventional way. Everything in my life was moving so fast that by the time my weekly session arrived, everything had changed and I spent the session catching my therapist up on my life VS actually making any real progress

Traditional therapy, in my experience, is not very effective in dealing with trauma because healing from a trauma requires intensive focused action.

Additionally, therapy and traditional healing practices have based their disciplines on the premise that you need time to heal which can elongate the process. Top-notch trauma therapists are actually very quick and they work systematically with a rigorous process to help people heal. When I did my PostGrad in Trauma, I was blown away by the pace at which the pros worked and quickly learnt that most therapists do not have the training to handle trauma.

I realise that the concept of needing time to heal is so ingrained in our society, that challenging this notion is usually met with an extraordinary amount of resistance, and in some cases, even anger or dismissal. The thought of healing quickly feels fake, shallow or unbelievable and could be misconstrued as a trivialisation of the healing process. I do however need to say that this notion is becoming antiquated. The latest technologies in healing all encourage a more proactive approach.

In my experience, time is actually a hindrance to healing, as over time the sense of urgency to take action dissipates.

Rosemary Kennedy (a renowned author and wife of Joseph Kennedy and the mother of President John F. Kennedy) shared her thoughts on time…

"It has been said, 'time heals all wounds.' I do not agree. The wounds remain. In time, the mind, protecting its sanity, covers them with scar tissue and the pain lessens. But the wounds remain."

> What I tell my clients when they say 'time heals all wounds' is:
>
> **❝ Time doesn't heal anything, time simply passes. It is what we do with our lives while time is passing that either helps us, heals us, or locks us in the past ❞**

Taking time to heal can lead to a false sense of healing

Scott M Peck coined the phrase, "Cheap Forgiveness" in his 1992 cassette series entitled 'Blame and Forgiveness'. He spoke of it being a cut-rate substitute, a quick and easy pardon with no processing of emotion and no coming to terms with the injury. What happens when people take their time to heal is they become resigned, complacent, and lazy; believing that the status quo is fine. False Healing to me, is synonymous with Cheap Forgiveness. It's the cut-rate substitute for true and real healing at a deep level. There is no processing of emotion and no coming to terms with the divorce.

There is also a real impact of False Healing...

1 False Healing can lead to illness

Case study: Nate

Please note: throughout the book, I make reference to case studies of my clients. Names have been changed to protect their confidentiality in all instances.

Nate is a client of mine who came to me after battling a brain tumour for three years. He had experienced a series of gruelling surgeries as well as extensive chemotherapy and was in clinical remission. The reason he came to do the 21 Day Programme was because he had gone through a divorce five years ago and felt that the anger and bitterness surrounding his divorce had made him ill. He was very focused on completing things with his ex-wife and releasing all the negative emotions which surrounded that experience. It was a very moving journey working with him on healing his past. He was so motivated and driven to leave no stone unturned. When we reached Day 9, he finally released 10 years of rage and frustration and slept for 36 hours after the exercise. During the Vow Break with his ex wife they both worked diligently through the steps and healed anger and resentment, promising to co-parent in a harmonious and cooperative way.

It's now 3 years later and Nate is still in remission and working harmoniously with his ex wife. His commitment to ensure that all negative emotions surrounding a traumatic time in his life were released was a contributing factor to his ongoing health and wellbeing.

Dr Deepak Chopra, author, renowned endocrinologist, and leader in the field of quantum physics and mind–body healing, formulated the theory of cellular healing. It has been scientifically established that cells inside the body regenerate at different speeds – liver cells in six weeks, stomach-lining cells in three days, eye cells in less than forty-eight hours. Why is it then, you might ask, that a liver riddled with cancer in January would still be riddled with cancer in June? Liver cells regenerate every six weeks they should already have regenerated several times, ridding themselves of cancer right?

Unfortunately not. Dr Chopra believes we all have what he calls *phantom memories* stored inside our cells. What he means is that inside each degenerative cell lies a traumatic memory and before that degenerative cell dies, it passes on its memory to the next cell. So the new cell is born as a replica of the previous cell. Thus the cells keep replicating themselves, passing on the degenerative memory from one generation to the next, and so on. Although the cells replicated, what they were replicating was the degenerative cell pattern stored inside.

Dr Chopra compiled thousands of case studies of the process successful survivors had used to heal themselves from serious diseases. He discovered that they were able to access the cell memory and the associated negative emotion, which they worked towards resolving and then releasing. When they did this, the degenerative memory was not passed on to the next cell generation and thus the next cell was born as a new, healthy cell. This process became known as cellular healing.

Dr Chopra's findings have since been backed by other scientists and the now late pharmacologist Dr Candace Pert, a PhD in cellular biology and biophysics from the United States, backed up Dr Chopra's research through laboratory experiments. Dr Pert unequivocally established that emotions and the body are neurologically linked and that there is a chemical expression for every emotion that we have. When we suppress an emotion the body releases a chemical into the bloodstream. This chemical travels to certain cell receptors and blocks them, leaving them incapable of communicating with the rest of the cells in the body. If those cell receptors remain blocked over a long period of time then there is a propensity for toxicity to build up and diseases to occur within the blocked areas.

Conversely, Dr Pert has also found that when you express emotions fully and in a healthy, non-repressive way, the cell receptors remain open. When you bury your emotions over time, it can have a very lasting impact on your health, wellbeing and happiness. It can also lead to premature ageing and illness.

Some of the symptoms of buried emotions include:-

➡ A feeling of extreme tiredness and general fatigue

➡ Losing hours in the day because you are preoccupied with daydreams

➡ Spending all day watching television or lying in bed sleeping

➡ Losing your lust for life and rarely wanting to talk about how you are feeling or doing

➡ Blowing up at the smallest of things for no apparent cause

➡ Focusing on keeping busy rather than on feeling things. If you battle to sit still and have to keep busy all the time, consider that you might be repressing your emotions

➡ An inability to concentrate for any extended period of time

➡ Focusing on your ex and what they're doing rather than focusing on how you are feeling

➡ Tumultuous relationships with those close to you

When you repress your emotions, your behaviour and reactions to events in the present are really reactions to past events too. This has a negative effect on your relationships. You can't be fully aware of those you love until you have released your emotions from the past. Not dealing with your emotions over an extended period of time can also lead to major illness in your body.

Dr Pert, Dr Chopra and other scientists like them have spent years researching the lasting impact of repressed emotion in the body. Some of this research appears to suggest that specific emotions can also lead to specific issues in the body such as:-

➡ Repressing Anger (as it rests mostly in the shoulders and upper back) can lead to an unexpected outbreak of acne, issues with the jaw (as you have clenched your teeth), back and neck tension, and at its worst: cancer and chronic fatigue

➡ Repressing Fear (as fear rests mostly in the stomach) can lead to constipation, Crohn's disease, irritable bowel syndrome and other issues of the bowel and colon

➡ Repressing Sadness (as sadness lives mostly in the heart/lung region) can lead to heart/lung problems, throat and voice problems, and issues with your eyes

2 False Healing can lead to resentment and bitterness

Many people throw themselves straight back into work or their lives after divorce, regardless of the complexity of their emotions. As a career person, you're particularly at risk of the soldiering on syndrome, which essentially means that you throw yourself into noble pursuits like working or taking care of children or doing something whilst inside you are crying out in pain and not acknowledging your right to those emotions. Pretending you are fine when you are not can lead to a breakdown or to harbouring deep resentment and bitterness, which will not only impact your relationship potential in the future, but the quality of your life today.

Resentment and bitterness can literally affect your face as it carves a nasty pointed look. This is often referred to as the 'Divorce look', when someone simply looks and behaves like they are divorced. Some people don't even know that people can sense their bitterness, but it is written all over them: the battle they did with marriage, and the resultant scars they carry with them. Whenever their ex is mentioned, a dark cloud covers their face which scrunches up with venom and anger whilst they calmly say that they are fine (whilst they wish their ex would burn in hell). These bitter thoughts have an ageing effect on the body too.

An old quote passed down from generation to generation goes something like this:

❛❛ *Holding onto resentment is much like taking poison and hoping someone else will die* **❜❜**

If you find yourself holding onto your anger and resentment, consider the impact on your life and even the wrinkles on your face.

Steve is to this day the angriest person who ever approached me to complete the 21 Day Programme. He had gone through a very bitter divorce a year prior to joining and was complaining that he struggled to focus in his business. To say he loathed his ex-wife was an understatement. Every conversation was a rant about this or that. His face would scrunch up into a pointed missile of derisiveness. No matter what conversations we had, his only focus was on what a terrible witch she was and how the whole relationship ending was her fault. He was unwilling to discuss anything beyond wanting to destroy her and making her pay for hurting him. We could not move beyond day 6 due to his total focus on hating her.

He is unfortunately one of only a handful of people who did not complete the 21 Day Programme because he was completely unwilling to take any responsibility for anything. To this day he is still stressed and unhappy. If you don't release bitterness, it can eat you up from the inside.

3 False Healing can lead to destructive behaviour post-divorce

Sometimes pretending you are fine when you are not can have long-term damaging repercussions. Take the story of Yin...

Yin is 55 years old and of Chinese descent. When his wife of 23 years left him he went through a very strange period of time and made some decisions which were completely out of character.

One of the decisions was to go to a very funky hair salon in central London. He wound up with a spiky haircut with the sides of his head shaven. He also joined a dating website and started emailing various ladies 20 years his junior. Needless to say his work colleagues in his Telecom job thought he was well and truly experiencing a midlife crisis.

He thought it was a good idea to cry publicly on various strangers' shoulders and leaned on his teenage children for support.

By the time he came to do the 21 Day Programme he said that many of his friends had told him he was behaving very oddly and that they were concerned for his mental wellbeing.

Whenever we feel stressed, as you will see in the Nourishment section of this programme, our hormones and neurotransmitters go out of kilter. In particular, excess dopamine can cause us to act a bit crazy. It's therefore important to sleep on any drastic changes you wish to make in your life so you don't regret decisions later.

4   False Healing can have a severe impact on those closest to you

Many people are overwhelmed by anger and frustration as a result of their divorce and have no idea how their attitude impacts their loved ones. I have heard countless stories of the brothers, sisters, mothers and fathers of those experiencing divorce who are exasperated because they don't know how to support their loved one going through a tumultuous time. They are so tired of hearing their endless complaints, and so desperate for this person to seek help, but are not sure how to address the topic for fear of reproach. Every family occasion and get together is plagued by tales of the break-up as the family has to suffer through the domination of their loved one's tales of woe.

If you are courageous enough to recognise that you may be burdening and dominating your family and friends with your divorce stories, then take a hold of the situation now. Stop the cycle of misery and begin the path of the Healing Formula today.

5   False Healing can lead to relationship baggage

Relationship baggage damages relationships. So even though you may be hurting from your divorce, healing is critical in terms of securing your future happiness. We all carry some emotional baggage but the question is – will you allow your troubles from the past to affect your current relationships? Not only is baggage unbelievably draining, it will impact your new relationship. If you are committed to your next relationship working out, you need to purge yourself of all your relationship baggage or make sure you manage it. Day 17 of the 21 Day programme is focused on healing from relationship baggage.

6   False Healing greatly impacts your children

Dr. Sara Eleoff, MD (Paediatrician in Rochester, NY) publishes research each year on the impact of divorce on children. Her research concluded that divorce is an intensely stressful experience for children, regardless of their age or developmental level. Many children are inadequately prepared for the event and its ramifications. Her research study 'An Exploration of the Ramifications of Divorce on Children and Adolescents' found that less than 10% of children had emotional support during the acute phase of divorce, primarily because their parents were so wrapped up in dealing with their own pain that they were ill-equipped to support their children.

> Before taking off in an aircraft, flight attendants brief passengers on the protocols to follow if there is a loss of cabin pressure and oxygen masks are required. The rule is that masks must be fitted to yourself before you help others. The same thing applies to healing. If you are experiencing the trauma of divorce, it is imperative to prioritise your healing and support to ensure you are emotionally available to support your children. If you're struggling with the concept of getting over this divorce for your own good, consider your children. The pain experienced by children at the beginning of a divorce comes from several factors; a sense of vulnerability as the family disintegrates, a grief reaction to the loss of the intact family (many children do not realise their parents' marriage is troubled), loss of the non-custodial parent, a feeling of intense anger at the disruption of the family, and strong feelings of powerlessness.

Sara's research has shown that younger children may experience disturbances with sleep, nightmares and sometimes bed-wetting. Older children may harbour fantasies about their parents reuniting or experience extreme anger towards one of the parents who become the source of blame.

The issue is that the older the children are, the more their anger is tied into the shattering of their paradigm of relationships and the illusion that there is a 'happily-ever-after'.

WARNING:

It's important to guard against hiding behind your children's needs as an excuse for not healing from your divorce.

The journey out of resignation

You may be feeling a bit stuck or have some resignation about what healing could look like for you. You may have some idea in your head that feeling different about your situation is not possible.

Wherever you are within the divorce or break-up healing cycle, the 21 Day Programme can work for you.

- You may find yourself in the middle of your break-up feeling the deep pain and sick feeling in your stomach. In this instance, you can achieve peace and completion EVEN IF the business-side of your break-up is incomplete. Those who have completed the 21 Day Programme whilst they are still getting divorced, found that they became less emotional, and they were less triggered by events and circumstances whilst handling the legalities of their divorce.

OR

- It may be that you got divorced months or even years ago and are still feeling stuck or unresolved. Perhaps you just feel ready to process all those emotions now. The **Naked Divorce** 21 Day Programme works in bringing up anything incomplete so you may heal those parts of yourself and move on.

Follow these simple steps to confront any resignation you might have and move on for good.

The journey out of resignation

STEP 1: Confront that you may be holding onto your suffering in some way

STEP 2: Become aware of the real impact of not healing from your divorce

STEP 3: Educate yourself on the Healing Formula

STEP 4: Take focused action and concentrate on healing

STEP 5: Take decisions on a daily basis to heal until you reach a momentum which leads to breakthroughs in your healing

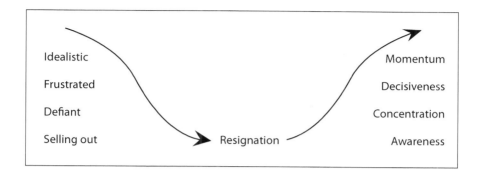

STEP 1: If you are taking your time, then you may be choosing to hold onto your suffering

You may not be sure about being ready to get over your divorce. Maybe you are not sure what to do or perhaps you picked up this book to see what will happen. Sometimes it's a question of commitment to the process, or being afraid of letting go. Perhaps you're still holding onto something.

Sometimes when we hold onto things, there is a certain payoff – some advantage or benefit that reinforces the cycle of behaviour – to not letting go.

But this payoff has high costs, whether to our vitality, self-expression, or sense of fulfilment in life. So if you are suffering but can see no way out of the suffering, consider that the benefit you are receiving for suffering is so juicy that giving up the suffering is simply inconceivable.

If I take my example with my ex-husband; he cheated on me many times and if I am truly honest, I enjoyed being the victim for a little while. It was utterly delicious.

"Poor sad and lonely Adèle who was wronged by this bad man. I feel so sorry for you."

I got loads of attention and lots of hugs and sympathy. I felt righteous and justified and had a gang of followers. We had 'Team Adèle' vs. 'Team Bruce'.

The problem was that inside I was still suffering. I was more interested in my agenda of getting attention, being the victim and feeling righteous instead of moving on, healing and living a happy successful life. So here is a little secret I will let you in on: **Your TRUE agenda always shines through.**

The problem for most of us is we have no idea what our true agenda is. We lie to ourselves and tell ourselves and others that we have good intentions, but if you are feeling dis-empowered in any way, shape or form, consider that your true agenda is revealed.

Your true agenda is in place so you can receive some hidden benefit in return.

Exercise:

Identify what the TRUE agenda has been in healing from your divorce. What do you think it might be?

What is the impact on your life of having this agenda?

What can you now see is possible?

What is a new agenda you are committed to having in your life?

Let's get something straight right away. There is nothing wrong with choosing to be single, provided you're having fun and not limping under tonnes of baggage, hurt and anger.

Picture yourself in the future. What do you see?

Do you see a lonely old person in the mirror? Do you see yourself angry at the world? In essence, most people tend to repeat the same situations in their lives over and over (unless something else interrupts this flow).

Exercise:

Picture yourself in ten or twenty years from now. Do you see the future you wish or hope for?

Are you being idealistic or hopeful?

Be honest with yourself. Are you taking actions today that are consistent with the future you desire and hope for?

STEP 2: Awareness of the real impact of your divorce

I was inspired in participating in the work of Landmark Education and there was an exercise in the programme called the Cost/Payoff exercise developed by Werner Erhard.

This exercise on the next page was inspired by the work of Landmark and Werner.

Real Impact of My Divorce exercise

There are three cards with some options on them. Imagine there is an angel on your shoulder and in contrast, a little devil residing in your head.

 The angel represents positive life-attributes which, include happiness, love in your life, health, vitality, self-expression, fulfilment, freedom, and sense of fun.

 The devil residing in your head represents your true agenda. You wouldn't be willing to give up all that you love in your life unless you were getting something back in return.

If you feel you're resisting what I'm suggesting, this is good. It means we've hit a nerve. There is always a true agenda running the show if you are experiencing a negative impact in your life. The true agenda may be hidden, but it's always there, ever present.

Instructions:

1   Take a moment to study these three cards on the next page

2   Pick the card that feels the most like the space you are in now

3   Circle the angel life-attributes which you feel have been sacrificed. The circled items are a representation of the negative impact that not healing from your divorce has had on your life

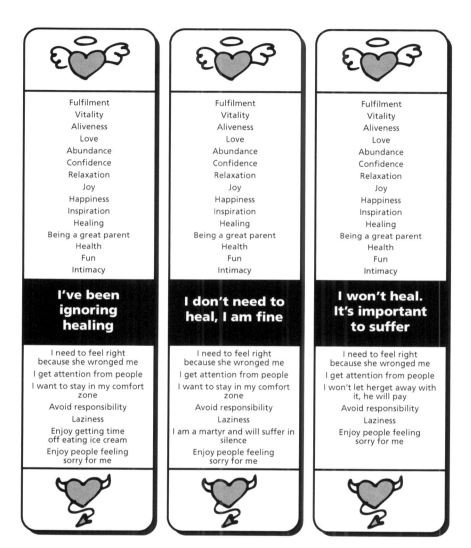

Fulfilment	Fulfilment	Fulfilment
Vitality	Vitality	Vitality
Aliveness	Aliveness	Aliveness
Love	Love	Love
Abundance	Abundance	Abundance
Confidence	Confidence	Confidence
Relaxation	Relaxation	Relaxation
Joy	Joy	Joy
Happiness	Happiness	Happiness
Inspiration	Inspiration	Inspiration
Healing	Healing	Healing
Being a great parent	Being a great parent	Being a great parent
Health	Health	Health
Fun	Fun	Fun
Intimacy	Intimacy	Intimacy

I've been ignoring healing	**I don't need to heal, I am fine**	**I won't heal. It's important to suffer**
I need to feel right because she wronged me	I need to feel right because she wronged me	I need to feel right because she wronged me
I get attention from people	I get attention from people	I get attention from people
I want to stay in my comfort zone	I want to stay in my comfort zone	I won't let herget away with it, he will pay
Avoid responsibility	Avoid responsibility	Avoid responsibility
Laziness	Laziness	Laziness
Enjoy getting time off eating ice cream	I am a martyr and will suffer in silence	Enjoy people feeling sorry for me
Enjoy people feeling sorry for me	Enjoy people feeling sorry for me	

4   Spend some time pondering what your true agenda has been in not healing from your divorce. In this process you might notice things about yourself that you haven't seen before. Use the true agenda on the card to prompt your own thinking. You might not like what you see. But I can assure you that facing up to these negative points could precipitate a significant turning point in your healing.

5   If you're struggling to find the true agenda, it's okay. This exercise can be confronting as most of the true agendas are wedged deep within our blind spot.

      One thing to try is to ask your family and friends (who are not afraid to tell you the truth) what they can see you get out of continuing your suffering. You may want to interview them.

6   Think of 20 points for each of these instances:

      •   What are you holding onto being right about?

      •   Why are you so angry?

      •   What are the reasons or justifications you are clinging to?

      •   What attention are you getting by holding onto this issue?

      •   Who are you dominating by holding onto this issue?

      •   Why are you refusing to let go?

7   Think of the negative impact this issue is having on your life. How much longer are you willing to sacrifice your life to hold onto your true agenda?

We have covered STEPS 1 and 2 in the journey out of resignation and I hope you are now clear on the impact of holding onto suffering and not healing.

Now let's look into STEPS 3 through to 5 which are covered within the remainder of the book...

STEP 3: Educate yourself on the Healing Formula and what it takes to heal

STEP 4: Take focused action and concentrate on healing

STEP 5: Take decisions on a daily basis to heal until you reach momentum in your healing

Those steps are coming up, so stay tuned!

part two

The healing formula

As my background is in change management and recovering from Post Traumatic Stress Disorder, I have a great amount of experience in what it takes to bring about sustainable change within people. Once I had healed from my own divorce, I was excited because I knew that the process I had created was amazing and transformational. In order to develop all of the facets of the programme, I had to go through a lot of trial and error. I used myself as a test subject and then I gathered a whole host of men to put my theories to work.

We discovered that healing is not a linear process or something that simply happens over time. Healing happens flashes whilst eating your Cornflakes in the morning or whilst walking the dog. Your thoughts suddenly become ordered and you realise something and suddenly you see everything differently. Those flashes of healing are unpredictable and many of us have no idea how to access them so we hope for those moments to find us over time. Scientists call those unexpected flashes, 'breakthroughs.' Complete healing is a sum of those flashes or breakthroughs and those who have healed successfully from their divorce or break-up sought out those breakthroughs in their lives.

So whenever we have to look for a new job, search for the right house or study to get through school, we need to take action. Even if you want to win the lottery, you still have to buy the ticket. In life, we have to take the initiative to do something to cause something else to happen. Healing is no different. To heal, you need to throw yourself into a situation where you have a clear goal to heal, where you set it up so it is inevitable, and where you focus completely on it. When you throw yourself into your healing you create an environment where the unpredictable flashes are more likely to occur because you are asking the right questions, analysing the situation in a different way, and taking actions to heal. By becoming intensively focused on your healing and taking daily actions, the breakthroughs which allow you to heal happen more predictably.

Out of all the trials we ran and work we did, we created a clear Healing Formula, which if followed, absolutely guarantees healing.

The Healing Formula is:

Healing Formula = Focused Intensity + 3 Specific Divorce Breakthroughs + 7 Foundations of Transformation

The Healing Formula Components

1. Focused Intensity

Ever notice how when you focus on something with intention and full concentration, it gets done quicker? This is why classroom trainings over a few days are more effective than distance learning over six months. When you take your time, sometimes you focus on the subject and sometimes you don't, so ultimately getting the work done takes longer. **Naked Divorce** works because you bring all your focus and intention towards healing AND you do this consistently over a 21-day period.

All it takes is dedicating approximately 90–120 minutes across each day of the 15 work-week days of the programme, plus no more than 12 hours across each of the three weekends to focus intensively on your healing. In total it's a 30 hour commitment to reclaiming your life and once done, you are done. We are also not saying, spend 21 days as a hermit - you can still dedicate your life to your work, your children, and other interests but your healing must take centre-stage for 21 days. If 21 days is too long for you, explore coming on a 7 or 10 day Haven Retreat and go through the whole process in beautiful surroundings. Check out www.nakeddivorce.com or www.nakedrecovery-online.com for more details.

❝ If you take healing steps daily, your healing will be faster than if you took those steps weekly or monthly. Miraculous healing happens with courageous action ❞

The 3 Specific Divorce Breakthroughs

Before discussing what the three key breakthroughs are, let's discuss the science upon which trauma healing is based. Here is an analogy...

I grew up in a town called Kimberley in South Africa.

Kimberley is known for its diamond mines. While growing up, I became fascinated with how diamonds are formed. It amazed me that something as dark and ugly as coal could be transformed into a brilliant diamond. My research uncovered that the journey from coal to diamond begins beneath the surface deep in the earth's crust. Coal can only transform into diamonds within an environment of extreme temperatures between 900°C and 1,300°C, combined with extreme atmospheric pressure.

- The extreme temperature and atmospheric pressure causes an explosion of magma which moves the coal at the speed of an uncorked champagne bottle, forming a 'Kimberlite pipe' through the path of least resistance to the surface. This resulting explosion is vastly more powerful than that of most volcanoes.

- The magma rises so quickly that the coal does not have time to convert to graphite, which is the more stable form of coal at the Earth's surface. But instead, the molecules are hugged together within the Kimberlite pipe and effectively skip some steps in the transformation, cooling down into brilliant and beautiful diamonds. This skipping of steps could not have happened without the Kimberlite pipe providing this strong container. The Kimberlite pipes are so strong that not only can they produce diamonds, they can handle the force of volcanic eruptions. The biggest deposits of diamonds worldwide are therefore found within these Kimberlite pipes.

- The diamonds that are formed are harder and more complex in structure than coal because they take on the properties of the heat and pressure they were exposed to. Due to the coal being held together, the molecules don't disintegrate, but transform into something stronger.

Ilya Prigogine, who won the Nobel Prize for chemistry in 1977, is widely regarded as the Isaac Newton of our time. In his work, Prigogine studied how biological organisms behave and transform when put under pressure, which gives us some insights into how human beings transform under pressure, too.

Prigogine's revolutionary research was adapted in the field of human behaviour by Marilyn Ferguson. In her book, 'The Aquarian Conspiracy', Marilyn explored the concept of transformation of human beings under pressurised conditions. She determined that how human beings handle those changes determine the journey of healing: either transformative healing or disintegration and chaos.

In the same way that coal is transformed into a diamond under pressure, a form of transformation is possible for humans who feel under pressure from a life change they are going through, provided they have something which supports them in being contained during the change.

The conditions for structural transformation are:

1   Intense environmental conditions need to be in place (heat, pressure, explosion or in the case of human beings – a strong, sudden, traumatic change – like the death of a loved one, losing your job, declaring bankruptcy, or experiencing divorce)

2   The organism is lucky enough to have a strong container or cocoon that holds it in place while it reconfigures itself into something more complex, to withstand the pressure being applied to it. Within this reconfiguration, the organism will actually take on the properties of the pressure being applied to it so will become stronger in the process

3   Conversely, if the organism is unfortunate so as to be left uncontained, then there is nothing to assist it in withstanding the pressure being applied, and it will move to a state of chaos or disintegrate. This process is known as entropy

When the conditions for structural transformation are met and a person is properly stabilised prior to commencing transformative enquiries, then transformation becomes inevitable and breakthroughs occur in abundance. These safety principles have been used for over 100 years in trauma therapy. However, we have created a new therapy adapting these trauma techniques and creating a unique environmental system so people have access to use these techniques themselves.

The unique application of these techniques is called **Perturbation Therapy** and it owes its success to combining several components together in a system.

In creating **Naked divorce**, I have outlined exactly what the three key break-throughs need to be, such that there is no mystery as to what it will take to heal:

 BREAKTHROUGH 1: Divorce Cocoon (days 1-4)

When you have a powerful container around you, you can withstand and use the strong forces and pressure from your divorce or break-up experience as a catalyst to transform yourself into anything you want to be. Through the first breakthrough and the first few days of the programme, you will create a strong solid foundation so you have a supportive environment to contain your transformation.

As an analogy, the first stage of the transformation of a caterpillar into a butterfly, the caterpillar's skin grows into a strong protective cocoon, so within the programme, this container is known as the *Divorce Cocoon*. Being cocooned leads to a sense of feeling invincible in life.

A person feels invincible when they:

- Are able to stand tall in the face of tough change and not be thrown off course.

- Are confident and have a healthy sense of self-esteem.

- Are able to hold position and withstand tough criticism, pressure and unfair judgment without being thrown off balance.

The first breakthrough is about creating this powerful invincible cocoon around you, and when it's in place you can withstand the strong forces from your divorce and use this time as a catalyst to transform yourself into anything you want to be. It also means you can heal faster. This transformation will make you stronger in the face of other challenges in your life.

 BREAKTHROUGH 2: Metamorphosis (days 5-14)

Once inside the *Divorce Cocoon*, the next phase called Metamorphosis begins. If we go back to our analogy of the caterpillar, from the outside of the cocoon, it looks as if the caterpillar may just be resting, but the inside is where all of the action is taking place. Inside the cocoon, the caterpillar is rapidly changing. During Metamorphosis, it's important for the caterpillar to stay in the cocoon. If the caterpillar exits the cocoon too early, the wings will not be strong enough and the caterpillar will not be able to fly. Similarly, it is essential for the caterpillar to struggle up against the walls of the cocoon so that the wings can become strong. Without your programme, apply the same principles. It's important once you commence that for your own safety, you remain within the confines, rules and safety of the programme until the transformation is complete. To achieve the second breakthrough you will be working on your old relationship, finding out what you learnt, what the source of your divorce was, getting over your ex, healing your heart and repairing relationship wounds. Rapid changes happen within a fairly short period of time.

 BREAKTHROUGH 3: Release (days 15-21)

Back to the final part of our analogy; the transformation from caterpillar to butterfly is complete and the job is to exit the cocoon. The process of exiting the cocoon takes some time as the butterfly needs its wings to dry before it can use them. Once Metamorphosis has been completed, you are ready to begin the work on your future, your desires for your next relationship, your relationship with yourself, and getting back in touch with who you are as a person. Your metaphorical 'wings' need time to dry and when you enter the final stages of Release, not only will you feel more alive but you will begin to feel free from making excuses to having the life you deserve and love.

The 7 Foundations of Transformation

The programme is designed to cover all aspects of mind, body and spirit so that the transformation is deep and lasting. Over the course of the 21 days, you will be working on mastering the 7 Foundations of Transformation. By simply following the Daily Checklist each day, you will be mastering these foundations.

Much like Stephen Covey's '7 Habits of Highly Effective People', the 7 Foundations of Transformation are key habits to adopt to ensure that your programme is a success.

The *Naked Divorce*
7 Foundations of Transformation

7 Game Plan
1 Ethics
2 Nourishment
6 The Right Support
5 Commitment
4 Work Performance
3 Emotions

The easiest way to do the 21 Day Programme is to do the online version on our website. You can do the version in the book but the web version has support. To sign up simply go to www.nakeddivorce.com/sign-up.

Foundation #1: ETHICS

There are some underlying ETHICS to adopt during the programme. They will help you remain on track.

Foundation #2: NOURISHMENT

The 2nd Foundation of Transformation will support you in your healing work by ensuring you eliminate foods and drink that aggravate your hormones, interrupt your sleep patterns or interfere with your ability to concentrate. With the correct habits in place, your emotional highs and lows will normalise, your stress levels will decline and healing will be ethical and healthy for you.

Foundation #3: WORKING WITH YOUR EMOTIONS

People often avoid feeling their emotions by keeping busy, numbing them-selves with alcohol, or adopting *Short Term Emotion-Avoidance Tactics*. This is largely because human beings inherently fear emotions and are unsure of what to do with them. For most of us, we don't understand our emotions, how they work, how to tame them, or what we can learn from them. Addi-tionally, with the dawning of 'Emotional Intelligence' concepts in the workplace, we are encouraged to keep our emotions under wraps, be calm, peaceful, and intellectualise them away.

When there is healing to be done, emotions are our greatest teachers and if harnessed, emotions can carve out powerful new ways of being. Within the **Naked Divorce**, there is a structured process for how to listen to your emotions, work with them as partners and harness their power as a catalyst for transformation.

During the 21-days I want you to try on no fear of your emotions. Let them out. Also don't engage in premature declarations of forgiveness unless you truly feel it to be true. Be real with yourself.

Learning the techniques of working with your emotions can transform your life in many beneficial ways.

Foundation #4: PERFORMING AT WORK

It's key to remain focused on your work and keep your head in the game throughout the 21 Day Programme. There are several techniques to follow to ensure that you have high energy and focus at work whilst at the same time you are being authentic in the processing of your emotions around your busy schedule.

Foundation #5: COMMITMENT

Commitment to the 21 Day Programme includes ensuring that you set up your life in a particular way so you are not distracted during the programme. Your commitment will be tested so to minimise these distractions, there may be certain things you could handle before doing the programme to ensure your success.

Foundation #6: THE RIGHT SUPPORT

Successful athletes have a coach who is rooting for them from the side lines. It is very tempting to burden your friends with your divorce troubles but those closest to you are often a hindrance to your healing without even knowing it. Bless them, they try their best, but often because they love you, they will let you off the hook. To truly heal, you need to confront some truths.

What you really need is someone who will hold you accountable – someone who will hold your hand and kick your butt if required. Your *Divorce Angel* is a critical component to your success.

Healing does not happen linearly or once a week. Healing at pace requires around-the-clock support so that whenever you need to call or contact your support person, you have someone who can assist you.

You will have an opportunity to choose your *Divorce Angel* carefully from your own life but if you get stuck, the **Naked Divorce** team of *Divorce Angels* are available to support you 24/7.

In the **Naked Divorce** 21 Day Programme, we have a great deal of fun doing the programme with groups of people like you, as the group-dynamic and sharing atmosphere is very supportive. That being said, you can do the programme without us, provided you have a *Divorce Angel* on hand. If at any stage, you feel stuck, you can contact our team for support by going to our website www.nakeddivorce.com.

Foundation #7: A GAME PLAN THAT WORKS

There is an intended structure for following the **Naked Divorce** 21 Day Programme and skipping steps is you simply doing the programme your own way. There is nothing wrong with doing that, but then do not expect the breakthrough results within the defined time period. For a complete transformation of your life and breakthrough results, I recommend you follow the structure of the programme exactly as it's designed.

For some of you, this will mean surrendering!

The 7 Foundations of Transformation ensure your success in healing from your break-up, so keep them in mind throughout the time you engage with the programme.

In Summary

The Healing Formula is:

$$Healing\ Formula = Focused\ Intensity + 3\ Key$$
$$Breakthroughs + 7\ Foundations\ of\ Transformation$$

part three

The 7 foundations of transformation

Foundation
#1 ETHICS

Like the spokes of a bicycle wheel, no spoke can be out of place or the integrity of the wheel will be compromised. The ETHICS of the are critical to the success of the programme. The ethics are:

1   Being self-expressed

2   Avoid *Short Term Emotion-Avoidance Tactics*

3   Establish a Grounded Routine

4   Sleep on any drastic changes you wish to make in your life

5   Say no

6   Cause vs. effect

7   Focus on yourself vs. your ex

1   Being self-expressed

Practice being honest with yourself about your break-up; how do you really feel about it? Many people act recovered. A false image or sense of recovery is the most common obstacle grievers must overcome if they expect to move on.

Putting on a brave face and pretending you're fine when you're not is exhausting. The cost in energy will be huge. Unresolved grief following divorce consumes tremendous amounts of energy.

Below are some things to avoid:

✘ Saying, "I'm fine" when you don't mean it

✘ Putting on your happy face

✘ Intellectualising your feelings

✘ Acting recovered

✘ Ignoring your feelings

✖ Focusing only on fond memories and building a pedestal for your ex

✖ Focusing only on what was negative about the relationship and being unwilling to let go of disappointments and anger

Here are some suggestions:

✔ Tell the truth

✔ Be real

✔ When your feelings come up, acknowledge and experience them

✔ Be authentic to yourself and how you're doing

It's important that you don't suppress your true feelings during the programme. You may build walls around yourself to block input from others. This means living with secrecy, frustration, anger and anxiety. If you have difficulty expressing yourself freely, it's possible you have been repressed a great deal, either in childhood or within your marriage.

When you're not fully self-expressed, you may feel as if you're not fully present, that you're a façade, rather than a whole person. Whenever you don't speak your truth (your feelings and thoughts), you shut down the powerful person within. When you do eventually speak, you may feel extreme anger or seek revenge for feeling muted for so long.

To practice full self-expression, start by journalling all your thoughts and all the things you have wanted to tell others about how you feel. Start slowly by expressing yourself to those around you, one person at a time. Concentrate on it. Take note of all the times you remain silent when you know you have something to say.

Exercise:

Where are you not fully self-expressed in your life?

Do you have a habit of bottling up your feelings?

How effective are you in communicating your frustrations?

Do you blow up? Over what?

Knowing what you know now, what are you committing to for the duration of the Naked Divorce programme?

----

2   Avoid Short Term Emotion Avoidance Tactics (STEATs)

John James and Russell Friedman, who wrote 'The Grief Recovery Handbook' talk about confronting your emotions rather than finding distractions that only provide short term relief. They tell the story of how a mother may deal with a child's crying by offering the child a cookie. The mother may say, "Don't cry. Here, have a cookie and you will feel better." Later in life, that child could associate fixing their feelings with food. Eating the cookie in the moment, the child gets distracted and may forget about the incident that caused the upset, but the fact remains that there was no emotional completion of the pain caused by the event. The event and all the feelings associated with it, were buried.

Short Term Emotion-Avoidance Tactics will help you feel better in each moment BUT the thing to be aware of is that you are not feeling better for real – it's a false sense of security - a false feeling of recovery. It fits into the False Healing category.

Short Term Emotion-Avoidance Tactics are things you do to avoid feeling the pain, numb the pain, or to take the pain away in the short term. They exist because human beings have not been taught to self-soothe, so they seek soothing capabilities outside of themselves. STEATs are often escapism-type activities where you keep SO focused and busy that there is no time to think about how you are feeling or doing. If you fill your life up with lots of STEATs, your healing will not progress.

The sad thing is that most people who struggle to get over their divorce are engaging in a cycle of feeling the pain, applying a *Short Term Emotion Avoidance Tactic,* feeling the pain, applying another *Short Term Emotion Avoidance Tactic* etc. until over time they feel numb and they think this numbness is them coming to terms with their divorce.

STEATs prolong the emotional rollercoaster of your divorce. So you never **fully grieve** for long enough or experience the loss critical to healing for real.

Your emotional rollercoaster will go up and down, up and down as shown in the diagram on the next page.

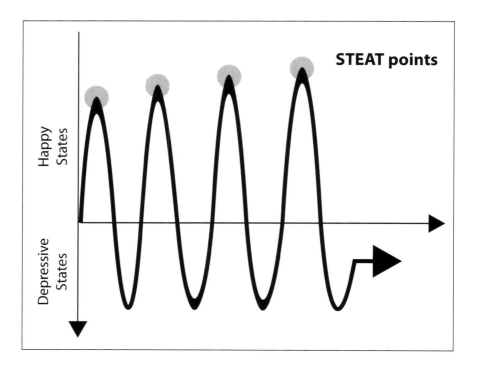

Short Term Emotion-Avoidance Tactics include but are not limited to:

➡ Excessive socialising

➡ Over-exercising

➡ Fantasy or escapism activities (books, TV, movies)

➡ Shopping/retail therapy

➡ Work and becoming a workaholic

➡ Ignoring feelings

➡ Pretending something hasn't happened

➡ Overeating

➡ Eating foods loaded with sugar and fat (comfort eating)

➡ Excessive drinking of alcohol

➡ Excessive use of recreational drugs

➡ Using prescription drugs such as tranquilisers or antidepressants

- Exercising compulsively

- Doing anything to avoid being alone

- Excessive sex with or without a partner

- Excessive busyness

- Constantly intellectualising and analysing situations

- Excessive reading or TV viewing

- Spending hours watching romantic movies or fantasising about the past

- Keeping conversations superficial

- Burying angry emotions under the mask of peace and love

- Spending countless hours with your children under the guise of being a good parent...

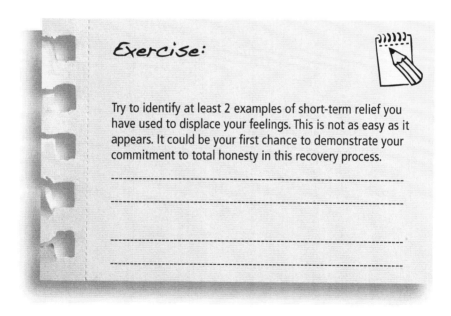

Exercise:

Try to identify at least 2 examples of short-term relief you have used to displace your feelings. This is not as easy as it appears. It could be your first chance to demonstrate your commitment to total honesty in this recovery process.

----

3   Establish a Grounded Routine vs. engaging in STEATs

Often, the first thing that goes out the window during a break-up is your routine. Many of my clients stopped eating, getting dressed, showering etc. The house descends into chaos as pizza boxes and dirty dishes pile up.

On a practical level, when something as earth-shattering as a divorce hits you, your number one priority should be to go back to basics and establish a Grounded Routine.

A Grounded Routine has a very particular purpose; the more aware and faithful you are to the rituals and routines that help you feel rooted, the more adaptable you will be when life throws you a curve ball. A Grounded Routine will prevent you from internalising the chaos, so that no matter what goes on around you, you'll be able to maintain your balance and stay solidly grounded.

You can establish a Grounded Routine by creating order, gaining support from key people and being honest and ethical in all your workings in your daily life. These steps will strengthen your resilience during divorce.

Trite as it sounds, it is the simple things in life that make a difference.

- ✔ Take up DIY or some creative activity
- ✔ Create routines which feel healthy for yourself
- ✔ Go to bed earlier
- ✔ Prepare your own meals, eat at a table and stick to established eating times
- ✔ If you like writing, then write in a journal every day
- ✔ Make an appointment with a nutritionist and improve your diet
- ✔ Eat loads of green, leafy vegetables
- ✔ Take a daily multivitamin
- ✔ Drink plenty of water; you need lot of water to re-establish balance in periods of emotional instability
- ✔ If you like baking, bake bread and spend some time kneading the dough with your hands
- ✔ Pay your bills on time
- ✔ Buy a leafy plant to care for daily

✔ Cook something from scratch. Cook something that takes hours to make

✔ If gardening is your thing, get into the garden and dig up weeds

✔ Volunteer or do something really nice for someone as a Random Act of Kindness

✔ Get to know your neighbours

✔ Establish exercise times and adhere to them

✔ Build something or dig up something

✔ Get in touch with an old hobby and try it again

✔ Go on a long bicycle ride

Whatever you choose to do in terms of establishing a Grounded Routine, the purpose is to create something to come home to. Even if your home is a physically chaotic place, find solace and comfort in your routine.

 Video: I created a YouTube video on the topic of **Grounded Routine.** To watch me explaining the concept in more detail, go to
www.youtube.com/nakeddivorce

4 Sleep on any drastic changes you wish to make in your life

I would highly recommend holding off on any drastic changes until at least one month after the programme has been completed.

I know it feels empowering and exciting to put the past behind you and do new things like change your look, get a puppy, buy a motorcycle or find yourself in Bali or quit your job BUT it's also important to make changes which are healthy and in tune with your life.

Prioritise your healing so limit any other drastic changes. It's all about timing and pacing the changes you want to make or you could find yourself in the same situation as one of my clients, Alex.

Case study: Whispers from the looney bin...

Alex went a bit crazy after his wife of 37 years left him. He decided three days after she left that he needed to try internet dating. Within a week he was dating six people at the same time and had very complicated relationship drama to contend with. He also completely changed his look, bought a Ferrari and wracked up a huge credit card bill. His desperation to fill the hole within himself could not be quenched. He kept filling every minute of the day with another date, another shopping spree or another crazy decision to fly somewhere or change something about himself.

After a while, his friends started to notice this madness was getting to him and raised the alarm. He eventually had to face the debts and returned the Ferrari, broke up with all the women he was dating and confronted that he had not healed from the pain of his divorce. Only then could his healing begin.

If you are doing any of these activities, you are in danger of making decisions which are not healthy for your life:

➡ You are obsessed with creating a 'new you' and you want to change everything such as your hair, your clothes, your behaviour

➡ You have decided to move house and maybe even take a backpacking trip and hide out in a jungle for five months

➡ You just put a deposit down on a new Ferrari

➡ You wrote a letter to the government declaring that you want to join the CIA or MI5

- The change is SO extreme that even you have trouble to believing what you have done

- Bills are drastically increasing or decreasing

- You are keen to quit your job tomorrow and change career completely

- Friends and associates are questioning these drastic changes and possibly talking about you behind your back

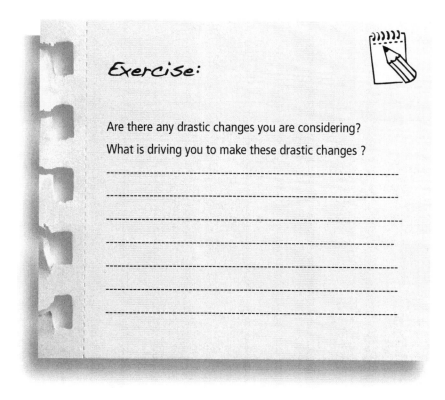

Exercise:

Are there any drastic changes you are considering?

What is driving you to make these drastic changes ?

Tip-

Delay making any major changes to your appearance or personality until you've completed the 21 Day Programme. Ensure that any changes you make are thought through, slept on, and congruent with the 'new you' and then still wait a month before making them...

5   Say no

Loving yourself is not simply about treating yourself well, taking care of yourself or having an inflated opinion of yourself. Love for yourself includes establishing healthy boundaries when it comes to other people, including your ex. It may feel hard to set limits with your ex or with other people in your life. You may feel ashamed or guilty. It's really important in the next few weeks to say no to things you don't feel comfortable doing and say no whenever you feel intruded upon.

A simple and direct, "NO, I am not able to help you with that" is the best solution. If you want to give an explanation you should keep it simple, "NO, I have already made another appointment for that time" or, "NO, sorry. I am afraid I have to decline because I have no spare time" or, "NO, it's not okay for you to pop in whenever you feel like it."

Other ways of saying NO:

➡ I can´t do this right now

➡ NO, thanks. Not this time. Thank you for asking

➡ Sorry, but NO

➡ Please accept that I cannot come

➡ I´d rather not

On Day 19 of the **Naked Divorce** programme, you will spend more time learning about setting healthy boundaries, but begin practicing from today onwards.

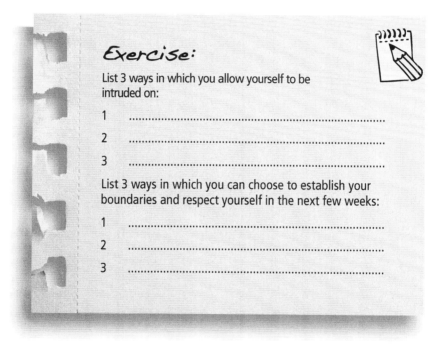

Exercise:

List 3 ways in which you allow yourself to be intruded on:

1 ....

2 ....

3 ....

List 3 ways in which you can choose to establish your boundaries and respect yourself in the next few weeks:

1 ....

2 ....

3 ....

6   Cause vs. effect

Many of us confuse responsibility with blame and blame is a hot potato that no one wants to hold. So you may feel that if you take responsibility for your divorce, you are stating that you are to blame which will force you to hold this hot potato in your hands. I want to be clear that **taking responsibility has nothing to do with blame.**

Responsibility is a way to regain power over a situation and stating, "yes, I had something to do with this happening."

The ultimate purpose of taking responsibility is to regain control over your life.

I remember thinking, "This divorce was forced upon me by Bruce so he is to blame." That may have felt very real and true for me at the time, but what I later learnt was that by blaming him, I gave up control of my life and turned myself into a victim of a bad situation. I had chosen to do that. I had chosen to become a victim so I didn't need to feel responsible for anything that was happening.

In life, you have a choice of either feeling at the *effect of life* or feeling in charge and like you *cause your life.*

Tad James, the founder of Timeline Therapy discusses the concept of cause vs. effect'. Here is a summary of his principles:

Feeling like you are at the effect of life

Do you feel like:

You are in a position where you are giving your power away to other people and you may believe that the answers, solutions to issues and power in life lie outside of yourself.

➡ You says things like "my ex ruined my life"

➡ You say things like "my ex makes me angry" or "my ex hurt me"

➡ It may feel like the divorce has all the power in your life and that you have lost control

➡ You may be feeling worried about what others think

➡ You might even be seeking someone or something to rescue you from your situation

Eleanor Roosevelt said, *"No one can make you feel bad about yourself without your permission.* You are in control of how you feel. You feeling angry or sad is you choosing to feel those things because only you can feel YOUR feelings" When we make other people or events responsible for our feelings, then we also give them control of our lives.

This way of living life is called *living at the effect of life.*

In a relationship, what is powerful is for both people to be fully responsible for themselves and their emotions. If you think it's your partner's responsibility to make you happy or it's their fault when you are sad, you are not living responsibly. Your job is to make yourself happy. Your partner's job is to top-up an already happy version of you.

Feeling like you cause your life

When you create your life and take full responsibility for your life, you acknowledge that you may have something to do with how your life runs, how your divorce will be, your emotional state and what actions you take. One of the biggest steps in healing is actually adopting the mindset that you are in charge and you have the power. Power statements include:

- I take the action

- I have the power

- They are my emotions and are not caused by anyone else other than myself

- I am responsible for my life and how it runs

- If bad things happen in my life, I don't allow those things to crush me, I rise up and find an empowering meaning from what happened, take responsibility for what I can be responsible for and learn the lessons that propel me forward

- I don't make excuses or argue for my limitations

- I am learning from this divorce situation and this is what I have learnt…

This will not always be easy to do when you are feeling low, however, it's all about practice. Just one simple thought like this every single day will make all the difference in the world.

Healing from your divorce now is all about taking ownership, being responsible and choosing to move on with your life. Practice living like you cause your life every day.

In the beginning it may be challenging but after 21 days of practice, it will come more naturally to you.

Exercise:

What part of your divorce can you take responsibility for?

Think of people you know who spend more time living at the cause of life (heroes, powerful men, billionaires):

What can you learn from these people?

What steps can you take today to demonstrate that you are practicing *living at the cause of your life*?

Tip-

CHANNEL YOUR HERO FOR A DAY:

Spend one day walking around as if you are your hero. For example, if you choose Martin Luther King or James Bond practice BEING him for a day. Think about how he would approach the situation you are in, what he would say, what he would do. Whenever you feel disempowered, try and channel your hero for a day.

7   Focus on yourself vs. your ex

Let me tell you a bit about one of my clients. I shall call him Edward.

Case study: Edward

Edward was obsessed with his ex-wife and spent copious amount of time talking about what she was up to. He was so fixated on how she was doing that he had not moved on from their divorce for five years. He was stuck. She had a new boyfriend, a new house and new hair and he was still walking around with the thought that she might realise that she missed him and come back to him. He was fixated on their love story and would not give it up.

What Edward wasn't aware of, was that by focusing on what she was up to was his way of escaping and avoiding dealing with his own emotions. Although a great deal of time had passed, time had stood still in his life and he was no further along in his healing.

Working with him, the key component which shifted him into healing from his divorce, was supporting him in shifting his focus from her onto himself. It was painful but once his grieving was complete, he found peace, harmony and a new life once he stopped fixating on whatever she was doing.

The last time I spoke to Edward, he had met someone new and was having a great time learning horseriding. He said he was the happiest he had ever been.

One thing which I see time and time again with my clients, is this concept of *Target Fixation*.

Target Fixation is a process by which the brain is focused so intently on an observed object that awareness of everything else diminishes.

This is a common issue for motorcyclists and mountain bikers as statistically most collisions are due to *Target Fixation*. A motorcycle or bicycle will tend to go where the rider is looking; if the rider is overly focused on something in the path ahead, the rider can collide with that object simply because of the myopic focus on it, even though the rider is ostensibly trying to avoid the object.

As a keen motorcyclist, I am well aware of the hazards of *Target Fixation*. In fact, on one motorcycle trip in the Himalayas, I collided with the back of another motorcycle I was fixated on in front of me. This almost led me to fly off a cliff so it was a pretty frightening moment.

Focusing on your ex and what they are up to leads to no good. You are in essence, fixated on them and end up having daily collisions with unnecessary pain and suffering over and over again.

When I observed this type of fixation with most of the people I worked with, I realised that tackling FOCUS inside of the programme was very important.

For some of you who have been divorced for years, it may be easy to not think about your ex however, do notice if you are constantly fixating on everything else except your healing. Perhaps you are constantly thinking of your job or your children as a distraction? The lesson is to think of yourself during this programme. It's time to be selfish and be fascinated in how YOU are doing and to grow your awareness and analysis of yourself, rather than something else.

Examples include:

➡ Whenever you want to think about what your ex had for breakfast or their new partner – think instead about yourself and your own eating habits

➡ Whenever you find yourself drifting off and wondering what your ex meant when they said x, y or z, think about you new DIY project

➡ Whenever you find yourself wondering why your ex said whatever they said, focus instead on your exercise regime

Training your mind to stop being preoccupied with thoughts of your ex and what she is thinking or what she is up to, OR to stop pointless thoughts of your neighbour or friend, or job, is a little like training a new puppy:

1) **Start by gently ignoring the yelps for attention.** If you notice your mind flashing to your ex or another unhelpful distraction, relax. Imagine that the thought is a soft, fluffy white cloud. Imagine this cloud drifting across your mind like a cloud floats across the sky. Just notice the thought and gently let it go. Tell yourself that this unhelpful thought is just floating across your mind. Engaging with this thought is like engaging with a puppy's yelps for attention and this is not constructive.

2) **If the yelps continue, keep a short leash.** If you find yourself constantly drifting into an amazing fantasy story or if you find yourself stuck in a cycle of analysis-paralysis, sometimes it's good to reign in that thought with one swift action. Immediately say to

yourself, "NO, enough is enough." Make a swift sudden action and stand up, telling yourself out loud that this line of thinking is not constructive. Become immediately fixated on doing something else like journalling about your feelings or going for a focused power walk. The key is swift, intentional action to jerk yourself out of the lethargy of daydreaming. If your leash is too long and you indulge negative thinking for too long, it takes longer to come back into the present.

3) **Reward with healthy treats if well behaved.** If you notice that it's been a few hours or days since you last engaged in unhelpful thinking, then reward yourself with a healthy treat.

In summary

Each day of the 21 Day Programme includes an exercise that reminds you of the ETHICS of the 21 Day Programme. Each day you have an opportunity to rate yourself and then devise actions you can take to move up a level (a rating of one is low on the scale and a rating of 10 is high on the scale).

The example overleaf is one a client completed while doing his homework:

ETHICS	Rate yourself on a scale of 1-10	Actions I will take to move this ETHIC to a level 10 in my life
Full self-expression	8	• I commit to stop hiding out and telling Patrick that Sarah and I are getting divorced. • I will call Bill and explain why I have been so distant.
Avoid STEATs	4	• STOP SHOPPING for random stuff • Will not hide behind the kids and will focus on getting a life • only 4 hours of video games per week. Need to get out and get some exercise!
Establish a Grounded Routine	6	• I commit to eating more healthily - no more take-out food • I will go home at a reasonable hour and make time to cook dinner. • I am going to take up squash again and join a league
Sleep on any drastic changes you wish to make in your life	2	• OK, will return the television system I bought on the week-end. I don't need it
Say no	5	• I will tell Paul tomorrow that he cannot come over before 3p.m. because earlier doesn't work for me
Cause vs. effect	10	• Feel pretty good just completing this list and proud that I haven't complained about my ex-wife once today
Focus on you vs. your ex	9	• Have not thought about my ex once today, so to reward myself, watching a movie with my mate Sam

Tip-

Whenever you feel lost during your divorce, come back to the ETHICS of the programme. Each day, take a look at actions you can take to put them back in place.

Foundation #2
NOURISHMENT

Whilst experiencing a trauma like divorce, a range of different responses are triggered; You may feel loss and pain and your feelings will dip and soar. One moment you long for your ex, desperate for them, and the next you want to rip their head off. This volatility and confusion add to the general sense of craziness.

Managing your health and diet

It is really key to take care of yourself when your life is disrupted by a trauma. To heal ethically, the first thing you need to focus on is re-establishing routines and taking care of yourself.

Getting divorced is a great opportunity to review your eating habits, your diet and your general health.

My story:

I used my divorce as an opportunity to really overhaul my state of health and general fitness. For two years prior to the end of my marriage, I was very unhappy with my weight and general health.

I decided that part of my healing programme would include an overhaul of my health and general fitness regime. I looked back to when I was nineteen and what I envisaged for my life and I realised that one of my dreams was to complete a triathlon.

It was a great goal during my own **Naked Divorce** because it gave me a lot of focus. I hired a trainer, reviewed my diet completely, and chose to become a vegetarian as a result. I trained every day and the weight fell off me, my skin glowed and my confidence soared.

I found the regular running, cycling, and swimming cathartic because I spent time thinking about my life, my future and what I wanted to achieve in the next phase of my life. I also rested a great deal and balanced out the cardio exercise with Pilates and Yoga. Completing my first triathlon was an incredible experience. I could not believe I did it. I inspired myself do more and be more in my life, and used my routines as a way to learn discipline and focus.

My friends and family didn't recognise me after my divorce because I became incredibly disciplined. I also noticed that a few times whilst entering a venue,

I was asked for my ID. I loved seeing the face of the bouncer when he noticed that I was born in the seventies.

This was not possible for me without learning about the value of focusing on my health and well being.

Regardless of whether or not you want to take on a personal physical challenge, it may be a great idea to consider treating yourself like an athlete during the 21 Day Programme. Changing your diet will even out the highs and lows.

Giving yourself the vitality and energy to complete the journey of healing will stand you in good stead.

Consider these principles of treating yourself like an athlete:

- ✔ A dedicated athlete never misses their workouts or practices
- ✔ An athlete is aware that success is underpinned by regular exercise, disciplined training, healthy eating, sleeping well, and taking care of their body
- ✔ An athlete will pace themselves, ensuring that they pay attention to their body during each exercise session. They don't want to overdo it or injure themselves during training
- ✔ An athlete participates fully in the process and in competitive situations. An athlete doesn't sit on the side lines or shrink back from the game

Thinking of yourself as an athlete and taking care of yourself in that way will produce extraordinary results in your life.

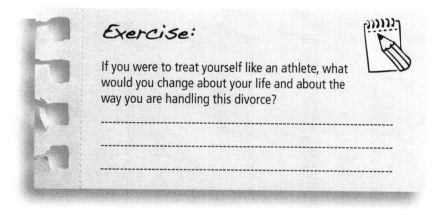

Exercise:

If you were to treat yourself like an athlete, what would you change about your life and about the way you are handling this divorce?

Nourishment Lesson #1: Our hormones and neurotransmitters go haywire during a trauma

The thoughts and feelings that make up our consciousness are linked to biochemical activities in our brain. These biochemical activities play a vital part in our behaviour. It's important to keep in mind that your body is going to have physical reactions to your divorce, because your brain is reacting to your emotional upheaval and trying to "fix" you. In our society, divorce isn't often labelled as "traumatic", but it's important to remember that you ARE suffering a trauma, and you need to be aware of what's going on physically in order to balance yourself out.

Hormones: Cortisol and Adrenalin

There is a part of our brain called the amygdala. The amygdala is where we think the 'fight or flight' response comes from. It responds best to the senses, like sight, sound and smell. It reacts fast, like an alarm going off, saying "That's dangerous, run away" or "That sounds worrying, go and look". The amygdala is not something we can control. To store memories in the brain, the hippocampus and the amygdala work together, with the hippocampus largely controlling when and where the amygdala fires. During trauma, however, the amygdala takes over.

When the amygdala gets overstimulated, it dumps out tonnes of adrenalin, noradrenalin and cortisol, also known as hydrocortisone, all hormones produced by the Adrenal Cortex. These hormones are released in response to stress or shock and with a bad break-up or divorce, a great deal of stress is impacting your body. Together with adrenalin, the primary function of cortisol is to increase blood sugar. It helps us store sugar in the liver as glycogen, aids in fat, protein and carbohydrate metabolism and suppresses the immune system. Mother nature equipped us with this hormone to assist us in fight-or-flight situations, such as having enough blood sugar in our body to give us the energy to run away from a lion. Its job is to quickly convert stored energy sources in the body into usable energy.

Although there isn't a lion coming at you, a divorce situation can be a major shock and your body believes that your life is in danger. So it pumps out cortisol to prepare you to run away from the perceived threat.

Cortisol also stimulates gastric acid secretion. This is why you sometimes feel nauseas or light-headed - almost as if you've sustained a blow to the stomach. This is also why many people don't eat much when dealing with heartbreak; they literally lose their appetite.

Elevated levels of adrenalin and cortisol also shut down the hippocampus in the brain – it seems to sort of 'fuse out' because of the increase in stimulation. This is why you cannot remember anything when you feel traumatised and can only handle simple tasks right in front of you (hence why we have a Daily Checklist!)

Heightened levels of cortisol is also associated with a weakened immune system. This is why chronic elevations of cortisol are detrimental to your health in the long term. Elevated levels of these hormones have been linked to adrenal fatigue, hormonal imbalances, heart disease, excessive blood sugar levels, elevated cholesterol, and pretty much anything else that stress precipitates within the body. Getting your adrenalin levels and cortisol levels under control is all about getting enough sleep, diet and exercising in the right way. The details are covered within the Trauma Diet which is complimentary as part of any coaching programme with the *Divorce Angels*.

Neurotransmitters

Neurotransmitters create and reflect your feelings, moods, thoughts, and behaviours. This powerful group of chemicals in the brain is responsible for physiological and psychological changes in how you experience your life. All behaviour has a corresponding chemical pattern in the brain.

There are more than a dozen neurotransmitters but Serotonin and Dopamine, play a crucial role in orchestrating your behaviour, thoughts, emotions, and experiences during a trauma like divorce.

When we're stressed, the increase in cortisol and adrenalin levels suppress Serotonin and increase our Dopamine levels. This change in chemical composition has the following effects with:-

1) Dopamine

Dopamine is responsible for making us more alert and attentive during the fight or flight response. However, when we're not releasing the Dopamine by fleeing or fighting, the elevation of this neurotransmitter causes a massive 'aching' feeling in your chest. The feeling of heartbreak – like your heart is being torn in two, is caused by elevated levels of Dopamine.

When your Dopamine levels are too high, you may be caught in distorted perceptions of reality, leading to excessive risk-taking and increased aggression.

The feelings below are all linked to higher-than-normal levels of Dopamine in the body:

- Feeling jittery and restless

- Urges to drive past your ex's house, to check their Facebook account, call them at three in the morning or talk to their friends

- Becoming obsessed with work, to the point of becoming a workaholic

- Feeling trapped and crazy, like a caged animal, or wanting to break things

- A feeling that you might just drive your car into a wall. The need to convert emotional pain into something you can actually feel is driven by excess Dopamine

- A fear of being alone and having nothing to do. An inability to tolerate relaxation or calm

- A feeling of hyper-vigilance or being overly controlling

- Feeling impulsive, with a short attention span, blocked and scattered, and may be prone to easily fly off the handle

- An urge to succumb to violence or aggression. A tendency to deliberately create conflict

- Avoidance in making connections with others

- A feeling of insecurity or paranoia

- A feeling of being chronically stressed, frustrated, and anxious

- Being overly competitive and determined to win at all costs

- An inability to concentrate, or feeling almost manic

Exercise:

Can you relate to any of these feelings above?
Which ones do you feel most intensely?

----

2)   Serotonin

Serotonin is the neurotransmitter associated with feeling good, peaceful or relaxed. Optimal Serotonin levels are required for all positive affective states and all balanced emotional conditions. When cortisol and adrenalin are released during trauma, Serotonin levels immediately drop as your body prepares for fight or flight. This depletion of Serotonin is why people become so incredibly emotional.

When Serotonin levels are extremely low, you may lapse into a cycle of struggle and hopelessness.

The feelings below are all linked to lowered Serotonin levels:

➡ A feeling of being reclusive and wanting to avoid situations that might create anxiety

➡ Avoidance of all conflict and a need to hide away

➡ Feeling overwhelmed, resentful or victimised by the circumstances

➡ Having a craving for sweets coupled with a tendency to overeat (especially comfort foods) in the afternoon or evening

➡ Suddenly prone to heat intolerance or feelings of panic

➡ A sudden experience of insomnia, or struggling to get to sleep

➡ Feeling depressed and hopeless and without any personal power

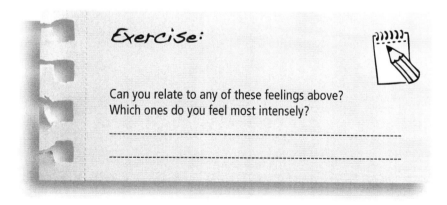

Exercise:

Can you relate to any of these feelings above?
Which ones do you feel most intensely?

Nourishment lesson #2: Rebalancing your hormones and neurotransmitters is about altering your nutrition and lifestyle

Your behaviour and experiences affect your biochemical profile and your biochemical profile affects your behaviour and experiences. By being alert to the red flags that tell you when your brain chemistry is out of balance, you can take steps to restore your equilibrium and be in charge again.

The sad thing is that for most of us, when we experience heartbreak, we go and bury our heads in a tub of Ben and Jerry's ice cream or indulge in crisps or drink alcohol or coffee. Those foods and drinks actually INCREASE the cortisol and Dopamine levels within our body and will lead you to feeling even more crazy and insecure. If you want to stop feeling the heartache, eating healthily is critical to stabilising your Dopamine levels and stimulating the release of Serotonin and oxytocin that will help you feel better. It's really important to note that what society teaches us in order to cope with trauma often makes us feel worse!

Under the section, **Foundation of Transformation # 7: A GAME PLAN THAT WORKS**, you will begin preparing effectively for the programme. There is a range of supplements to take which combat or reverse the effects of cortisol, boost Serotonin and decrease Dopamine back to normal levels. There are also dietary tips as all these chemicals can be affected by your diet.

➡ Use cortisol-reduction supplements (shopping list section under Foundation of Transformation # 7: A GAME PLAN THAT WORKS)

➡ Serotonin levels can be controlled through diet and supplements. In particular, focus on getting more vitamin C and omega-3 fatty acids, and eating more complex carbohydrates instead of eating sugary foods. A complete **Trauma Diet** can be purchased on the **Naked Divorce** website and is complimentary with any of our coaching programmes

➡ There are specific tissue salts to use, which are effective for restoring the salts in your cells. These can be depleted through the hormonal imbalance precipitated by stressful events such as divorce. They can be found in most health food shops

➡ Eat at regular intervals throughout the day. Don't skip meals or your body will release cortisol

➡ Avoid too many carbohydrates as they trigger a cortisol release in response to constantly–elevated insulin levels

- Get to bed earlier and try a bath with Epsom salts for a magnesium boost

- Avoid all stimulants (nicotine, energy drinks that contain ephedra-like compounds, and caffeine) or restrict yourself to only one–two per day. Stimulants shift the body into sympathetic dominance, in other words, the fight or flight reaction so they increase the levels of adrenalin and cortisol in the body. Stimulants can also disrupt your sleeping patterns. If you must have your daily coffee, try decaffeinated, or ensure you don't drink coffee after midday

- Keep your workouts under one hour. At the one-hour mark, your testosterone levels begin to decline and cortisol levels rise. 45-minute workouts are even better

- Maca Root Powder is also known to reduce cortisol levels and restore the adrenal glands to health

- Use stress reduction techniques. To calm yourself and restore your hormonal balance, listen to the **Naked Divorce** break-up Reboot. It is a relaxing audio programme designed to refocus your mind on your HEALING GOAL (discussed on Day 0) and realign the neurotransmitters in your brain. Listening to it every day for 21 days will dramatically increase your healing process and reboot those feel-good emotions. The **Naked Divorce** break-up Reboot is part of our online 21 Day Programme which you can sign up for on the www.nakeddivorce.com website

- Massage therapy can reduce cortisol as well as stabilise Dopamine levels

- A study by a Japanese cosmetics company in 2006 showed that taking care of your grooming actually reduces cortisol levels in a mentally stressful situation. So it's important to keep getting up in the morning, having a shower, getting dressed and looking your best, even if you don't feel like it!

Optimising you brain chemistry and neurotransmitter profile not only supports you in healing faster after divorce, but the spin-offs include improved well-being, the achievement of your goals and dreams, and the attainment of the successful, healthy and integrated life you aspire to.

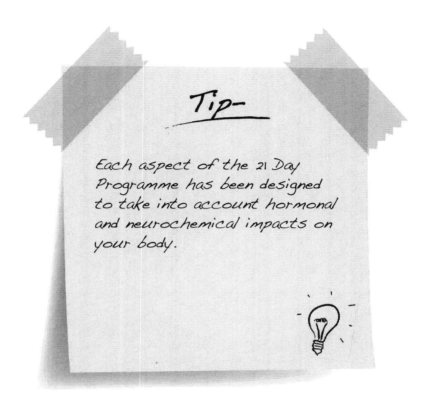

Tip-

Each aspect of the 21 Day Programme has been designed to take into account hormonal and neurochemical impacts on your body.

Nourishment Lesson #3: Be cautious of antidepressants

I completely agree that in many circumstances antidepressants are lifesavers and make an important difference in people's lives, but I am very concerned about the increase of antidepressant use in today's society.

A report written by Dr. Mark Olfson, a professor of clinical psychiatry at Columbia University/New York State Psychiatric Institute in New York City in 2009 showed that antidepressant use among US and UK residents almost doubled between 1996 and 2009, along with a concurrent rise in the use of other psychotropic medications.

"Over 10 percent of people over the age of six are receiving anti-depression medication" said study author Dr. Mark Olfson. According to background information in the study, antidepressants are now the most widely prescribed class of drugs in the United States. The expansion in use dates back to the 1980's, with the introduction of the antidepressant Prozac (Fluoxetine).

Although I will concede that there must be times when antidepressants are considered useful, many doctors are prescribing them left, right and centre — particularly if patients look vulnerable or display signs of stress.

The long-term effects of antidepressants are unknown. I know from my own personal experience of taking antidepressants in my first few years at university that it took me years to fully get the drugs out of my system once I started coming off them.

I would caution you to be wary of your doctor subscribing antidepressants when you're feeling low during your divorce.

Although antidepressants offer temporary relief while you get back on your feet again, studies have shown that they are not good in the long run. Charly Groenendijk who conducted his research into antidepressants showed that in some instances, antidepressants can actually increase cortisol and suppress Dopamine completely so that you don't feel like doing anything.

What you ideally want is Dopamine to return to normal levels vs. manic levels but the total lack of Dopamine creates lethargy and lack of ambition and drive which has long term repercussions for your life. Antidepressant medications artificially increase Serotonin levels at the synapse by blocking the re-uptake of Serotonin into the presynaptic cell.

Moving off antidepressants can also be very difficult in the future as your body has to get used to producing its own Serotonin once again.

If you can, try to get through your break-up naturally and following the methods prescribed in the **Naked Divorce** programme. Ensure you use the **Trauma Diet** as it has been designed to help you get through the pain of divorce quickly, healthily and naturally.

If you need support, please go to www.nakeddivorce.com or consult with your medical practitioner for more information.

Foundation #3 WORKING WITH YOUR EMOTIONS

> *« I feel like a piece of fabric fraying at the edges, one piece of thread at a time. I can only really handle what is right in front of me. Almost like I have tunnel vision »*
>
> Debbie, 42

My story:

It was within the first four days of my divorce. At 02:30 am I was on my third glass of wine and hadn't eaten in three days. I had been in my tracksuit for 36 hours straight and had chain-smoked 40 cigarettes (and I'm not even a smoker.)

There was a pile of laundry on the couch waiting to be ironed and used tissues everywhere. The house was in absolute chaos and I didn't feel like doing anything. I wasn't answering my phone or talking to anyone else. I had a vision of being found dead of a broken heart at the age of 65, still wearing pyjamas, with no love in my life.

The only time I left the house, I was so distracted, I almost drove into a wall. I thought that if I could convert my emotional pain into physical pain, I could take a pill for it. How bizarre my thoughts were!

The reality is that I was in despair. I felt completely out of control. For someone who is usually organised and structured, this was a very new feeling.

Nothing helped and I remember thinking, "Why the hell is this happening to me?"

I had read 27 books on breaking up in two weeks. I had spoken to two therapists. I listened to music. I listened to a personal development CD. Nothing helped. I was going crazy. I was so uncomfortable in my own skin. The pain felt unbearable, I just wanted to feel normal again.

If this sounds familiar to you or you can relate in any way, welcome to the club. If you have been acting super weird, just know that you are completely normal and you will be okay. Here are some completely normal responses to divorce:

➡ Numbness – numbness can be physical, emotional, or both. The numbness lasts for different periods of time for different people

➡ Disrupted sleep patterns – not being able to sleep or sleeping too much is completely normal

➡ Changing eating habits – it's normal to have almost no appetite or a need to eat nonstop, or both, alternately

➡ Rollercoaster of emotional energy – extreme ups and downs. As a direct result of these emotional highs and lows, you may feel emotionally and physically drained

➡ Depression – feeling low and depressed is normal

➡ Despair, desolation and desperation

➡ Reduced concentration

➡ Feeling hopeless

➡ Feeling helpless

➡ Feeling strong anger or rage

➡ Experiencing dramatic mood changes

➡ Exhibiting a change in personality

➡ Losing interest in most activities

➡ Experiencing a change in sleeping or eating habits

➡ Performing poorly at work

You will feel low for the first few weeks, even months. That's normal. After that, you'll start to feel more like your old self. You'll start to rationalise things and you'll begin to work out what to do next. This is a turning point, and it means you're thinking about your future. The pain will still be there, but it will become easier to bear and in the **Naked Divorce** programme you'll find many things you can do to work through the pain and speed up your recovery.

You may feel it tempting to keep busy and avoid being alone. However, if you want to heal, the key is to face your emotions and process them. I know this may sound like a frightening idea and possibly not something 'a man should be doing'. I remember thinking that my own sadness and grief would swallow me whole. What I did realise after a few days was that every single emotion I experienced had another emotion underneath it, almost like there were layers of emotions which needed to be peeled off. My job was to simply move through each emotion, find the boundary or ending of the layer and move onto the next emotional layer. There was actually a natural ending to each emotion but only when I truly experienced and acknowledged the preceding emotion. And none of the emotions lasted particularly long and they certainly didn't swallow me up whole. I realised I had nothing to fear by feeling them. When you resist your emotions and avoid being with them by indulging in *Short Term Emotion-Avoidance Tactics*, you prolong the healing cycle unconsciously. You will consequently have no say about how much time your healing will take or what will happen.

Ben's emotional journey: This graph tracks the healing experience of one of my clients prior to meeting him. It illustrates the first year of the past five years of his life as drawn by him.

Ben's rollercoaster started off with a big shock stage, an initial paralysis at hearing the bad news of his wife leaving him. He described it as a big kick in his stomach and an indescribable ache.

This was followed by a denial stage where he spent days trying to avoid the inevitable, telling himself it was not happening. This was followed by an anger and betrayal stage where he was very angry with his ex. Unsure of how to process the emotions he simply ignored them, and spent weeks pleading for her to return, promising to be a better husband. When he realised that she wasn't coming back, he again felt anger. He shouted and screamed at her. When she didn't retaliate he felt humiliation and disgust with himself. This disgust soon turned into despair, closely followed by more anger, which he didn't process and more pleading with his wife to take him back.

He momentarily felt grief and loss then went out and slept with a colleague from work. Afterwards he felt numb, briefly angry, then numb again. When the colleague didn't call him back, he was overcome by loneliness and more grief and loss. He then started drinking more alcohol and soon returned to numbness. As the divorce came through, he felt momentary happiness. His life continued along this path for several years. In the second and third and forth years, he continued the cycle of up and down. The numbness lasted days, then weeks, then months. He said for years, he simply went through the motions in his life. Almost feeling like he was dead inside.

When we started working together five years later, he was feeling very numb and resigned. He told me that life since his divorce was a series of ups and downs and that over time he just felt quite numb and had understood the numbness to be a form of acceptance. Upon examination, we actually found that deep sadness, resentment and anger were still very much present in his life. The numbness was masking the deep grief and upset over his wife leaving him. He had fallen victim to being passive over time and thought that simply the passage of time would cause his healing. We also discovered that he made use of *Short Term Emotion-Avoidance Tactics* (STEATs) like alcohol, food, sex with random strangers, and spending hours and hours at work to avoid feeling the pain of his heartbreak.

He realised then that although he had learnt a great deal during the past five years, he had not healed from his divorce and did not know what to do to heal. He commenced the **Naked Divorce** journey and achieved the inner peace he had been seeking all those years.

Ben's emotional rollercoaster is not too dissimilar to any of my client's emotional rollercoasters after divorce. The problem for Ben was that there was no knowledge of which emotion was coming next or how long the emotional ride would take. He realised that although he achieved moments of happiness, they were often fleeting and shallow like a mirage in a dessert. He would then jolt back to earth as if awakening from a dream.

> **" Go towards the pain. It will hurt but not for long. Be brave, you can do it! "**

Ben's healing cycle also didn't stop, it kept going for five years and just when he thought he had healed after an extended period of revenge, numbness or false acceptance, he would get knocked back by something that happened in his life and the emotional rollercoaster would speed up again, revealing another emotional dip or bend or loop. To avoid feeling the feelings at each point, he sought out *Short Term Emotion-Avoidance Tactics* (STEATs) to bring him instant relief, and what he didn't know at the time was that those *Short Term Emotion-Avoidance Tactics* just prolonged the cycle of the rollercoaster ride. He felt extremely stuck in his life and that there was no way to get off the emotional rollercoaster, or exercise any control over decreasing the time on the ride. He was simply strapped into his seat and needed to hold on for the duration of the journey.

I could tell you hundreds of similar stories and to me this is the saddest part about divorce healing – the years of your life that are spent in purgatory or in a departure lounge. Because there is no clear process to follow to overcome the emotional grief, no grief cycle which maps out what emotion might come next, and no structured support along the way; everyone deals with divorce as best they can. This can often lead to long-term depression and a lack of contentedness with life. Ben was very brave when he stopped stepping over things and proactively confronted and dealt with his revenge and grief emotions so they didn't hang around polluting his life.

The Grieving cycle vs. Healing cycle

The Grieving cycle is something I created based somewhat on the work of Elizabeth Kübler-Ross, my experience as a change management consultant, the invaluable lessons I learnt from my divorce, during my PostGrad in Trauma and Post Traumatic Stress Disorder and from studying numerous cases as a Divorce Angel. The emotional highs and lows experienced after a divorce can feel very extreme as they alternate between activity and passivity in our very human and desperate efforts to avoid the change.

If you can learn to truly FEEL each emotion and stand strong within it, each layer of emotion will pass and a new emotion will arise and eventually this will lead you into the Healing cycle.

The difference between Ben's emotional journey and the Grieving/Healing cycle is that by taking the right courageous steps throughout your healing journey, you are in the driver's seat of your divorce and are not allowing your life to be buffeted around by your emotions.

And then, in the calm of this relative paradise, a bombshell bursts...

Grieving cycle

1 **Denial stage:** Trying to avoid the inevitable

2 **Anger and betrayal stage:** Frustrated outpouring of bottled-up emotion

3 **Panic and negotiation stage:** Seeking a way out. Making deals with your ex. A strong sense that if you could only change X then your ex would stay

4 **Humiliation, fear of failure or looking bad stage**: Gradually sinking into a spiral, feeling embarrassed and avoiding seeing people

5 **Despair stage:** Realisation that something awful is coming your way and you're strapped into the rollercoaster and helpless

6 **Loss, grief and depression stage:** A final realisation of the inevitable, surrendering to the grief

Healing cycle

7 **Space and nothingness stage**: Once you have grieved and experienced the associated loss and pain, you're left with a feeling of nothingness. It's different to numbness because you feel very present

and can notice things around you. Your senses are heightened. You may also find that you cannot cry anymore. You experience an emotional vacuum

8   **Acceptance stage:** Seeking realistic solutions and finally finding the way forward, it's not a feeling of resignation. It's a feeling of profound understanding of the way things are and the way things are not

9   **Responsibility and forgiveness stage**: Taking responsibility for where you may have caused cracks in the relationship and contributed to its subsequent breakdown and divorce. Forgiving your ex and yourself for any failings during the relationship is a critical part of true and real healing

10 **Gratitude stage:** Transformational experience. Learning from your divorce and seeing positives and negatives from the experience. This stage completes the healing

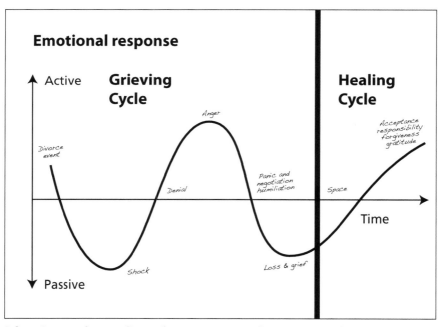

Often, just understanding where you are in the process and accepting that it is a process that you will get through, really helps. It's important to keep in mind that although the graph looks linear, you will bounce between the first six stages many times.

One minute you may be feeling angry and the next minute you're back in despair. But by feeling the emotion deeply and profoundly, it will pass and reveal the next emotional layer. If you avoid *Short Term Emotion-Avoidance Tactics* whilst processing your emotions, the emotional rollercoaster will end sooner. It's only when you're finished grieving authentically, to the point of being aware of only space and nothingness around you that will you be truly ready to move through to the advanced stages.

By the time you complete the 21 Day Programme you'll achieve those most advanced stages of the Healing cycle.

Acknowledging and truly feeling your emotions is the key to your healing

In describing the importance of acknowledging our emotional states, American psychologist Dr Maurice Elias says, "emotions are human beings, i.e. warning systems as to what is really going on around them.

Emotions are our most reliable indicators of how things are going in our lives. Emotions help keep us on the right track by making sure that we are led by more than the mental/intellectual faculties of thought, perception, reason and memory."

In her article titled 'How to Understand, Express and Release your Emotions', author Mary Kurus, a renowned psychologist based in New York, writes that emotions control our thinking, behaviour and actions. If you ignore, dismiss or repress your feelings, you're setting yourself up for physical illness.

The most advanced trauma therapies and techniques in the world use techniques to tap into those emotional memories and bring them into the foreground. There is no short-cut: healing happens THROUGH feeling your emotions.

> **"** *The unconscious mind is the domain of your emotions. To truly heal on an unconscious level, you need to pay attention to your emotions and sensations.* **"**

You cannot control your emotions BUT truly acknowledging them and feeling them, allows them to move on

Think of the people who trundle along day after day, seeming to function normally. And then one day they'll suddenly explode over something trivial and ram someone with their shopping trolley. This example of behaviour is a result of a pressure-cooker syndrome where the simple application of a little heat in the form of a tense situation causes repressed emotions to boil over. It's not popular in today's society to express negative emotions in public. Seeming 'out of control' is interpreted as a sign of weakness. We're often uncomfortable around people who express strong emotions. As a society we're taught to hide our emotions, to be ashamed of them and to be afraid of them, so we talk about our emotions instead of simply feeling them.

It's easy to want to judge our emotions and make some emotions bad or some good. The interesting thing that I have observed in working with so many people is that you cannot turn down the dial of one emotion and simply turn up the dial on another. You can try, but it will feel fake and can kill your true aliveness.

Suppression of anger means your ability to express deep love or peace is also suppressed. Suppression on any level impacts your ability to be truly vulnerable or truly connected with someone else.

There is no dial on your emotions so you cannot turn up your happiness whilst turning down your anger. Suppress one emotion and you suppress them all.

To feel MORE in life, you need to turn up the dial to ALL of your emotions – even the undesirable and not-so-nice emotions.

Orb of Emotions

Your **Public Persona** is the image you portray to the outside world. It's a thin, delicate layer, a facade used to mask the emotions you are experiencing below the surface.

To reach the underlying **Core Issue** which rules all your relationships in life, you will need a relationship coach to help move you through the many layers of the **Presenting Emotions**.

Lasting and profound change can only take place at the **Core Issue** level.

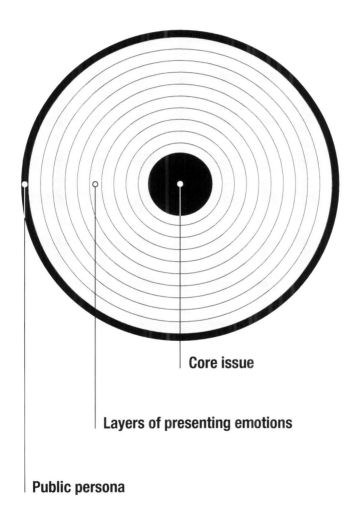

Core issue

Layers of presenting emotions

Public persona

Allow yourself to heal THROUGH truly experiencing all of your emotions. All of my clients who experience Day 9 of **Naked Divorce** later say that they are no longer afraid or confronted by their emotions and feel a sense of freedom and ease in being with their emotions. They stop fearing being alone.

My story:

> I was staring into my coffee mug when it dawned on me. I had been experiencing a very deep and anxious depression for over a week. I realised that the depression stemmed from trying to run away from how I was feeling and that it was the running away that was delaying my healing. I was trying to avoid feeling sad, crazy and depressed. The avoidance was debilitating me. After this realisation, I began letting go of avoiding all the emotions I was feeling and began to truly feel them. Don't get me wrong – it hurt like hell - but it's still the most profound experience of my life: knowing that my emotions didn't kill me, they made me stronger.

We are emotional creatures and we must learn how to know our emotions, be with them, and release them. The journey to becoming more powerful includes having the capacity to BE with strong emotions of others. The only way to achieve this state of being is by having the compassion to BE with your own strong emotions.

> **“** *Healing from divorce is about surrendering to the feelings surrounding the event. Let go and feel each emotion. You will note that each emotion, once truly experienced, does not last much longer than 30 minutes* **”**

The steps to releasing your emotions

The more you try to control your emotions, the more your emotions resist. Eventually you lose emotional control. You cannot control your emotions arising when they do. They arise regardless of your attempts to suppress them.

When you try to ignore them, it causes a chemical to be released into your bloodstream which blocks your cell receptors which can lead to illness. So what should you do when your emotions arise?

I developed these steps to releasing emotions over many months of trial and error, using a myriad of techniques I'd learnt over the years. They've not only worked for me but they've been effective for my friends and clients.

 Video: I created a YouTube video on the topic of Releasing Emotions. To watch me explaining the concept in more detail, go to **www.youtube.com/nakeddivorce**

STEP 1: Start by reminding yourself that you have control. You are not the victim of your emotions. You can't stop them from appearing, but you can decide how to react.

STEP 2: Don't ignore the emotion. Notice it. Identify it. Tell yourself that it's ok that you have it. Articulate what the emotion is that you're feeling

You start by labelling your emotion. You've heard the expression, "I just don't know how I'm feeling anymore." The programme provides a daily exercise to articulate your emotions by selecting the emotion label that mirrors how you're feeling from the table below. Begin by identifying the emotion as best you can. For example, feeling fidgety and bored can be an indication of anxiety and panic and at the heart of those emotions is unexpressed despair.

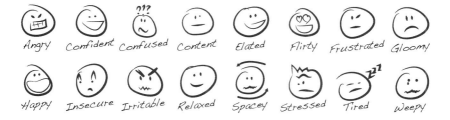

I have drawn up an emotional chart for you to assist you in articulating your emotional state. It's not a definitive list as each of us are different, but the list can be used as a prompt to help you think about your feelings and work out which emotion your physical sensations represent. Understanding your emotions is key to really getting to know yourself better.

Possible Physical sensations	What you may be telling yourself	Possible Emotions
Pain in the chest, nausea, numbness against the skin, an inability to concentrate or stomach anything.	• This is not really happening. • This cannot be happening.	Denial, shock, heartbreak.
Fiery feeling in the chest, heartburn, feeling fidgety accompanied by a need to shout or scream, like you cannot sit still, fists want to clench, tightness in throat.	• How could you? • Why is this happening to me? • Why does this always happen to me? • Why me? • This is not fair! • I feel so much rage! • You will pay. I will make it my life's mission to completely destroy you	Irritability, anger, sense of betrayal, revenge, cunning manipulation
Feeling fidgety and restless accompanied by an ache. Cannot sleep, pain in your chest, feeling that you will hyperventilate, panic sensations across your skin, fluttering in your throat, heart palpitations, stomach ache, feeling crazy.	• I can fix this. • If I just do X and Y, my ex will come back to me. • Explanations for what happened and making excuses. • Bargaining with her to come back. • The feeling that my ex is like a drug accompanied by wondering how I will get over my addiction to this person. • Strapped into the rollercoaster, helpless. Total panic and feel like melting down. • Feel completely out of control. • Want to run away/numb the pain with alcohol/ drugs/seeing people/food. • Restless/not at peace. • House/routine descends into chaos. • Feel like going crazy and driving car into a wall.	Anxiety, desperation, craziness and despair accompanied by a sense of needing to bargain and negotiate.

Cannot get out of bed, don't like bright lights, want to run away and hide.	• Withdrawal/hiding. • Beating yourself up. • Can't talk to anyone about this. • Pretending everything is fine when it's not. • Doing things out of character to prove you are fine.	Denial, humiliation, shame and a fear of failure.
Pain in chest, can't stop crying, can't sleep/eat/function normally. The feeling that you are dying inside.	• Oh no, this is really happening! • My heart feels ripped out. • I think I may do something to myself. • Moping around the house. • Feel like a zombie. • Feeling desperate and lonely. • Morose thoughts. Will I ever recover? • Emotions are overwhelming. • Can't function. • It's all my fault, I failed.	Loss, grief and depression.
Feel quiet and empty, but not grieving any more. Feel alert and present. Can't cry any more. Feel nothingness. Noticing things around you: cars, birds, trees, washing not done.	• No thoughts. Your mind is quiet. You are present and feel at peace with everything. • Getting into action again.	Space and nothingness.
No more pain in your chest or body, a feeling that life goes on and everything will be ok.	• I am OK. Went through hell and I am still here. • I can cope and haven't died of a broken heart. • Realising that the relationship was actually not that good for me. I am able to see both sides. • The fairy tale is gone and I am actually OK with that.	Understanding everything accompanied by feeling victorious, proud and accepting of the situation.
Head up, shoulders back, standing tall.	• I failed in the following areas... • I can acknowledge and take ownership of my part in the divorce. • I can see how I contributed to the divorce without beating myself up.	Taking responsibility. Being courageous, strong, peaceful and clear.
Relaxed body posture, a sensation of gliding rather than walking.	• This has happened and I am so grateful it did. I have learnt so much. I am in a better place.	Grateful, happy and at peace.

STEP 3: No matter how hard it is, commit to accepting the emotion, rather than denying its existence.

STEP 4: Imagine that the emotion is a person. Tell it that you see it and recognise it, but right now, you need to get on with your day.

Now that the emotion has been "contained", carefully and deliberately take action – or just tackle your normal tasks – while it's still there. Don't let it take over, but don't suppress it or wait for it to leave. You're in charge of how this goes. Don't let the emotion dictate or delay what you need to do.

STEP 5: When you're finished your tasks for the day, sit down with that emotion and have a serious chat.

Ask the emotion why it's here and what it wants to tell you. Make notes about what it actually wants you to do.

STEP 6: Ensure you're in a private place before expressing your emotions

You shouldn't be at work or in a public place. You need a private space where you're free to let go and express yourself. Find a room or a quiet location to let go. I alternated between driving my car to a remote location, using a back room in my house and the stairwell in my office.

STEP 7: Fully feel your emotions but don't make rash decisions

There's no need to fear your emotions. Don't fight them, run away from them or block them. Regardless of what they represent, welcome them in, hug them towards yourself and be with them. Emotions dissipate and slowly disappear if you feel them and allow yourself to be present with them. Close your eyes and feel them as deeply as you can. You know that sensation when you've been in the water too long and your skin becomes 'pruny'? In the same way, feel your emotions until you have nothing left to feel and are naturally ready to let them go. Whilst feeling your emotions, keep your heart open. What this means is FEEL the emotions deeply but allow each emotion to wash over you and not become stuck anywhere in your body or in anger within your heart. Keep feeling the one emotion till it moves onto the next emotion, allowing a natural movement.

There are several ways you can begin to release your emotions, especially those related to anger and hurt.

1. Punch something. Or go for a drive alone, pull over at the side of the road and shout it all out. Do it as loudly as you can. Shout the words, "I hate you!", or whatever it is you're feeling. So many people have never screamed out their hurt or their rage. Continue to do this as long as it feels right inside. And allow yourself to cry your feelings out.

2. If you don't have the space to scream aloud, imagine you are screaming out your rage, hurt, and pain. Imagine it completely. See it, and hear it and feel it as deeply as you can.

My story:

I remember screaming for 20 minutes. I kept shouting, "Rage! Rage! Rage!" I fully felt every part of that rage in every part of my body. I did not stop until it felt like the emotion was gone. By doing this, I released the emotion to ensure no blockages occurred within my body. It was exhausting but felt fantastic.

3.   If you're a physical person, take a pillow, take a stick and hit something, feeling your hurt every time you lash out. Each time you hit out, say the words, "I hate being hurt!" or, "I'm so f*&^%^ upset!" or whatever it is that you are feeling.

4.   If you like to write, write about your anger, your hate, sadness, upset, frustration or disappointment.

Tip-

One of the most important things about releasing an emotion is to concentrate on the emotion rather than what caused the emotion. Forget who did what to you. Concentrate on the emotion or act that you hate, rather than the person. For example,
" I'm SO angry" or,
" I HATE it when you ---"

STEP 8: Acknowledge yourself and drink water

Expressing emotions is thirsty work. You may even lose your voice a little. When you're done expressing your emotions, stop, breathe, and then drink a big glass of water. Sit quietly and notice what you're present to. When you've fully expressed your emotions, you will probably be feeling a sense of what I call space, or nothingness, which is step seven in the Healing cycle.

Foundation #4
PERFORMING AT WORK

Your career vs. your divorce

Keeping your career on track while coping with a trauma is like juggling eggs: you have to remain focused to continue performing, and falling apart is not an option.

The 21 Day Programme has been designed to provide a structure for your healing while you work and even whilst you manage your family. In the **Naked Divorce** you will proactively tackle your healing every day, in the mornings, in the evenings and over weekends, so that your emotions do not sneak up on you. The office is no place to vent your repressed feelings, but if that's where you find yourself when a rage attack threatens, there's an exercise at the end of this section that will help you remain calm and at peace.

The etiquette for dealing with your divorce at work

The general rule of thumb when facing divorce is that you should take leave from work to gather yourself. If you cannot take two weeks, even three or four days will do. Not only will you need this time to be alone to think, but you'll need privacy to do so.

Some people find they need a routine to carry them through a crisis and the comfort of routine is one thing, but be wary of throwing yourself into work as a distraction too soon. When you do go back to work, there are some tips that are helpful.

General tips:

➡ It's very common to feel foggy and unclear during the first few weeks of a divorce, as your mind is preoccupied with feelings. It's therefore a good idea to write down all action points and notes from meetings so that you have a reference. Pay special attention to requests being made of you. Remember that with all the adrenalin and cortisol in your bloodstream, the hippocampal (memory store) function in the brain is limited, so write everything down

➡ Ensure you communicate clearly about what you are willing to take on and what time frame you can commit to for those outputs. Add on a buffer of 30% to all deadlines as you won't be your usual, productive self

➡ Make a point of taking a lunch break each day for a few weeks. Leave the office and take a walk. It's important to take time out when you're under severe stress

➡ To remain calm at work drink some herbal tea. Peppermint or chamomile tea is very effective

➡ A great way to remain calm and focused at work or to relax when heartbreak threatens to overwhelm you is to listen to the **Naked Divorce** break-up Reboot

 Video: Listen to more tips about handling your career during divorce by watching the videos at: **www.youtube.com/nakeddivorce**

❝ Take eye drops and good, soft tissues to work. If you find you are feeling hyper emotional or weepy, use the eye drops so that your emotional state is not overly obvious to everyone. ❞

➡ If possible, don't discuss the details of your divorce with your colleagues. Even if they're good friends, discuss details outside of work and only with those you know will not make your divorce the office gossip of the day. Avoid crying sessions with your colleagues at a bar or in the parking lot or kitchen area. I know that it can feel 'delicious' to win the sympathy vote, but this strategy is not easy to come back from.

Having the details of your divorce batted about the office will only add to your stress and this could therefore count against you if you are looking to climb the corporate ladder later on

The etiquette for handling your boss at work

➡ Firstly, tell your boss what you're dealing with. Do this in a brief and matter-of-fact way. Don't give your boss the gory details just ask for a few days off. Deal with any urgent matters that won't wait until your return to the office. If you think you might get overly emotional, write a formal email or letter

➡ No matter how evolved your workplace may be, most working environments are not equipped to handle an employee's personal issues. Divorce is a personal issue. HR departments are often unsympathetic and do not offer adequate support. Their job is to minimise company risk and you crying in their office is something they are obliged to report to your boss (certainly in the cases I have seen and experienced)

➡ Keep in mind, although it's hard to hear, you are hired to do a job. All your company cares about is whether or not you can do the job you are hired to do. Your company does not owe you anything as most companies expect their employees to leave their personal issues at home. Therefore, try to remain professional and as unemotional as possible whilst at work. If you feel yourself getting emotional, excuse yourself and leave the building for 10 minutes. A personal tip from me is don't let others see you being overly emotional if possible, they might judge your competency based on your ability to handle strong emotional stress so are the wrong crew to lean on for support

Tip-

Delegating during your divorce is not only a stress reliever for you, it's a great opportunity for others to shine and take leadership in your team.

Empower them with new responsibilities.

➡ Communicate very clearly with your boss about what he or she can and can't count on from you. Give deadlines and try your best to stick to them. However, if it looks like you are struggling to meet a deadline, communicate with your boss immediately and recommit to what is possible

➡ Your colleagues and boss will be looking to see if you are working less hours. Therefore, unless you have permission to work less, work the full-allotted time you are hired to work. If it looks like you might arrive late to work, communicate immediately that you are going to be late AND ensure you work later to make up the time

➡ If you have the option to work from home, do so. It's easier to maintain professional etiquette via email than to be around the colleagues and people you work with everyday when you're dealing with raw emotions

➡ Inform the accounts department as soon as possible about your pending divorce as your tax code may change. If you feel nervous about calling and aren't feeling organised, prepare a list of things to communicate and email these through. Ensure that you include your current tax code in the email

The etiquette for handling your divorce at work if you are the boss

➡ If you are the boss going through a divorce, the key thing is appoint someone you trust to delegate responsibilities to. Explain to this person that you are dealing with some personal issues at home (don't get into specifics) and that you will require some extra support in the coming weeks

➡ When you delegate, be very specific about what outcomes need to be achieved. Have a discussion with this person or people about what you envisage and what the end game is and ask them to build plans for how those outcomes are to be achieved. Ask them to break the tasks down as much as possible

➡ Once everything is handled and you have a structure in place to achieve the outcomes laid out, take some time off to handle your personal situation

➡ If you have a very close-knit team share with them what is going on, but keep it brief. This is not the time to get the sympathy vote or try to get everyone to feel sorry for you. It's important to remain powerful and grounded in their eyes. This will win their respect and regard in more ways than one

➡ Even if you have close relationships with clients, I wouldn't recommend telling them about your divorce. Simply mention you are taking some time off and who their contact person is whilst you are away

➡ If necessary: check in with your team whilst you are away to ensure that the delegation has worked successfully. This will give you peace of mind

The etiquette for handling your divorce if you have your own business

➡ This is the tough one and I can tell you from personal experience, that driving ways to earn money whilst feeling raw emotions is not an easy thing to do

➡ I recommend getting the healing over with as soon as possible so you can get back to earning money. If you delay your healing, you may begin attracting all kinds of negativity to your business. So in a nutshell: prioritise getting over your divorce as soon as possible so you can get back to work. You may want to consider the **Naked Divorce** 10-Day Divorce Retreat in Thailand. Take a break, heal and come back hitting the ground running again

This is what I recommend:

1) Focus on the **Foundation of Transformation #1: ETHICS**. In particular, establish a Grounded Routine and avoid *Short Term Emotion-Avoidance Tactics* so you can prioritise your healing

2) Focus on **Foundation of Transformation #2: NOURISH-MENT** and get yourself onto the Trauma Diet as soon as possible

3) Prioritise starting the programme so you establish the *Divorce Cocoon* and manage it being in place. Personal performance is a function of stability and routine. Not having this in place will make your mind scatty and keep you unproductive

➡ For entrepreneurs, **Naked Divorce** really comes into its own as we are the people who cannot afford to lose pace with our businesses. Keeping your mind in the game is essential to success so following the steps in the programme will assist you with this. If you don't have time to do the 21 days then consider joining the 7 or 10 day Haven retreat

➡ It really depends on how big your business is. If you have a team (even if it's small), try to delegate wherever possible but check in with your team as often as you can to ensure objectives are still being met. Follow the tips above for managing your divorce if you are the boss

If you don't have a team and you are self-employed, what I recommend is to:

➡ Take some time out if possible, to ensure your living arrangements and personal situation is stabilised again

➡ Communicate with your clients that you have a personal emergency to deal with and when you will be back at work. Let everyone know how your accountabilities will be handled in your absence

➡ If you cannot take time out, get clear on all your revenue and expenses and work out exactly what your financial requirements are and by when

➡ If you don't think you can keep to your financial commitments, then get into immediate communication with your creditors and work out a plan, ensuring you lower your expenses as much as possible to ride the storm

➡ Follow the general tips covered earlier

➡ Ensure you sleep more, eat healthily and take care of yourself

The exercise for handling your emotions whilst you are at work

When you feel you need to put your emotions aside to focus on your work, practice the following exercise. Cycle through the four 'A' words:

Be **A**ware of the emotion

Accept the emotion

Acknowledge your right to your emotion

Act normal

This is how it works:

1. When feeling overly emotional, stop

    1. Stop doing anything
    2. Just sit
    3. Be still

2. Breathe

    1. Breathe long and deeply, right into your belly
    2. Let the breath fill your lungs like the ocean surging up the shore
    3. Breathe like this for 20 breaths. And if you cry, you cry

3. Become **aware** of what is happening. It's simply the increase of cortisol and Dopamine combined with the depletion of Serotonin which are contributing to feelings of depression or craziness. It's an uncomfortable feeling, but it will pass if you let yourself be with it and keep taking your daily supplements and following the **Trauma Diet**

4. Visualise. Liken the erratic emotions to a puppy that has run off without a leash. Understand that your emotions cannot be controlled,

whilst at the same time you do not need to engage with them. Allow the emotions to simply be. Just notice them. Watch them and remain calm whilst breathing deeply. Try to describe the emotional form. What is the emotion's colour, texture and shape? Give that part of yourself that feels crazy a label, or a name like Red Dragon, or Mad Dog. Ask the emotion, "What am I to learn from you? What will set me free from you?"

5.   **Accept** and acknowledge the craziness and anxiety. If you allow yourself to see the emotions as visitors, they will eventually pass

6.   No matter how you're feeling at that moment, behave normally. **Act completely normally**. Even if it feels fake, it doesn't matter. You will have time to process these emotions later in the day when it's appropriate. You know that the craziness will pass. (Acting normal whilst feeling crazy emotions is a great Cognitive Behavioural Therapy technique and works very effectively)

7.   Make yourself a hot water drink. Chamomile or peppermint tea is very soothing. Alternatively, add some lemon and two teaspoons of honey to a cup of boiling water. Drink it slowly. With each sip, sense the craziness retreating, like a tide. Calm down

8.   Take a walk outside if you can. Walk slowly as if you're gliding. While walking, cycle through your five senses and ask yourself, "what do I see, hear, touch, taste and smell?" Keep the focus outside your mind and on what's around you. Stop for a moment whilst walking and study the plants around you or the ants in the grass. Be vigilant about looking at your surroundings rather than listening to the voice in your head

9.   Remind yourself that there will be an opportunity to feel your emotions when you're in a quiet space later

10.   Remind yourself that everything will be okay. Think of all the things that people have overcome in their lives. Think of someone who has overcome immense obstacles to achieve greatness. This can be you

Foundation #5: COMMITMENT

Commitment = Results

When you make a choice to heal and let nothing else stand in the way of your success, something fundamentally changes and your choice begins to shape your future, and ultimately, your destiny.

Until one is committed, there is hesitancy, the chance to draw back, always ineffectiveness. Concerning all acts of initiative (and creation), there is one elementary truth the ignorance of which kills countless ideas and splendid plans. The moment one definitely commits oneself, then providence moves, too. All sorts of things occur to help one that would never otherwise have occurred. A whole stream of events issue from the decision, raising in one's favour all manner of unforeseen incidents and meetings and material assistance, which no man could have dreamed would have come his way. Whatever you can do, or dream you can, begin it. Boldness has genius, power and magic in it. Begin it now.

Johann Wolfgang Von Goethe

What we tend to do in life is check things out, see how you 'feel' before committing. We try something out for a while, and if we like it and it sits comfortably with us we will commit to it. We rarely just choose what we want to do and once committed, do whatever it takes to succeed with the commitment. To truly get over this divorce and move on requires commitment. You need to commit first and then work out all the logistics, issues and factors inside of that commitment.

In life there are many logical reasons why you should delay healing from your divorce, "I have to get the kids to school", "I have an important board meeting coming up, and deadlines" or, "What? No alcohol for 21 days, what about my beer after work?" or "I don't have time to do this programme, I am far too busy." These reasons, excuses and factors are actually running the show vs. you running the show. What is powerful is not letting these things rule your life. If you CHOOSE to heal, then you will be willing to do whatever it takes to achieve your goal. If you focus on how hard your life is and how you cannot fit the programme in, then you will give up the moment it gets tough. If you make a powerful choice, you will be propelled towards the inevitable: healing completely from your divorce within 21 days.

Commitment assumes the courage to make declarations you don't know how to fulfil and then working out how to make those declarations come true.

My story:

I think it was the day I found I'd broken every glass in my kitchen that I realised I didn't want to feel like a basket-case any longer. I wanted to get over my divorce. I'd run out of reasons and excuses. I wanted to take action. I'd reached a place of recognition; I knew I was going to move on, come hell or high water. You will arrive at this place of recognition when you know you're willing to do whatever it takes to move on.

So, my question to you is this:

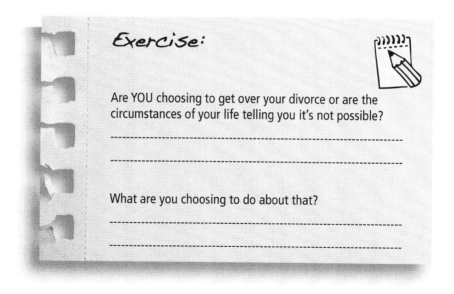

Exercise:

Are YOU choosing to get over your divorce or are the circumstances of your life telling you it's not possible?

What are you choosing to do about that?

Set yourself up for success

Minimise contact with your ex

If you are just getting divorced and still feeling raw from your break-up, minimise contact with your ex, particularly during the first 15 days. Continued contact with your ex during the **Naked Divorce** programme could lead to confusion and may lead you off the track, feeding your needy side.

Minimise contact with your new love interest

Likewise, if you have just started seeing someone new and are not sure if it's a rebound thing or not: take a breather. Your ability to attract the right person into your life is diminished when not thinking clearly. If the person is the right person for you, they will wait. To do the programme, you need SPACE to truly think, feel and connect with yourself vs. run away behind *Short Term Emotion-Avoidance Tactics*.

Help yourself first

To ensure that you're ready and able to support your children through the trauma of divorce, or get back to managing your team at work or leading a project again, help yourself first. Without helping yourself first, you'll be in no position to help anyone who relies on you.

Foundation #6:
THE RIGHT SUPPORT

Why your friends and family are sometimes the worst support during your divorce

Although your friends and family are an important part of your life, you may find that they're ill equipped to support you through your loss. I found that even though my friends and family were well meaning, they didn't know what to say to me and I often didn't feel better around them.

Before you chuck this well-meaning lot, remember that although they're trying hard, they're just not equipped or trained to help you. Society has conditioned them to deal with loss in a particular way. It's not their fault. They care for you and hate to see you suffering. They'll try to distract you or take the pain away and will do whatever they can in every moment to achieve this.

Whenever I hung out my friends they would try to distract me or unknowingly invalidate my emotions and my right to feel lousy. I'd leave feeling superficially better but also feeling as if I'd moved two steps backwards. I soon realised that I'd have to get divorce support elsewhere.

Bear these in mind about some of your friends and family (you'll probably recognise some of the points below.)

They may say weird or inappropriate things

We've all been there; the awkward moment where you say something you wish you didn't say. Family and friends often succumb to some old clichés in their struggle to try and make things better. They are all attempts to move you out of your emotional state but these statements are often damaging to your overall healing.

Common phrases my clients have heard include:

*   "Thank goodness this happened before you had children"

*   "God will never give you more than you can handle"

*   "There are lots of fish in the sea"

- "There's someone special out there for you"
- "It's better to have loved and lost than not to have loved at all"
- "Be grateful you were once married and knew love"
- "Now you are free to relive your teenage dreams of being single"

These are awful platitudes designed to make you feel better. But they don't!

You cannot fix matters of the heart with intellectualisations of the mind. These statements do not encourage your healing.

They have no idea what to say, so sometimes they change the subject

When I was young I attended my friend's mum's funeral. I felt so awkward. I was standing next to my friend and her face was a picture of despair and grief. We'd been playing dolls a week earlier and now I had no idea what to say. I stared at my shoes. I couldn't wait to get out of the church and away from the coffin and her pain. I looked at her and cracked a joke, trying to lighten the atmosphere. She didn't look up. She simply turned and walked away.

You've probably experienced this with one or two of your friends. When you talk about your divorce, they change the subject, pretend not to hear you, or crack a joke. They do this because they love you, they want to make things better for you, but they have no idea what to do. Understand their ineptitude.

Some want to revel in the drama

Some family and friends love the drama of your situation. They will ask to know everything about it so that they can revel in the excitement and intrigue of your divorce as a distraction from their own lives. Be wary of these people because getting into the drama of your divorce will not help you.

Some don't want to talk about divorce

After a while you'll realise that some of your friends and family simply don't want to talk about your divorce and will encourage you to do things to get over it so that hanging out with you is fun again. The bottom line is - you need to talk. You need to be heard. You do not need fixing. There is nothing wrong with you or the fact that you're emotional or struggling.

They are afraid of catching this disease called divorce

I remember coming home after a night out with a girlfriend, feeling awful and deflated, like an insect that had been squashed and scraped across a pavement.

I had just recounted my divorce story (okay, it was the second time) but halfway through, she looked out the window, absorbed in her own world. I was shocked. Had I said something wrong? Was I boring her? Was she disinterested?

She then changed the subject to talk about her new curtains. While I sat listening to her rattling on about the curtains contrasting with the walls in her lounge, the conversation in my head went something like this:

- "It's okay for everyone that I feel the pain, but I cannot appear to be floundering"

- "I am expected to discuss the divorce with my friends only once (don't overdo it as no one wants to hang around with a basket-case)"

- "I mustn't mope around because it's not healthy. It also makes people feel awkward"

- "But while falling apart I can't seem too happy either. That would brand me as insensitive or immature"

I realised that I was alone in my divorce. I had caught the disease called divorce and as I walked around with a scarlet letter D on my forehead, this made me persona-non-grata. When I mentioned my ex husband's indiscretions, I knew she was wondering about her own husband. I could see that all she wanted to do was go home to check that they were okay. (Months later she admitted my presumption was true.) I excused myself and gave her the opportunity to do that. I know my friend felt awkward. She wanted to help but didn't know what to say. I remember the same feelings of inadequacy at my friend's mother's funeral. The simple fact is we are not trained to deal with traumas.

Myths about getting over your divorce

Friends are fantastic, but they all have their own lives and issues.

Here are some common phrases that my clients have told themselves in the past or have heard others say.

Myths about getting over your divorce	The deeper 'meaning' you may have taken on board about loss...
Don't cry	Don't feel bad
There are many fish in the sea	Replace the loss with something else quick
Be by yourself	Grieve alone
Time heals all wounds	Just give it time and the numbness I feel is actually acceptance
Be strong for my children/mother/brother	Be strong for others and don't show my emotions
I must stay active	Keep busy and distract myself from my emotions
I mustn't fall apart	Don't drown in my emotions
Don't mope around	I must bounce back quickly or I will have no friends left
Don't bring my emotional baggage into the office	It's not OK to express my emotions
Don't fall in love with anyone else too soon	Rebound relationships are bad

WARNING:

Be wary of buying into any kind of intellectual theorising. Ban all these phrases from your head.

Give your family and friends a *Weirdness Pass*

Give the people in your life a Weirdness Pass which is a ticket allowing your loved ones to say weird or inappropriate things while you're dealing with your divorce.

They don't know any better and no one trained them on how to deal with the situation.

Remember not to take on board anything that they say. Remain aware of what they are saying, and of the myths and possible generalisations in their comments, to guard against becoming embroiled in their intellectualisations.

Weirdness Pass

This card gives the bearer a Pass for Weirdness

Simply hand over this card to anyone, to give them the right to be weird around you

Exercise:

Are any of these myths, intellectualisations or thoughts shared above familiar to you? What myths about divorce have you found yourself buying into?

Which friends or family members have you noticed are being a bit unsupportive?

Can you find it within yourself to give them a *Weirdness Pass* so you can forgive their ineptitude?

Divorce Angel

Appoint a *Divorce Angel*. This should be someone who is preferably not a close friend or family member but someone you can discuss your **Naked Divorce** experience with.

Your *Divorce Angel* is your champion who will walk alongside you in the darkness of your divorce, back into the light. If you are feeling vulnerable or have anxieties, it's best to work with a trained *Divorce Angel* from www.nakeddivorce.com. If you work with someone from your own life, be careful whom you choose. If you select someone who dislikes your former partner or has any kind of agenda for you or your life, each discussion could turn into a rant session. Also, someone you know too well could feel too much empathy for you. This could impede your progress.

When choosing your *Divorce Angel*, avoid a person that:

✖ has tumultuous personal relationships

✖ likes to talk about themselves a great deal, is opinionated or bossy

✖ likes to tell you what to do

✖ will feel sorry for you or see you as a victim in a bad situation

✖ dislikes or hates your ex

✖ is so involved with their own life that they will abandon you

✖ has a hidden agenda where you are concerned

Your *Divorce Angel* should be someone that:

✔ you don't necessarily know that well, someone who won't buy into any of your drama

✔ is wise and has it together

✔ has successful and healthy personal relationships

✔ is not afraid to tell you the truth

✔ cares about you and is willing to commit to you being empowered

✔ will stick with you through this programme

It's important to understand that your *Divorce Angel's* job isn't to be your therapist or a shoulder to cry on. They're there to help you stay on track and to ensure you're taking care of yourself.

Make a list of five potential *Divorce Angels*. Pick the first one and make a time to talk. Be honest. Show this book to your possible angel and ask if they will be available for discussions and some of the homework exercises.

Ask if it's okay for you to check in with them once a day, for no more than fifteen minutes, during the 21 Day Programme.

If they agree (well done!), ask them to read through the guidelines for the *Divorce Angel* and ask them to sign the declarations and commitments at the end of this section.

If they don't agree, don't take it personally. It is a commitment and a responsibility that some might not have the time for. Move on to the next person on your list until you find your *Divorce Angel*.

WARNING:

I don't recommend doing Naked Divorce without a *Divorce Angel*. **The programme was designed to be done with a** *Divorce Angel* **at your side.**

If you wish to have an impartial super-trained **Naked Divorce** angel to be your personal *Divorce Angel*, feel you require any additional support, or just want to do the programme with people like you (so much more fun) you can join the many support programmes by checking **www.nakeddivorce.com** for more information.

The *Divorce Angel* guidelines

So your friend asked you to be their *Divorce Angel*. That's a fantastic honour and says a great deal about you. If you're thinking it's a big responsibility and you are accountable for your friend's healing, relax. This is not therapy and you are not their therapist. All you need is a pair of listening ears, some patience and a commitment to follow the guidelines below during your 21 days of support. The most important thing is to check in with them daily and watch out for the warning signs.

I, _____

☐ understand that it is NOT MY JOB to get my friend over their divorce. They have to do the **Naked Divorce** on their own

☐ know that my job is to listen and not to offer any advice

☐ commit to be vigilant and watch out for any warning signs (covered at the end of this section) and am aware of the Notice of Important Information and Health Warnings (at the end of the section called **Time to Choose**). If I notice anything out of the ordinary, I will notify their doctor, family or the **Naked Divorce** team immediately. I have their contact information

☐ understand that it's okay to set limits. I have a life, too, and I don't want to be taken advantage of. If 15 minutes on the phone is all I can do, then that's cool. I will let him know when I am available and what to do in case of emergency meltdowns

☐ will put aside any personal feelings I have about his ex. I will focus on how he can heal from his break-up or divorce and how he can bounce back within 21 days

☐ will take a stand and be honest with him. I will not allow him to sink into bitterness, resentment or victim-type behaviour. My job is not to be nice. My job is to challenge any negative thoughts and instead of giving solutions, I will ask open questions about the impact of his behaviour on his life

☐ promise to keep everything they share absolutely confidential. Absolute confidentiality means that I carry any personal information they shared to the grave with me

☐ understand that the 21 Day Programme is designed to be the duration it is designed to be. I will support him to push themselves through the eye of the needle but if he needs to slow down, I will support his wishes

☐ will not compare my healing to his. I understand that he is an individual and it's essential for him to heal from his break-up or divorce in his own way. I will endeavour to respect his individuality

☐ will be vigilant about his use of dis-empowering language. I have read this entire chapter and will guard against offering general, intellectualised encouragements for healing

☐ understand that people struggle to stay committed to something big in life. I will endeavour to support him in completing **Naked Divorce**

Naked Divorce participant

Date

Divorce Angel

Date

The warning signs

It is completely normal and appropriate to feel extreme sadness and a complete loss of control as the result of a bad break-up or divorce. It is normal to feel hopeless and helpless. It is normal to feel you want to withdraw from life to grieve and get over your lost relationship. It is also normal to feel numb and to wonder about dying, but only if this is a passing thought.

If you're dwelling on morbid thoughts, you need to address them. Below are the warning signs to watch out for. Contact your doctor, family or the **Naked Divorce** team if you suspect you're moving into dangerous territory.

My story:

I lived very recklessly for a few days after my divorce. I was driving my car, feeling very numb to everyone and everything around me. I wanted to feel alive again so I hit the accelerator. The car went faster and faster. I didn't care. Suddenly the road curved to the left. I was seconds from colliding with a wall and even though I saw it, for a moment I wondered how it would feel to crash. I pulled over and sobbed, knowing that I had hit a metaphorical wall. I vowed at that moment to take better care of myself and stop being reckless with my life. I also chose to forgive myself for the rash behaviour, understanding that the numbness I was feeling was part of the healing cycle.

www.suicide.org advises a full list of warning signs that you can review. I have re-written this list as I believe the behaviours described should be red-flagged only if they are above and beyond what is reasonable for someone dealing with divorce.

Please review the warning signs below with your *Divorce Angel* and ensure that when you check in with them, that your *Divorce Angel* keeps these warning signs in mind.

Normal feelings that should be monitored if they continue longer than 7 weeks:

➡ Feeling hopeless and helpless

➡ Experiencing dramatic mood changes

➡ Exhibiting an extreme change in personality

➡ Losing interest in most activities

➡ Experiencing an extreme change in sleeping habits

➡ Experiencing an extreme change in eating habits

➡ Performing poorly at work

If you experience these symptoms, please seek help from your doctor immediately:

➡ Appearing depressed most of the time

➡ Talking or writing about death or suicide OR planning your death

➡ Withdrawing completely from family and friends for an extended period

➡ Feeling trapped; feeling there is no way out of the situation

➡ Abusing drugs or alcohol

➡ Exhibiting a change in personality – above what is reasonable for your divorce

➡ Giving away prized possessions

➡ Feeling excessive guilt or shame

➡ Acting recklessly. Emotional loss will already have impaired your concentration levels. As a result, impulsive behaviour could place you in danger

Be responsible for your well-being during the **Naked Divorce** 21 Day Programme and keep a vigilant watch over the above warning signs.

Foundation #7:
A GAME PLAN
THAT WORKS

It's important to have a game plan for the 21 Day Programme so you are ready for it and have scheduled it in.

This is what you need to know

People are creatures of habit. Research shows that those who participate in a daily routine are three times more likely to stay on course than those who participate in the same routine six days a week. They also fare five times better than those who participate three, four or five days a week.

Therefore, for best results, work daily for all of the 21 days. If you miss a day, simply start again the following day.

Be kind to yourself. The mind does not like change and your divorce, as well as tackling the **Naked Divorce** programme, represents change.

Your mind may tell you that it doesn't like the programme, that it won't do any good, or that you don't have the time. Don't listen! Simply tell your mind, "Thank you for sharing that" and do the programme.

The programme will take approximately 90-120 minutes each day during the week and a bit longer over the weekends, supporting your healing process after the break-up. Each exercise will take as long as it takes.

The programme has been designed to run over 21 days. You may take longer than 21 calendar days, just ensure you follow the order of the days and don't skip over any exercises.

If you need a day off, that's okay too. Provided you complete all the exercises in whatever timeframe works for you, you will find yourself bouncing back quicker and feeling better about yourself and your past relationship. Your ability to move on will be accelerated.

The best way to use the **Naked Divorce** is to read through each of the days carefully. Do this a couple of times so you're quite clear about each step.

Then work through it methodically, putting 100% of your concentration and commitment to work for you.

Remain open and watch for miracles. If you find yourself feeling lucky at any time during this programme, make sure you acknowledge your good fortune and yourself for all the good work you've done.

What you must do PRIOR to commencing the programme:

STEP 1: Go to the end of the book and print out the Daily Checklist 21 times and paste into a book. Alternatively, go to www.nakeddivorce.com and sign up for one of the online programmes where there is an online portal with the workbook as well as other important components to keep in mind during your programme

STEP 2: Go to www.nakeddivorce.com and do the 21 Day online programme to get the break-up Reboot which is a healing journey that will end the hurt, speed up your recovery process, and open your heart to love again. Listen to this recording daily for 21 days during the **Naked Divorce** programme to help you heal faster.

STEP 3: Go to the end of the book and print out the Daily Declarations and laminate them. Buy all the items in the Shopping list and handle all the elements within the Things to Handle list

STEP 4: Ensure you have a *Divorce Angel*.

STEP 5: Overhaul your eating habits and diet as per the book. Ensure you use supplements to help you. The Trauma Diet is included within the online programme.

Please note: Make it easy for yourself and purchase one of the Naked Divorce packages that include all the components you require plus break-up Reboot, Daily Declarations coaching support, extra downloads and much, much more!

WARNING: Do not proceed with the programme without the Daily Checklist. It is critical to do the exercises, the reading and follow the Daily Checklist daily. **Naked Divorce** is designed in a very particular way to achieve certain objectives.

Tip-

SHARE ANY MIRACLES

Either at
www.nakeddivorce.com

Or by emailing
info@nakeddivorce.com

We would love to hear what you
are creating!

What you will be doing daily

Daily Instructions

1. Begin each day by taking your recommended supplements and drinking a hot cup of water and lemon. This will rejuvenate you

2. Open up your Daily Checklist for the day and fill in the date

3. Read the lesson for the day and read the exercise to be done. Allow your mind to think about the answers for the exercise during the day

4. Complete the Daily Conditioning Processes for that day

5. Take your **Naked Divorce** journal with you wherever you go so you can work on your homework during the day. Alternatively if you are doing the online programme, you can update each component of the programme on your mobile phone or mobile device and print everything later on

6.   In the evening after dinner, avoid television and spend time working on your homework for the day.

Daily conditioning processes

The 'I feel' process

You can become numb to your emotions while healing from your divorce. It is vital that you remain present to your feelings (even if this concept is foreign to you). Give yourself permission to feel and be deserving of your feelings, whatever these are. This exercise is designed to make you aware of how you are feeling and what those emotions are. The exercise works especially well in the mornings and gives you an opportunity to take time every day to keep track of how you are feeling.

Daily Declarations

This exercise also works well in the mornings. I recommend getting the Daily Declarations (available at the end of the book) laminated and sticking them up in your shower. Complete the Daily Declarations in front of the mirror or while you shower each morning. Put your hand over your chest like you mean it. Read the declarations out loud and with conviction. After some time you'll notice a shift in how you feel about yourself. Almost all of my clients are completely addicted to their Daily Declarations now.

The 'acknowledge your successes' process

This exercise works well in the evening before bed. Like-attracts-like and success-breeds-success. The more you feel that you are wonderfully made, and awesome partner material, the more amazing things will come your way. You cannot feel fantastic about yourself if you do not look for and acknowledge your successes. The successes can be major or minor. It doesn't matter. What matters is that you acknowledge yourself for whatever you've done. Look specifically for the progress you made in any arena, be it financial, business, health, fitness, relationship, loving yourself, hobbies, etc.

Checking in with your ETHICS

ETHICS	Rate yourself on a scale of 1 - 10	Actions I will take to move this ETHIC to a level 10 in my life
Full self-expression	8	• I commit to stop hiding out and telling Bob that Sally and I are getting divorced.
Avoid STEATs	10	• I am SO proud of myself for being so healthy and focused at the moment. I even caught myself almost hiding behind the kids and it didn't happen. WOW!
Establish a Grounded Routine	2	• I commit to getting to bed earlier so I don't stay awake all night worrying. • I will go home at a reasonable hour and make time to cook dinner. • I just called Myra to help me with the washing and ironing, which was piling up – feel SO much better
Sleep on any drastic changes you wish to make in your life	2	• Hmm. I sucked at this today as I almost quit my job. I will focus on being calmer tomorrow
Say no	5	• I will tell Paul tomorrow that he cannot come over before 3p.m. because that time doesn't work for me
Cause VS effect	10	• Feel pretty good just completing this list actually
Focus on yourself vs. your ex	10	• Didn't think of my ex once today

What to do when you are feeling overly emotional at inappropriate times

When you're feeling overly emotional at work and you feel you need to put your emotions aside to focus on your day, practice the Exercise for handling your emotions while you are at work, featured earlier in the book.

Daily exercises

If you follow **Naked Divorce** to the letter, you will not only heal more meaningfully, you will be happier and more fulfilled. Remember, be kind to yourself. If you fall off the wagon, simply begin again, get back on track and focus on completing the programme.

Although the exercises and techniques can bring about immediate, radical change in your life, they will not let you run away from or obscure whatever life is trying to teach you.

These techniques allow you to leave the pain of heartbreak behind. But life may give it back to you if you don't learn from what it is showing you.

The purpose of the pain is to teach you so you learn and you are protected in the future.

Exercises to establish the Divorce Cocoon (days 1-4)

The first four days are all about establishing the *Divorce Cocoon* that is the cornerstone of becoming invincible during the programme.

During *Divorce Cocoon* you will:

- Get grounded in the ETHICS of the programme
- Get grounded in the STRUCTURE and Grounded Routine of the programme
- Find ways to handle your emotions and find out where you are within the Grieving/ Healing cycle

- If you feel particularly vulnerable just stay on Day 4 and repeat it until you feel ready to proceed

Exercises during Metamorphosis (days 5-14)

Metamorphosis begins by surrendering and truly feeling your emotions. You will start to work through how you feel about your ex and your divorce.

There will be a TEST that you need to pass checking that your *Divorce Cocoon* is in place before you commence with Metamorphosis. Do not move into Metamorphosis until the *Divorce Cocoon* is established.

During Metamorphosis you will:

- Write your relationship story
- Get clear about everything you learnt from your old relationship and list what you will do better in the future
- Find out what generalisations you have made about your ex
- Restore a balanced view of your ex (whether that means falling out of love or putting an end to the hatred you might feel)
- The anger exercise (a day to just go crazy)
- Find out all your past patterns from past relationships so you can be aware of them
- Hear the sorry you have always wanted to hear from your ex
- Diagnose old patterns which existed within your relationship
- Find the true source of your divorce

Handling your ex with respect is a core value within the **Naked Divorce** programme. We are just not that big into bitter and twisted people (besides it will make you have a pointed face). In the long run, the friends you have in common will admire you for not lowering yourself to revenge levels.

Exercises during Release (days 15-21)

The final seven days are all about you rebuilding yourself emotionally.
During Release you will:

- Forgive your ex
- Do a Vow Break

- Dehypnotise yourself from false beliefs and rid yourself of the ex-hexes of relationship baggage

- Work on your values and who you are now that you're no longer married or in a relationship

- Work on setting boundaries

- Develop a personal manifesto for your life

- Get back in touch with the dreams you had for your life and put plans into action to live some of those dreams, starting today

- Acknowledge yourself and celebrate your achievements

This is the home stretch. For me it was the most exciting and personally moving part of my journey. This is also the part I enjoy the most when working with clients.

Schedule your life around the programme

"Failing to plan is planning to fail." – Alan Lakein, author on personal time management. To get through your divorce you have to dedicate daily time to your healing. This requires planning and preparation.

Tip

Do not try to fit the 21 Day Programme into your life - this has no power.

Fit your life around the 21 Day Programme and have it be the centre of your life for 21 days.

This way, you know you will succeed.

Planning is an up-front investment in success so that you can:

- Avoid wasting effort

- Consider and include all factors, focusing on the critical ones

- Identify all the changes that will need to be made. If you know what these are then you can assess in advance the likelihood of being able to make those changes, and take action to ensure that you will

- Gather the resources you need in advance

For the duration of the programme…

☐ Plan the start date for your 21 Day Programme. The programme has been designed to start Day 0 on a Thursday. Give yourself at least a week to handle some of the things on the **Naked Divorce** Things to Handle list and the **Naked Divorce** Shopping List within this chapter before commencing the programme

☐ If at all possible, try not to arrange nights out during the week so you can focus on your healing work for the day. (It's only for 21 days - it's worth it!)

☐ If at all possible, try not to arrange any social engagements during the three weekends of the **Naked Divorce** programme. This will enable you to focus on the healing work

☐ Schedule at least one massage within the 21 days

☐ Schedule your days so you get to bed earlier than normal (aim for no later than 22:30)

☐ **DURING WEEK DAYS:** Set aside at least 90-120 minutes daily to work through the **Naked Divorce** exercises and daily checklist. Schedule a morning healing routine of approximately 20-30 minutes and then schedule 60-120 minutes later in the day (either at lunch time or in the evening before you go to bed). Each day's exercise has a time estimate on it based on years of trials with people - this is to give you a good indication of how to fit your work and home routines around the homework tasks wherever possible. The most important thing is to establish a routine and stick to it

☐ **DURING WEEKENDS:** Set aside enough time on weekends to do your intensive healing work. (Arrange a babysitter for your children if you need to)

- **Weekend number 1**: Schedule in six hours on Saturday and six hours on Sunday - Schedule to spend the first weekend of **Naked Divorce** arranging your living arrangements or spring-cleaning and tidying your existing home AND sorting out your finances and foundational integrity (for more details on what this will entail, you can look at Days 2 and 3 of the programme). It may be a good idea to invite a few people to assist you in sorting out your finances or spring cleaning your home

- **Weekend number 2**: Schedule in 4-6 hours on Saturday and 3-5 hours on Sunday

- **Weekend number 3**: Schedule in 2-3 hours on Saturday and 3-4 hours on Sunday

☐ Schedule in exercise, time to cook meals, and administrative tasks, too. Because there will be a lot to handle, it may be a good idea to take a step back from administrative tasks for a few days to give yourself space to do the programme

Take the time right now to add these activities to your diary or schedule.

Now, schedule in handling the following activities in the week prior to commencing the programme...

The Things to Handle list

Ensure you remove these items from your home during the programme:

☐ Alcohol, drugs and stimulants. (Alcohol, drugs and stimulants remain in your body for five days and keep you numb to your emotions, so eliminate them at least five days prior to commencing the programme)

☐ Chocolates, sweets, cakes, candy, crisps and sugary products

☐ Junk food

☐ Coffee and carbonated sodas

☐ Television, going out and fantasy/escapism

Ensure the following items are available for your use and are arranged:

☐ A baseball bat or axe. (I am serious about this one. But don't worry, you won't be harming anyone!)

☐ An iPhone/Samsung or other .mp4 player

☐ Print the 7 Foundations for Transformation to be found at the end of the book. Put them up in a place where you will be reminded of them daily

- [ ] Print out the Daily Declarations to be found at the end of the book and if possible, laminate them to put up in your shower cubicle

- [ ] Appoint a *Divorce Angel*. If you get stuck, appoint someone from our team

- [ ] Your ex. If your ex is used to hearing from you regularly, let your ex know that you are doing a programme to heal from your divorce. Request support and let your ex know you won't be seeing much of them while you do the programme as you need to focus on your healing

- [ ] Friends and family. Tell them that you're doing the **Naked Divorce** programme. Request their support and let them know you won't be seeing much of them either as you'll be focusing on your healing

The Shopping List

It's important to assist your body in its healing too, so I describe this as healthy and restorative retail therapy.

You should have available:

- [ ] A journal to write in every day (although if you do the online programme, it's already online for you to access anytime, anywhere as well as print out)

- [ ] 10 bags of ice to keep in the freezer or a big bag of wood for Day 9's exercise

- [ ] Green Tea and a bag of lemons

- [ ] Some herbal teas like peppermint or chamomile tea

- [ ] Several bottles of water

- [ ] Nutritious (and preferably organic) food. Focus on foods that are rich in colour, for example: green leafy vegetables, red tomatoes, strawberries and grapes, yellow pumpkin, peppers, fresh oranges, fruits in season, and fresh fish

Cortisol reduction supplements:

Purchase the following:

- [ ] A good complete multivitamin and mineral supplement

- [ ] Magnesium–C, one capsule three times a day

- [ ] Advanced essential minerals, two capsules three times a day. (Mineral absorption and assimilation can be impaired by stressed adrenal glands. Minerals are essential for energy metabolism)

- [ ] B5, one capsule a day

- [ ] B6, one capsule a day

- [ ] Vitamin C and Omega-3 fatty acid-rich foods with more complex carbohydrates (Serotonin levels can be controlled through diet and supplements and these foods will help)

OPTIONAL: Tissue salts, which are wonderful for restoring the salts that live in your cells but which can become depleted because of the hormonal imbalance precipitated by the stress of divorce. They can be found in most health food shops. Tissue salts are available in homoeopathic tablets that dissolve on the tongue. They are available individually as described below.

- [ ] Tissue salt # 12: SILICIA: This tissue salt will sooth irritation and excessive anger

- [ ] Tissue salt # 6: KALI PHOSPHATE: This will help if you are feeling mentally and physically exhausted, sleep-deprived, anxious and stressed

- [ ] Tissue salt # 4: FERRUM PHOSPHATE: This will boost your immune system

- [ ] Tissue salt # 2: CALCIUM PHOSPHATE: To alleviate that pale and gaunt look, palpitations, sadness and poor healing and recuperation

Time to choose

This is it. Your moment of choice. The programme will take commitment. There is no secret as to why I spent so many pages preparing you for it. It works if you do it EXACTLY as its designed. You need to be honest if you want it to work. I can try to motivate you, and I can give you the tools – but you're the one who will have to be ready to get rid of the excuses and commit to doing the whole programme without skipping any of the steps.

You know how it goes right?

You can take the path most travelled, allowing your divorce, with all its attendant pain, suffering and loss of time, to overtake your life. You can deal with it as best you can and hope to feel better in a few months from now. You can soldier on and hope for the best.

> **WARNING:**
>
> **Focusing on avoiding your pain will simply give you more of what you have right now because resisting your emotions doesn't make them go away.**

OR

You can take the path less travelled and commit to do everything it takes to get you over your divorce in a focused and healthy way. Sometimes it will be painful, and human beings don't like pain. We will do anything to feel good, even hiding behind denial. HOWEVER, the power of this programme is once it's done, it's done. You can go on and have a wonderful life, free from relationship baggage and grief. It's time to dig deep, be a warrior, stop complaining and sort your life out.

Life is short and precious. I don't want you to waste one minute on suffering. I don't want to see you trapped in a cycle of anger, anxiety, suffering or misery.

Let's think back to the earlier analogy of the dislocated shoulder; consider that perhaps popping it back into its socket in one go can have its benefits, rather than ignoring it over time.

So here is a test that will establish how ready you are to commit to healing from your divorce.

The Naked Divorce Readiness Test

Complete the following questions. The best way to honour yourself right now is by being brutally honest.

#	Question	Yes	Not ready	I am not sure	Not applicable to me	Not yet	No
1	Am I ready to begin healing from my divorce?						
2	Am I willing to do whatever it takes to heal and set aside 90 minutes each day during the week and 3 weekends to complete this programme?						
3	Do I have the courage and determination to be open to forgiveness and letting go?						
4	Am I ready to stop focusing so much on what my ex is up to and focus on what my life could be about in the future?						
5	Am I ready to stop the divorce topic dominating my conversation with my friends and family?						
6	Am I ready to stop having the divorce affect my children negatively?						
7	Am I willing to stop telling myself I am fine when I am not? Am I ready to be honest about how I am doing?						

☐ If you answered **Not ready, I am not sure, Not yet** or **No** to three or more of these questions, you're probably not ready to get over your divorce and you're probably holding onto your suffering. If this is the case, complete the Real Impact of My Divorce exercise earlier in this book so that you have a clear picture of the actual toll this divorce is taking on your life. If you find you are still not ready, then put the book aside. Come back to it when you feel you are ready. Whatever you do, do not start the programme in a half-baked way. It will not lead to any breakthrough results

☐ If you answered 'Yes' or 'Not applicable to me' to all of the questions above, then you are ready to tackle your healing wholeheartedly. If this is the case, read on

What you will learn in the 21 Day Programme
By walking this path with me through the Naked Divorce programme:

- You will learn to build a strong foundation in your life to contain your emotions and contain the pressure you will experience as you heal from your divorce

- You will learn about the science of healing. I researched healing from divorce and will share everything I have learnt

- You will learn how to deal with the emotions and the processes you will encounter

- You will learn to how to feel calm and to re-establish emotional equilibrium

- You will find out why your marriage didn't work and how to get over your ex

- You will learn to change bad habits and eliminate destructive psychological patterns

- You will learn to build a great relationship with yourself, your children, friends, family and community

- You will learn to regain self-confidence and open the door to new love

I will be alongside you through this. I will hold your hand but I will also kick your butt when necessary. So, if you're ready to accept that, let's go!

Notice of important information and health warnings

Some people experience some heightened levels of stress during the 21 Day Programme. Although stress is a part of life, for some people, this stress is abnormal if they have a history of mental illness or emotional problems. If you have a history of emotional problems or mental illness, you may find yourself more vulnerable during the programme. If at any stage, this heightened level of stress is a cause for concern, seek medical attention immediately. If you have a history of mental illness or emotional problems either personally or within your family OR if you have concerns about your ability to complete the programme or handle the daily commitment of the programme or handle the stress of examining your relationship, whether temporary, occasional or intermittent, and whether treated or not, do not participate in the **Naked Divorce** 21 Day Programme. If you are not sure about your ability to participate in the programme then discuss your participation with a mental health professional or contact one of our trained staff at www.nakeddivorce.com. It is ultimately your choice but I have been advised that you do not participate in the 21 Day Programme if you:

(a) are uncertain about your ability (either mentally, emotionally or physically) to participate in the 21 Day Programme or are currently in therapy and your therapist has advised you to not participate in the 21 Day Programme;
(b) have a history of manic-depressive disorder which is also known as bi-polar disorder either personally or within your family, are taking, have taken or been prescribed to take within the previous 18 months any medication to treat bi-polar disorders; any drugs or medicines, whether prescription or non-prescription, intended to treat or affect mental processes or mood or to treat a chemical imbalance (such as Lithium, Gabapentin or Depakote); or anabolic steroids;
(c) have considered suicide, self-harm or harm to yourself or another or have a history of depression (acute or chronic), whether or not this has ever been treated or diagnosed; are taking, have taken or been prescribed to take within the previous 18 months anti-depressants (such as Celexa, Cipram, Prothiaden, Elavil, Prozac, Zoloft, or others);
(d) have a history of any psychotic disorder (an example would be schizophrenia), (either yourself or within your family) whether or not you or your family are being or have ever been treated or hospitalised; are taking, have taken or been prescribed to take within the previous 18 months anti-anxiety drugs (such as Klonapin, Xanax, Dormicum, Librium, Ativan, or others); anti-psychotics (such as Stelazine, Risperdal, Zyprexa, Dogmatil or others);
(e) have a history of drug abuse (including steroids and cannabis) which has not been treated or have used any drugs or steroids in the past 12 months.

My declarations and commitments to myself

I, _____

☐ have carefully **read the notice of important information and health warnings** and understand the recommendations and instructions

☐ I acknowledge and understand that the 21 Day Programme was designed for people who clearly understand they are responsible for their own health and well being before, during and after the 21 Day Programme

☐ I represent that I am not participating in the 21 Day Programme to handle any emotional problems better handled by a medical professional and I fully understand that no portion of the 21 Day Programme is delivered or supervised by medical or health professionals

☐ I understand that I alone am responsible for my choice to participate in the 21 Day Programme

☐ I warrant that I am responsible for my own health at all times prior to, during and after my participation in the 21 Day Programme

☐ I promise to do the programme EXACTLY as it is designed and not to do it my own way

☐ I promise to commit to apply the Healing Formula of the **Naked Divorce** programme wholeheartedly

☐ I promise to keep the 7 Foundations of Transformation in my mind throughout the programme. I will go back to restoring them whenever I feel a loss of power

☐ I promise to work diligently at my healing every day

☐ I promise to put both feet into the programme. Even when there are days I don't want to do the work, I will do the work because I am committed to myself and my healing

☐ I promise that if I do skip a day, I will get back on track as soon as possible. I won't allow it to mean anything where my healing is concerned

☐ I promise I will complete all steps of the **Naked Divorce** programme and will not take any shortcuts

☐ I have read through the warnings earlier in the book and I validate that it's safe for me to do this programme

☐ I promise to love myself and to be kind to myself throughout the programme. I am wonderfully created

☐ My *Divorce Angel's* name is _____. My *Divorce Angel* has signed the guideline sheet. I promise to check in every day

☐ I promise to take care of my health and nourishment during the **Naked Divorce** programme

☐ I promise to guard against becoming a workaholic, having meaningless sex, indulging in retail therapy, and excessive socialising or partying as I understand that during this intensive healing process I need to take good care of myself

---------------------------------   ---------------------------

Signed   Date

part four

21 Day Programme

day

0

HEALING GOAL

Write your HEALING GOAL

In your journal, write about where you see yourself at the end of the 21 Day Programme.

We shall call this your HEALING GOAL. This HEALING GOAL is used in conjunction with the **Naked Divorce** break-up Reboot.

The HEALING goal is not a simple paragraph. It is also not a conceptual thing. Avoid saying things like 'I am happier and free-er'. This is not something measurable. The HEALING goal is a little daydream. It has a beginning, middle and end and it's something you escape into which makes you feel good. I want you to think of a daydream which incorporates healing elements within it. Make a movie in your mind...

1. Choose a very specific movie in your mind that you will work with on a daily basis. Make sure that this goal is something that is really important and meaningful to you. It should make you feel good imagining yourself having achieved that goal. The goal is not a conceptual thing, it is a movie with a beginning, middle and an ending

2. Create a specific scene in your mind's eye that would indicate to you that your goal has already been accomplished. For example, if your goal is to heal from your past relationship and be even better off than you were before, your inspiring outcome might be that you are walking down the street, your head held high, looking your best and feeling empowered, amazing, light and free. Your ex walks past you and calls your name. You feel relaxed and powerful. There is no worry or angst remaining as you go over to say hello. Your inspiring outcome is the end result. (You don't have to have your ex in your goal, this is just a common example)

3. To find your inspiring outcome, ask yourself the following three questions:

   a. "How will I know that my goal has been accomplished?"

   b. "Where will I be and what would I be doing when my goal has been accomplished?"

   c. "What will I see, hear, and feel when my goal has been accomplished that will indicate to me that my goal is realised?"

4. Write out your HEALING GOAL describing in exact detail what you will see, hear, feel (emotionally and physically), taste and smell when your goal is complete

5. Go to the www.nakeddivorce.com website and if you purchase the online programme, you will receive the break-up Reboot which you can listen to as often as you like, imagining the same goal for at least 21 days consecutively. Make sure you will not be disturbed while you listen to the programme. (NOTE: it's okay to fall asleep whilst listening to it as it works on your subconscious mind)

6. The break-up Reboot contains powerful suggestions specifically designed to gently suggest affirmations to your subconscious mind. As you listen you'll hear dual voice commands at one particular point in the recording (two very different voices, one in each ear), which distracts the conscious mind whilst your unconscious mind is supported in making positive changes

Note: You can hear each suggestion and can RELAX in the knowledge that YOU are making POSITIVE changes to your subconscious mind.

Express your goal in all five senses:

- V - Visual (sight)

- A - Auditory (sound)

- K - Kinaesthetic (feeling, both touch and emotion)

- G - Gustatory (taste)

- O - Olfactory (smell)

As your mind experiences reality, it filters reality through your five senses i.e. it receives input from what you are seeing, hearing, feeling, tasting and smelling.

The purpose of listening to the break-up Reboot, is to help you imagine your HEALING GOAL using the five senses. Every day as you listen to the break-up Reboot, you will imagine your goal in all five senses – as if it was really happening, like a movie in your mind.

Research shows that when you use your imagination like this, you can create an imagined experience so real that your mind cannot tell the difference between your imagined experience and reality. When this happens and your mind believes that your imagined experience is actually real, chemical reactions take place in your brain, effectively storing your imagined experience into your memory banks as if it were a real memory.

As you repeat this process of imagining using the break-up Reboot over time, you can programme new false memories into your mind. Your mind can then use these false memories as the basis for creating your reality. The end result of all this is that you can begin to think, feel and behave in new, more productive ways that will lead you closer to your goals. New ways of thinking, feeling and behaving have you attract new opportunities and resources into your life to help bring your dreams and goals into reality.

Note: Before you programme your mind, it is important to get specific about what you want to program your mind with. Fill in your HEALING GOAL using single words or short phrases.

An example of what a completed HEALING GOAL looks like can be found on the next page.

Example HEALING GOAL

I see myself walking on the beach, feeling powerful and relaxed. I don't feel anxious or lonely. I just feel really calm. I see my ex but there is no emotional pain or longing. I just feel really happy with my own life, and their presence does not negatively affect me or my mood.

Here is an example of what you might write down describing your HEALING GOAL.

Visual: (Sight)

Beach, soft sand, blue water, waves crashing, seagulls in the sky, I see my ex in the distance, I see my feet in the water, throwing a frisbee with my dog

Auditory: (Hearing)

Sound of waves crashing on the shore, seagulls in the sky, children laughing, dog barking as it chases after the frisbee

Kinaesthetic: (Touch)

Feeling the water on my feet, sand between my toes, clothes on my skin, warm sun on my body, wind in my hair

Kinaesthetic: (Emotions)

Happy, contented, empowered, at peace, very chilled and unfazed by life

Gustatory: (Taste)

Salty as I lick my lips

Olfactory: (Smell)

Crisp sea air

VAKGO sensory elements

To help you extract the VAKGO information from your HEALING GOAL, I have included a list of some sensory elements that make up each of your five senses.

If you find yourself having difficulty creating some of the sensory information in your HEALING GOAL, go through the list below for the particular sense that you are working on, and see if it jogs your imagination.

Visual elements:

Objects around you – what are they?

Are there people around? Who are they?

What are the shapes of the objects around you

What are the sizes of the objects – big / small

Colours

Brightness

Contrast – light / shade

Texture of the landscape

Auditory elements:

Volume – loud / soft

Distance – near / far

Quality – clear / distorted

Background sounds

Kinaesthetic (Touch) elements:

Temperature – hot / cold

Wind / water / rain against skin?

Texture and pressure

Clothing – how your clothes feel against your skin.

Are you holding anything in your hands? / Are you touching anything?

Are you sitting or lying down – if so, what does that feel like?

Movement and posture

Kinaesthetic (Emotional) elements:

Emotional quality – e.g. joy, excitement, pride, gratitude etc…

Intensity – strong / weak

Location in your body – e.g. heart area, solar plexus area, head area.

Gustatory Elements:

Texture

Intensity of taste

Hot / Cold

Sweet / Sour / Salty

Olfactory Elements:

Pungency / intensity of smell

Smells good / bad

Distance – close / far

MY HEALING GOAL

Date: ....

My HEALING GOAL is (no more than a simple paragraph):

....
....
....

My Inspired Outcome is…

(write one or two sentences summarising your outcome):

....
....
....

NOW, break down your goal into the five senses to expand on each part:

Visual (sight)

....
....

Auditory (hearing)

....
....

Kinaesthetic (touch)

....
....

Kinaesthetic (emotions)

....
....

Gustatory (taste)

....
....

Olfactory (smell)

....
....

The Divorce Cocoon

The next four days are about establishing a supportive and grounding *Divorce Cocoon*.

day
01
COCOON

TIP FOR THE DAY: *If your best friend was going through the pain of divorce, think about what you would do for him or her and then look at how you can be your own best friend during this time.*

Rule #1: *Be gentle with yourself.*

Theme: Be gentle with yourself

Date: Friday, _____

🕐 **Estimated time to complete the exercise: 60 minutes**

Remember to go through the daily checklist

Tick when done

☐

Read through the thought for the day:

Today is about you. Decide to focus on yourself and how you do today. If you are going through a divorce right now, then ensure you follow the principle of no contact with your ex. Let's not concern ourselves with what your ex is or isn't doing. Understand that any feelings of angst are just your Cortisol and Dopamine levels playing up again. When you are at work, practice the four A's from the **Naked Divorce** exercise for handling your emotions whilst at work. But if you get a break and you feel like crying, do so. When you get home tonight and need to shout out loud, find a pillow and shout into it. Indulge the ups and downs of your emotions. Experience them fully, and then gently let them go. It may feel strange to feel them if you are not a 'feeling' sort of guy, but healing involved feeling your feelings.

If you went through your divorce some time ago then the next few days are about looking after yourself and setting up the foundational structure of the *Divorce Cocoon*.

Your brain may tell you things in the first few days about it all feeling a bit fast: this is your natural human resistance to transformation. Your psyche may feel under threat so if it feels too fast, try to push through the discomfort as the programme was designed to be done within 21 days for a specific reason. If however, it's all too overwhelming, there is no pressure: you control the speed of your transformation and you can start the programme when you feel ready.

BREATHE.

Read through the exercise you'll be doing later today.

Allow yourself to think about it during the day.

Exercise:

Go to http://nakeddivorce.com/ and complete the test to find out how messed up you are.

Make a note in your journal about where you are in the grieving process and how you feel about where you are.

Think about what you will tackle this weekend, whether it be your finances or your home to lay a solid foundation for your **Divorce Cocoon**.

day

02

COCOON

*TIP FOR THE DAY: Divorce is extremely unsettling so establishing a **Grounded Routine** and solid foundation is key to your healing. Focus on your home and finances for the next two days and work hard at clearing out junk and restoring order. The order, structure and routine will be grounding.*

Theme: Home clean-up

Date: Saturday, _____

🕑 **Estimated time to complete the exercise: 6 hours**

Remember to go through the daily checklist

Tick when done

Read through the thought for the day:

The next two days are all about establishing order around your home and in your finances. You want to get stuck in and sort out any key matters concerning your foundation and base. Your outer environment is critical to your mind's inner peace. Here are some overall considerations for the next few weeks. This weekend is all about tackling a few basic things to give you stability to complete the **Naked Divorce** programme.

If you are going through a divorce right now, then read the three sections below. If you went through a divorce some time ago, it might be more appropriate to skip to the exercise.

If your living situation is still unresolved

When you're splitting up, your home can often be a refuge in a sea of uncertainty. You may yearn to hang on to your house after the divorce. But is it practical to stay there, will your ex be okay with you staying there when they move out and does it make financial sense?

Weigh up the expenses involved in keeping the house against your desire for emotional stability for you, and if applicable, for your children. What will you gain if you move? In some areas, rentals and housing prices are so high that even a smaller house or condo may be out of your price range. Also, it may not be possible to find an affordable house in the same area, or in another high-quality school district.

Property division is one of the most important decisions during a break-up. "The property division in a divorce is final and you can't undo it even if you realise later that you made a mistake," says Carol Ann Wilson, a certified divorce planner and author of 'The Financial Guide to Divorce Settlement.' "Other areas of a divorce decree can be changed, such as child support or visitation, but not the property settlement."

While the property settlement is final, there is flexibility in crafting it. One option is co-ownership between you and your ex for a set number of years. Taking sole possession and refinancing to keep mortgage payments reasonable is another possibility. If you do choose to stay, consider contacting all the companies you have bills with and changing occupier details.

Some people have an intense emotional connection with their house. Be careful to make decisions about your future based solely on how you feel. If the house is not affordable, be honest and downsize. You can create a home anywhere...

In some cases, it makes sense to downsize immediately to a smaller place, especially if the expenses involved in keeping the house are more than you can afford. Some people associate the house with their failed marriage and are anxious to start fresh somewhere else.

Make an effort to sort out your living situation this weekend so that you have a place you can call home. It is likely that you will not complete all this work over the next few days but do make an effort to make a dent in it. The idea is simply that your living situation should not be occupying your mind or stressing you out whilst doing the programme. Other than the obvious things to pack, see the list below for some ideas:

➡ Bills, medical and legal documents

➡ Useful telephone numbers

➡ You may need to arrange putting your stuff into storage if needs be

➡ Redirect your mail. Contact your local post office and ask them to redirect your mail for a month or two

➡ Notify your doctor, dentist and school of your new address or change in circumstances. Your doctor may be able to refer you to other organisations for help. It's also a good idea to have a general health check

➡ Contact everyone you have bills with and ask for final bills to be sent to your new address

WARNING:

Focus on what you can do with your home within reason. Ensure you create a budget and stick to it! This is not the time to plunge yourself into debt.

If your living situation is already resolved

➡ Make a list of all items in your home that need repairing or altering

➡ Work out a budget for the small things you can do to make you feel you're claiming the home as your own. How much of the work can you do yourself?

➡ Make a list of family, friends or DIY specialists who can help you with other jobs

➡ If you don't have the money to repair or redecorate, then spring clean. Use today to clean out junk and sort out cupboards and spaces you have left untouched for years

➡ Get clear on the real maintenance costs of your home

➡ In addition to the regular bills, budget for unexpected repairs and regular maintenance. You don't want to be caught short if you need a new water heater

➡ Consider household insurance that covers unforeseen problems with the heating or plumbing

➡ Hire a building inspector to evaluate the house and list any major repairs that may be on the horizon

➡ Identify potential trouble spots. If, for example, the house needs a new roof, then make plans for that to happen

Tip-

HOUSE PARTY

OPTIONAL: Organise a cleaning/redecorating pizza party and ask people you know to help you redecorate your bedroom.

You buy the pizza, paint and paintbrushes and they provide the manual labour!

Exercise:

1. From the reading above, spend today making a list of all the things you need to do to sort out your home or your living situation over the next 6 months.

2. Whether it's a spring clean, redecoration or moving furniture around, plan to do a chunk of this work today.

3. Create a schedule to complete the rest of the work over the coming weeks and months. The goal for the end of the day is to feel physically exhausted, as well as to feel clearer in your mind and more on top things.

day
03
COCOON

TIP FOR THE DAY: Besides the immediate decisions around your home and finances, defer any major decisions about your life for at least six weeks. Sleep on it. Your emotional state could cloud your decision-making abilities.

Theme: Financial clean-up

Date: Sunday, _____

🕐 **Estimated time to complete the exercise: 5 hours**

Remember to go through the daily checklist

Tick when done

Read through the thought for the day:

Today is about handling your finances. Just think how amazing it will feel tonight when you review the progress you've made with sorting out all your finances.

Whether you are going through a divorce right now or some time ago, read through this entire section.

Complete your daily homework – start this in the morning.

Dealing with your finances

"I find that when both partners feel they are fairly treated, they will have a good relationship in the future," says Sally Coullahan, a certified divorce financial analyst in London.

Even if you are good at managing your finances, it's important to ensure that nothing financial will trip you up during your 21 Day Programme. Take today to resolve anything which might come up in the next month and take a moment to ensure you make some good financial decisions. Even if you don't resolve everything, at least have a clear list of what there is to do.

"Financial issues carry over into parenting, so if the wife made bad decisions in the divorce and didn't get enough financially, it affects the kids, too."

Video: I have done several interviews on the topic of handling your finances during and after divorce. Watch these here: **www.youtube.com/nakedrecovery**

Here are some considerations for handling your finances during and after a divorce:

➡ Look through all your bank accounts and bills. Make notes on what has to be handled each month

➡ Avoid living off your credit card or getting into debt

➡ Draw up a budget, working out what you can spend and how much money you have coming in. Work out an action plan to correct anything you wish to correct

➡ Consider making an appointment with an accountant, financial advisor or trusted family friend to advise you on your financial situation

➡ Start a savings account and work out a savings plan (even if it's a few extra pounds or dollars per month)

➡ If you need help with bills, ask friends or family for short-term loans rather than to get into consumer debt

➡ Be proactive and communicate with all your creditors

➡ Write down a list of things to discuss with your ex and agree on a time to talk. You'll need to think about the house, car, children, debts, finances, any pets and your shared possessions

➡ Get advice on your mortgage if you have one. Be absolutely clear on any additional charges on the property or any attached investments you need to arrange

➡ Contact your local council or state to enquire about any benefits or social assistance you qualify for

➡ While arranging your divorce, consider drawing up all the correct documentation to resolve your matrimonial finances

➡ Notify your bank of changes. If you have a joint account, can you withdraw your share of the money and cancel the account? If your ex also has access to other accounts you may need to change their access

➡ Get a copy of your credit report. Check your local credit agency in your country so you can see if there are any debts in your name

Credit Guru (http://www.creditguru.com), Experian (www.experian.co.uk), Equifax (www.equifax.co.uk) and Transunion USA (http://www.transunion.com/) are good places to start

➡ If you feel daunted by finances, take a class on accounting or basic bookkeeping at your local college. Be proactive and draw up a filing system for your bills

➡ If you are based in the United Kingdom, visit: www.moneysaving-expert.com which is a great resource for how to save money on all your bills, credit cards and insurances

➡ Schedule time to draw up your last will and testament

➡ Pension. Meet with a financial advisor to discuss your pension plan

Exercise:

1. From the reading above, spend today making a list of all the things you need to do to clean up your finances over the next six months.

2. Whether it's some filing, sorting, or budgeting, plan to do a chunk of this work today.

3. Create a schedule to complete the rest of the work over the coming weeks and months. The goal for the end of the day is to feel physically exhausted, as well as feel clearer in your mind (because things are noted down) and more on top things.

*TIP FOR THE DAY: If you're tempted to contact your ex, don't. It is better that you put some distance between yourself and the situation. If you feel a burning need to call for answers about how this all happened, etc. note that you're probably in the panic/negotiation stage of the **Naked Divorce** grieving cycle and still have a lot of dopamine kicking around in your system. Stay off the caffeine, alcohol and stimulants, eat lots of green, leafy vegetables and stick to your supplements. The panicky feeling will pass.*

Theme: Get grounded inside the Divorce Cocoon

Date: Monday, _____

🕑 **Estimated time to complete the exercise: 60 minutes**

Remember to go through the daily checklist

Tick when done

Read through the thought for the day:

It may seem extremely basic but establishing a solid foundation is critical to ensuring the success of the programme and ensuring you have a *Divorce Cocoon* in place so when you start with Metamorphosis, then you are ready to handle whatever comes your way.

Work through each of **The 7 Foundations of Transformation** and ensure that each element is in place and you are clear on how to work with each foundation.

Confirm that you have gone through all the introduction sections of this book.

In particular:

1 ETHICS – Spend some time today ensuring that the ETHICS of the programme are intact and that you score at least a five on each item in the table on the next page. Then make a list of some actions you can take tomorrow to move this ethic up to a level 10 in your life. Then schedule those actions in your diary and get them done!

#	ETHICS	Rate yourself on a scale of 1 - 10	Actions I will take to move this ETHIC to a level 10 in my life
1	Being self-expressed		
2	Avoid STEATs		
3	Establish a Grounded Routine		
4	Sleep on any drastic changes		
5	Say no		
6	Cause vs. effect		
7	Focus on yourself vs. your ex		

Work through each of **The 7 Foundations of Transformation** and ensure that each element is in place and you are clear on how to work with each foundation.

Examine each foundation and check the following. If anything is missing, put it in place:

2 NOURISHMENT - are you in a routine of taking your healing supplements? Have you changed your diet to ensure you are eating healthier (an increase in green and red foods)? Have you decreased your intake of sugar and stimulants?

3 WORKING WITH YOUR EMOTIONS - are you clear on how to release your emotions in a healthy and ethical way?

4 PERFORMING AT WORK - have you had key conversations with your boss and/or staff at work? Do you feel able to work and process your emotions at another time? Have you practiced the exercise for handling your emotions whilst you are at work?

5 COMMITMENT - can you categorically say that you commit to completing the programme and that you will do whatever it takes to complete it?

6 THE RIGHT SUPPORT - have you been having check-in sessions with your *Divorce Angel* and do you feel you have the support you need to complete the 21 Day Programme?

7 A GAME PLAN THAT WORKS - have you purchased everything required, handled everything there is to handle and scheduled in the time you need to complete the 21 Day Programme?

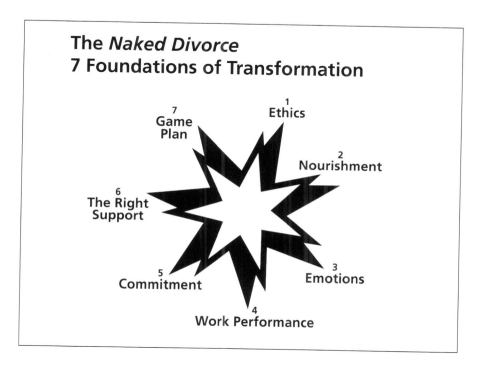

Test

Call your *Divorce Angel* and discuss the work you have done in the past four days.

ONLY IF your *Divorce Angel* agrees that you are ready to move into *Metamorphosis*, will you be ready to move into Metamorphosis.

Ensure YOU feel ready to move too!

Metamorphosis

Metamorphosis begins once the *Divorce Cocoon* is in place. This phase lasts for 10 days.

TIP FOR THE DAY: Whilst working on your relationship story if you notice that you've been living in a dream world, be calm. This is very common during a trauma. Keep in mind that living in a romantic dream world is you wanting to avoid reality around you. Inhabiting that day dreaming world is problematic. It keeps you stuck in a childlike way of being. Facing reality is what transforms boys into men.

Theme: Your relationship story

Date: Tuesday, _____

🕐 **Estimated time to complete the exercise: 90-120 minutes**

Remember to go through the daily checklist

Tick when done

Read through the thought for the day:

Today is all about your relationship story. Writing a chronicle of your love life and marriage is very important to your healing. Tomorrow, you'll read the story to your *Divorce Angel*, so schedule time with him/ her for Wednesday.

My story:

In my relationship story I noticed that I was like a princess living with my prince in our castle. Life was perfect. I was one half of the perfect couple and life was a dream. The story went on and on for pages and pages about how we were destined to be together and how we were cruelly ripped apart by my friends who slept with him. It was only when I read the story back to myself the third time that I realised that in reality, things were not so good between us. I told myself and the outside world that we were the perfect couple. I felt an inner drive to maintain the illusion because I couldn't handle the thought of failure in my life. My romantic needs weren't being met within my relationship so I became addicted to romantic movies. I spent hours daydreaming about Prince Charming and how he would rescue me from my marriage. I cried hopelessly during movies that showed love-torn, passionate couples. It was only when I read the relationship story I had written back to myself that I noticed that I didn't pay attention to these obvious signs that my marriage was in trouble. I was living in my fantasy world of dinner parties, playing house and being the perfect wife. The break-up of my marriage was accompanied by complete denial and shock within me as I refused to acknowledge that we had split up. It was only when I committed my story to paper that I realised how my life with him had been unreal and that things were broken almost from the very beginning.

Your relationship story is the key to unlocking how your relationship began but also how your relationship got to this point of divorce. Strive to be brutally honest with yourself.

Read through the exercise you'll be doing later today. Allow yourself to think about it during the day.

Exercise:

Write down your entire relationship story. Write down the whole thing: how you met, all the romance, events, drama, and hurt. Ensure you distinguish the exact moment you 'died' a little in your self-expression or happiness. Those moments are key to working out where things started going wrong. Make sure it's as long as possible and write it like you would a best seller. Don't skip any key details.

- When done, read it to yourself five times. Make sure you re-read it until you know it intimately.

- Make a note in your journal of what happens each time you read your story. How does it feel?

- Remember to schedule time with your **Divorce Angel** tomorrow to read them the story.

day

06

METAMORPHOSIS

*TIP FOR THE DAY: You are making great progress. Now, notice any **Short Term Emotional Avoidance Tactics** that may be creeping in to sabotage you. Anything you're considering doing that could side track your healing will only slow down your progress. Because your mind is afraid of change, it will plot to take you out of the game. Remain vigilant and guard against STEATs.*

Theme: Lessons from your relationship story

Date: Wednesday, _____

(L) **Estimated time to complete the exercise: 90 minutes**

Remember to go through the daily checklist

Tick when done

Read through the thought for the day:

☐

Today is all about reading your story to your *Divorce Angel*, looking for the signs that pointed to your divorce. Focus on what you can be responsible for.

Responsibility is not about assigning blame, it's about looking at what you contributed to the break-up, what you learnt from it, and what learnings you can take into your next relationship. Today is about learning for the future.

Read through the exercise you'll be doing later today. Allow yourself to think about it during the day.

Your exercse is to read your story to your Divorce Angel. Discover the patterns and look at what you can be responsible for.

day
07
METAMORPHOSIS

TIP FOR THE DAY: We all have a little critic in our heads telling us bad and unhelpful things about ourselves. Whenever this critic has anything to say about how you should or shouldn't be handling your divorce, I would like you to practice saying this, "Critic, thank you for sharing. Now SIT DOWN AND BE QUIET."

Theme: Considering your relationship from different points of view

Date: Thursday, _____

🕐 **Estimated time to complete the exercise: 60-90 minutes**

Remember to go through the daily checklist

Tick when done

Read through the thought for the day:

It's very common during your relationship to become stuck in rigid thoughts about your ex or about your relationship. It's also normal to make glib generalisations about the relationship, for example, "My ex never loved me and I was never good enough" or, "We were happy for years and then suddenly everything fell apart."

When we make sweeping generalisations, we can get stuck and unable to move forward. We can also become very angry if anyone challenges the validity of those fixed thoughts and emotions we hold so close.

I'm particularly talking to those who have been holding a grudge against their ex (or their new partner) for some time. If a little voice in your head is vehemently denying this, you probably don't even realise you're holding a grudge.

If you do have a grudge and are feeling very angry or upset about the end of your relationship, it's okay. It's normal to be upset.

But to heal, it helps to take a step back, test your assumptions and to be open to considering different points of view. Was your ex really that bad? I know it might seem tough but try to stop imagining your ex as this evil person that deserves only the worst in the world. Changing perceptions can be difficult. It takes great humility and courage to fight through your resistance.

When you hold a grudge you see only one side of the coin, and that's the message you deliver to your brain. That becomes your reality. If you change your frame of reference by looking at the same situation from a different point of view, you can change the way you respond to situations in life. You can change your representation or perception about anything. In the same way, you can change your states and behaviours.

We tend to see a situation in one frame. A frame can refer to a belief, which might limit our view of the world. If we let this limiting belief go, new ideas, interpretations and possibilities can develop.

Being open to healing

Be open to the possibility of forgiving your ex and all those involved. This doesn't mean you have to do it. Just begin to be open to the fact that someday soon, you will forgive your ex. Forgiving does not condone what they did or even what happened; it simply releases YOU from the pain of their actions. It's a way of untying yourself from those negative perceptions so you have negativity draining your energy every single day.

Consider making a place for the event in your life within your head and then put this experience in this place filed away. It's important to remember that whatever happened in your past did happen and it did affect you. At the same time, its place is in the past, much like a chapter in a book you have read and choose not to read again.

Read through the exercise you'll be doing later today. Allow yourself to think about it during the day.

PART I of Rebalancing your view of your ex

In the space below, describe a central problem you've experienced in your divorce with regards to your ex and then complete the table below.

Example: I am angry at my ex for parading her new partner around in front of me.

1. Reframing the context of your ex's behaviour

#	Write down ten things that describe how this problem is a stumbling block to you (here are five):	What is another context for this behaviour where the meaning may be different?
1	I feel embarrassed and want to hide away.	Her moving on so quickly shows how much she hates to be alone. I am a stronger person emotionally than she is and willing to heal vulnerably and authentically.
2	I feel our children will get upset because it's too soon to introduce her new boyfriend.	I have shielded and protected our children all their lives. Maybe it is a good thing that they fend for themselves now.
3	I feel lonely and alone.	This is probably a good opportunity to get out there and start playing tennis again. I have actually been feeling lonely for a decade.
4	I cannot believe he is only twenty-two! I feel so embarrassed that I am being replaced by someone so young.	Her dating a 26-year-old guy demonstrates my feeling that we were never really on the same wavelength. Maybe it is time to find a more mature woman who will appreciate all my qualities.
5	I will never find anyone again.	Ok, ok, I know this is slightly dramatic. Someone at work already asked me out for a drink. My friend literally just met someone new so if it's possible for him, it's possible for me!

Now, it's your turn!

In the space below, describe a central problem you're experiencing in your divorce with regards to your ex:

....

....

....

....

....

#	Write down ten things that describe how this problem is a stumbling block to you:	What is another context for this behaviour where the meaning will be different?
1		
2		
3		
4		
5		
6		
7		
8		
9		
10		

2. Think about your divorce from different angles

- What are the generalisations you've made about your ex?

- Why is your point of view so biased?

- Now imagine a famous person you really respect watches a movie of your life. Watch the movie through their eyes. What point of view might this famous person have about your situation?

- Now imagine an alien lands on our planet and they watch a movie of your life. Watch the movie through their eyes. What point of view might this alien have about your situation?

- Notice the differences between what generalisation you made vs. what the famous person and the alien noticed. What are they?

3. The critic in our heads

We all have a little critic in our heads BUT it is key to challenge the validity of what your little voice tells you. This exercise will help you to find other meanings in what is happening in your life which can be more empowering than the dis-empowering meanings you may have in place today.

The little critic in your head is not you.

You are the one who notices the little critic.

The little critic is just your worst thoughts, worst meanings and worst night-mares voicing their negative commentary. To help me with my little critic in my head, I gave it a name.

My little critic's name is Jane. Whenever I hear it say, "Adèle, you are ugly, you are unattractive and you are going to wind up alone" I just say, "thanks Jane, but your opinion is not valid, so shut it."

Sometimes I have amusing moments where I notice Jane rattling on about something, but since separating my 'Jane' from the real me, my ability to control the negative chatter in my head has improved.

Give a name to the critic which operates in your head. Whenever the critic has something to say in the next 5 days, practice telling it to be quiet...

day
08
METAMORPHOSIS

TIP FOR THE DAY: "Whatever you do, you do to yourself. To judge others only compounds your own faults."
~ Buddha

"A pedestal is as much a prison as any small, confined space."
~ Gloria Steinem

Theme: Perception is projection, and Pedestal Shift

Date: Friday, _____

🕐 **Estimated time to complete the exercise: 120 minutes**

Remember to go through the daily checklist

Tick when done

Read through the thought for the day:

It is dangerous to put anyone on a pedestal, but it is equally damaging to hate or loathe them.

All people possess both positive and negative traits, even your ex. It's normal if you are feeling very strong negative emotions about your ex. You may be feeling like they are the most hated person in your life or perhaps you are completely indifferent.

In contrast, it's also completely normal to be pining for your ex and experiencing very strong, positive feelings, almost as if you have placed your ex on a pedestal and are struggling to get over the relationship.

Today's exercise is about rebalancing any highs and lows you're experiencing in this regard. Returning to a neutral space where you can see that both the positive and negative traits are critical to your healing. There are two parts to this exercise: one part is if you are feeling strong negative emotions and the other is if you are feeling strong positive emotions. Pay attention to which part of this exercise you will be doing.

Undertake this exercise, even if you feel you feel just 'fine'. It's natural to want to avoid confronting these issues BUT I can assure you, you will feel emotions one way or the other. Keep focused on the end game and keep moving forward.

Read through the exercise you will be doing later today. Allow yourself to think about it during the day.

PART II of rebalancing your view of your ex

If you are feeling very strong negative emotions about your ex, balance out those strong emotions by doing the Perception is Projection exercise.

1. Perception is Projection

Perception is Projection is a concept developed by Richard Bandler (the founder of Neuro-linguistic programming). In everyday life there are millions of bits of information per second that our unconscious minds are aware of-- but our conscious minds can only process 134 bits of this data at any one time.

How we choose what information to delete and which to 'see' comes from our beliefs and perceptions about life. Essentially, you cannot see anything outside of what you can perceive, unless it exists within you.

Your ability to see and acknowledge a character trait in another is only possible because on some level: **you possess this character trait within yourself.**

Have there been times in your life when you reacted very strongly when you met someone and thought, "they are so bitter" or, "they are so superior".

In order to actually SEE or recognise bitterness, superiority or any other character trait, you must possess or have experienced these traits to some extent within yourself. Either way, I want you to acknowledge that it is unjust to label people according to your own perception, and work to expand past using snap judgements to label others.

Complete this exercise on the next page...

Think of a situation in which your ex is pressing your buttons	Describe their behaviour	Do you ever do the same thing? Be honest.	How would you prefer them to behave in that moment?	How can you behave better when you display the same behaviour?
Example... She spends hours on her laptop.	Engrossed in her laptop and totally oblivious to me.	Sometimes I can become engrossed and not want to be interrupted. I get that.	Turn around when I talk to her and listen intently to what I have to say.	I can listen more to others. I notice that I tend to think more about what I will say vs. truly listening to others when they speak.

To keep yourself from falling into toxic situations and relationships in the future, it is important to work on being self-aware of the situations, behaviours and character traits that set you off. For example, if one of your pet peeves is spending money on new fads or fashions, it might be best to avoid women in the future who love shopping and having a closet of the latest designs. At the same time, you need to work on this pet peeve so that when you encounter a situation where you would normally be set off, you know how to react appropriately, understand where the other person is coming from, and explain your frustrations without blowing up or losing patience.

It's important to remember that when you are emotionally tied to someone – whether it is out of love or hate – you're giving them rent-free space in your head, and spending your energy and emotions on them. By taking charge and addressing your own projections, you take control of the situation and can choose how much emotional space that person takes up in your life.

2. Pedestal Shift

If you are feeling very strong positive emotions about your ex (you've allowed your ex to stay on their pedestal), balance out those strong emotions by doing this exercise.

If you are struggling to get over your ex, it may be because you have banished all negative thoughts about the relationship, what your ex was really like, and can only remember and see positive aspects of their personality– whether those aspects were truly positive or not.

If that is the case, it's time for a little reality check because if your relationship was so wonderful, you would still be in it. There HAD to be things that did not work about the relationship and about your ex that it's time to be honest about. It is time that you move your ex off the pedestal!!

  Note: if you struggle to do this exercise alone, contact your **Divorce Angel** and request to do the exercise together.

Answer these questions:

- Was I truly happy in my relationship? And if so, why? Was the happiness real or was it simply what I told myself was real?
- Did I feel like the BEST version of myself when I was with my ex?
- Was my ex definitely feeling like the BEST version of herself with me?
- What about my ex was irritating that I have glanced over?
- Describe 10 events in detail that hurt me in the relationship
- What characteristics came out which were undesirable traits that I am willing to acknowledge (close your eyes and replay each of those events in your mind. Turn up the brightness of each event in your mind's eye as you replay them)

After replaying each event, journal how you feel about your ex now?

For the rest of day, question if you were in reality about your relationship and whether your ex truly deserves to be put on a pedestal.

day
09
METAMORPHOSIS

TIP FOR THE DAY: According to countless research studies mentioned within the Bibliography of this book, a leading cause of depression is often the suppression of emotions over a long period.

Let go, surrender to all your emotions and feel them fully. When you do actually feel your emotions fully, none of them last more than 30 minutes. It's the resistance to feeling emotions that often leads to depression.

Theme: Releasing strong emotions

Date: Saturday, _____

🕑 **Estimated time to complete the exercise: 6 hours BUT take the whole day**

Remember to go through the daily checklist

Tick when done

Read through the thought for the day:

Today is about exorcising your negative angry or sad emotions and fully expressing any major emotions that are locked within you. Even if you think you have healed or can consciously rationalise why your marriage ended, the thoughts in your subconscious mind are the ones that actually decide your future. Relationship baggage, insecurities, doubts, jealousy and all dis-empowering thoughts arise unconsciously within your subconscious mind. Your subconscious mind is ruled by your emotions. To truly heal on an unconscious level, you need to pay attention to what your emotions are telling you. Emotions are there as warning signs that something is not quite right. Most of us ignore our emotions or rationalise them away. This is the time to feel them fully.

Day 9 was the most important day in my healing. Here's why…

My story:

> This was the day I truly let go. I was sitting on the edge of my bed and the rage began building up like a volcano about to erupt. I felt it trapped in my stomach. I wanted to scream.

> My body started shaking. I was so mad with anger that I stood up with one clear thought, "I am going to wreak havoc on our house." I looked around my bedroom. First, I grabbed the picture frame with our wedding picture in it and smashed that on the floor. Next was the vase he'd bought

me for our anniversary. As I worked my way from the bedroom into the kitchen, I broke anything and everything I could get my hands on. I was like a hurricane but with each item I destroyed, my anger subsided. I broke nearly everything I could find in the kitchen, thinking that I'd want to buy new crockery anyway. After an hour of mayhem, I was standing in the kitchen, surrounded by broken glass and crockery and felt totally alive. I wanted to destroy more. Releasing this anger, rage and fury was a new experience.

I opened the freezer and took out a bag of ice. I went in search of my baseball bat. I couldn't find it. I grabbed my squash racket, put a photograph of our wedding day on the ice and then beat it, screaming until the ice had shattered. Exhausted, I collapsed on the floor and cried. My anger transformed into a sadness I had never known before. I surrendered to despair completely until I felt it would swallow me. It was unbearable, but I stuck with it, knowing that in time it would pass. The sense of failure was overwhelming and I cried out, "How could I have been so foolish?", "Why did I marry him?", "How could he do this?" At the core of everything was my absolute terror of being alone, unloved and unwanted. I knew that this was the final emotion I had to exorcise. I was so afraid. I hugged my legs, sobbing like a little girl.

The emotion changed again and moved into grief. I spent 20 minutes crying and lying on the floor. The grief soon changed into despair, followed by panic and then shaking fear. The pain of each layer was almost unbearable but I kept drawing it towards me and felt every layer of it. All the way through, I kept my heart open. I did not shut down. I felt every part of it knowing that my emotions would not kill me – they simply needed to be expressed. After six hours or so, I felt nothing. There were no strong emotions left. There were no more tears to cry. I was spent. There was this eerie space all around me. I sat in silence in a pool of shattered glass, ice and debris.

I walked to the lounge door and opened it. It felt like everything was moving in slow motion. I stood outside and took in a deep breath of fresh air. I sat on the grass outside and noticed birds, noticed the wind caressing the shrubs in my garden. I watched ants making their way along the grass. I sat like this for what must have been a few hours. No thoughts went through my mind, I was simply present to nothing except nature around me. After a few hours, my first thought was that I was thirsty. I walked through the garden and tiptoed through the glass on the floor of the house to a cupboard in my kitchen. I managed to locate one lone mug that had not been destroyed and made myself a fruit smoothie with whatever I could find of the crushed ice in the bag I had decimated. I even found a little tropical umbrella in the drawer left over from a party years ago and stuck it into a piece of pineapple on the side of the mug. As I made the fruit smoothie, each piece of fruit I sliced was cut in slow motion. I was astounded at how present I felt. When done, I carried my mug with me and slowly walked over to the sofa in the lounge. As I sat there I was present to silence. Emptiness. There was no more anger, no more sadness, no more despair, and no more depression - just nothing.

I felt like I was standing at the beginning of something. Almost like I was standing in an empty white room ready to be created. It was a life transforming moment and life has never been the same since then.

Over those hours I'd not only destroyed everything breakable in my home, I'd killed the old married-Adèle. Like a phoenix rising from the ashes, a new Adèle emerged from the broken glass. The emotions I had unleashed every day in the preceding nine days culminated in today's final outburst of emotion. It felt like a purifying hurricane. Previously hidden from me, a new door opened. Letting out those emotions on the ninth day was the key.

Sure, that evening there was some mess to clean up. I do remember wondering what the hell had I done to my house, but it was an amazing moment of clarity and peace. I encourage you to let out your strong emotions today. Sitting with your anger, resentments, sadness and not expressing it can eventually lead to resistance, resignation and depression. Holding on to those emotions will eventually kill all aliveness in your life because your ability to allow your anger to be expressed is linked to your ability to be vulnerable and connected with others. This is the day you must walk this path alone. If you surrender to all your emotions, experiencing them fully, you'll find that inside the core of your anger is sadness, despair and regret and inside the sadness is fear. Fear is at the core of many negative emotions. Be comforted by the fact that few emotions last longer than 30 minutes when fully experienced and embraced.

WARNING:

I don't advocate releasing emotions 'at' anyone. This is called ranting and is not a responsible action. Be responsible for the timing in terms of releasing your emotions.

Complete your daily homework – start this in the morning.

Exercise:

Release your strong emotions like anger/upset and despair

This exercise is designed as a catalyst to help you trigger your emotions into action. Even if you are not feeling angry, you can tap into your anger with this exercise. It is healthy to feel your anger. There is no judgment and this exercise is not about being enlightened or positive, just be angry.

You need:

1 baseball bat/squash racket/cricket bat or sturdy stick or axe if you are chopping wood. 5-10 large bags of ice or bags of wood, and WEAR gloves and goggles! (This exercise is about unleashing your anger responsibly, not about injuring yourself in the process).

A large, open space that is easy to clean afterwards and where you can smash the ice and not be heard or disturbed. Wear loose clothing and shoes.

Make cards for all the things that make you angry in your life.

Steps:

- Clench your fists and teeth and breathe angrily to get into the mood
- Lay out the bag of ice or wood on the ground and look at it. Lay the cards, photographs or symbols of your anger on the bag of ice.
- Think about all the things you're angry or upset about, everything that should have happened in your marriage, in your life, in your divorce. Allow yourself to embrace these emotions and then allow yourself to feel them, express them through shouting or swearing or screaming.
- There is no need to think, just feel and express.
- When you're ready, beat the living daylights out of the ice or wood
- Roar, yell, scream. Don't stop until it has been destroyed.
- Feel and release any other emotions that arise. Allow them to be. They will not last for more than 30 minutes to a few hours if you surrender to them (then they are done).
- You will know you are done feeling your emotions when you can feel no more and are simply present to nothingness and the feeling of 'space'.

When done:

- Ensure you drink water or juice. Releasing emotions is thirsty work!
- Clean up any mess.
- Rest. You'll probably feel very tired.

SPECIAL NOTE: If you did not complete Day 9's exercise, then delay progressing with Day 10 of the Naked Divorce until you have completed the exercise from Day 9.

day
10
METAMORPHOSIS

TIP FOR THE DAY: There is a temptation to think that the reason your relationship failed was because of your ex and who they were. Be careful of falling into this trap. The common person in all of your relationships is you.

If you have the courage to find out where you can be responsible for your relationships not working out, then you have the power.

Theme: Completing your past relationships

Date: Sunday, _____

🕐 **Estimated time to complete the exercise: 5 hours**

Remember to go through the daily checklist

Tick when done

Do the reading and exercise for the day in one go:

☐

The first step is to complete Day 9 and think of everything you learnt from your past relationship. Your emotions now released, you'll be left with some things you have learnt from your past relationship.

Completing Day 9

- Underneath your anger are needs you had within your marriage or relationship that you never communicated. What did you need in your marriage that you never received? Write down those needs.

- List the things you have learnt from the relationship and that you will never repeat or do again

- Keep going until you have a list of fifty things you have learnt

Completing your past relationships

When done working on everything you learnt from your marriage, it's important to look into the source or reason your relationship ended. HOWEVER, the key is to look at this from the perspective of what you can be responsible for.

In this exercise, it's important to view your marriage in the context of all your relationships in the past, as this helps you remain impartial. It may be tempting to say, "Yes, but what about my ex taking responsibility?" Unfortunately this kind of thinking will not help you. Your ex is on their own healing path. The common thread in all your relationships is you, so look within yourself for the things you know contributed to your relationship not working out.

Why? Because if you can be responsible for the source of your part in the marital breakdown, you are in control of changing this pattern in the future. You are not in control of your ex's thinking or their relationship patterns. What goes around comes around, so focus only on yourself and your own happiness. Your ex will have to deal with their own emotions and lessons in their own time.

My story:

It would have been easy to blame Bruce for the failure of our relationship. He did have so many affairs that it would clearly appear to an external observer that the failure of our relationship was his fault. This thinking was enjoyable for a while but it made me feel powerless.

When I did this exercise, I realised that I was responsible for marrying him knowing we didn't have real chemistry together. Even though I was crazy about him, I knew he wasn't crazy about me and I ignored my own intuition which said that he was lying to me about his affairs. I discovered that I was responsible for emasculating him on many occasions because I earned more money than he did and it annoyed me so I unconsciously rubbed it in his face. I was responsible for putting up with an unworkable situation in my marriage. My lack of standing up for myself and what I deserved in a relationship contributed to the relationship carrying on much longer than it should have.

My need to be claimed and walk up the aisle superseded my feelings that something was not quite right. I did that. I was responsible. Taking responsibility not only set me free, it gave me back my power.

When I did the exercise for Day 10, I realised that my pattern with my ex was not an isolated event. My previous relationships ended in a similar way. I had a pattern of attracting men who would leave me emotionally and then I would either dump them or have them cheat on me. I unconsciously sought out men who would leave.

Harville Hendrix, author of 'Getting the Love You Want' believes that we all have a **core issue** (for want of a more accurate term) that emerged in our lives as a result of growing up.

If you look back at all your previous relationships, you'll probably notice a pattern. Often the relationships end in the same way or for similar reasons. Once you see your pattern in relationships, you'll see those patterns everywhere in your life. Your patterns are driven by your core issue. The good news is that this pattern is your mind's unconscious desire to help bring your core issue to the surface of your awareness, so that you can heal it once and for all and create the life you want. The problem is that most of us have no idea what our core issue is and how to resolve it.

Below is an example pattern discovered by one of my clients in reading back the stories of his past romantic relationships:

1.   *Most of my relationships have ended with my partner leaving me*

2.   *Most of my relationships have ended because I became attached to the relationship not ending. I didn't want to feel abandoned, so the minute I felt like my partner was withdrawing from me, I would take my focus off my own life and put it on saving the relationship. Often, the relationship didn't actually need saving because nothing was wrong, I'd just interpreted it that way (e.g. when my partner would withhold communication or go quiet or show an interest in other men, I'd perceive that they were going to leave, so I'd go straight into, "save the relationship" mode). This change of focus would make my partner feel that something was wrong, and instead of communicating my fear to her, I'd become needy and go into pleasing her to try to make her stay. Neediness is never attractive and it repels people and so I would unconsciously drive my partner away and eventually my partner would leave...*

3.   *Whenever this pattern has played out in my life, I have ALWAYS (as in every time) felt abandoned (my core issue and biggest fear)*

4.   *I seem to always attract people who abandon me and who are not actually suited to me*

What my client acknowledged after completing this exercise was that he was unconsciously attracting people who would abandon him because of his core belief that all women would eventually abandon him.

He could therefore ONLY attract what he could perceive which, were women who would abandon him.

What he later realised and proved was that if he widened his perception to include people who would love and cherish him, he would be able to see them when they came along.

Name of the person?	How did you meet them?	How long you were together?	How it ended?	Who ended it?	What do you believe ended it?	What did you decide about yourself at the end of this relationship?

Discover your own unconscious patterns in relationships and your core issue

The important part in discovering your core issue is to identify what you feel whenever you play out your pattern. Your feelings will point in the direction of your core issue. Take a moment now and do this exercise:

1. Write a brief story of all your past relationships using the table below. Make a note of everyone you can remember. Write down what happened to end the relationship and the feelings you felt when it ended. (be more honest with yourself than you've ever been before)

2. Now, read all your stories back and if you haven't already, find the common threads in what you wrote. Perhaps you have abandonment issues, perhaps you consistently attract cheaters or emotionally cold women. Perhaps it always ends with an argument. Maybe you can't commit because you feel like committing is a sure path to feeling hurt if your partner leaves. Maybe you don't speak up because you don't like conflict

3. Look over what you wrote in the previous step and identify the common feelings you felt in most of your relationships. Usually these feelings surface as fears, particularly when you perceive that you are somehow under threat. These fears will point you to your issue that you keep on inviting into your life

   My pattern in relationships is that I always go back to doing ....(describe your repeating pattern keeping in mind that how you do ANYTHING is how you do EVERYTHING). The reason I do this is ....

When complete, journal what you noticed...

Can you find any patterns within your past relationships?

If so, list all the patterns you have found.

Keeping those patterns in mind, what choices do you now make for your future?

Drink at least six glasses of water during the day.

day 11

METAMORPHOSIS

KEEP THIS IN MIND FOR THE DAY: To get complete emotional release from your marriage, you might need to hear your ex say sorry. Realistically, very few of us will ever get the 'sorry' we need to help us heal.

The exercise is all about how you can be in the driver's seat when it comes to hearing the perfect apology.

Theme: Hear the 'sorry' you have always wanted to hear

Date: Monday, _____

🕐 **Estimated time to complete the exercise: 90 minutes**

Remember to go through the daily checklist

Tick when done

Read through the thought for the day:

My story:

I got to a point in my healing, where I needed to hear Bruce say sorry. Unfortunately at that point I knew I would not hear it from him in the way I needed to hear it. Consequently, I designed this exercise with the help of my friend Olwen and her experience in resolving a past relationship.

Try it. It really works!

It began with writing a letter from Bruce to me, titled: **What I really always wanted to hear from my ex to move on.** I didn't hold back and wrote the most elaborate apology letter I could create. In the letter, I literally had him apologise for everything I ever wanted him to apologise for. In short, it was a fantastic process. I designed this exercise to be dramatic and over the top. The idea is not to be responsible or enlightened in this letter. Just let go, be self-indulgent. Have fun with it. Before you write yours, here is an excerpt from a client to inspire you:

My dearest lost love Trevor (the most perfect guy on the planet ever.)

You are sexy, gorgeous and I completely desired you and if I ever said otherwise I was lying to you and to myself. I married you because I loved you completely and you were my soul mate. And whatever happens in the future, that was really why I married you and whatever I did or said later, that was the truth. For some reason I was a complete idiot and I cheated on you. I cheated on the guy I loved the most in the world. I am so sorry for taking you for granted. I never appreciated you as I should have. I will never ever find someone like you again and I have ruined my life.

I never wanted to hurt you. You are the closest, dearest person in my life and what saddens me is that I will probably never have anyone again who will get as close as you did.

Etc. (I went on for 22 pages. It was great fun.)

. . . .

I hope you forgive me.

Love

Anne

Spend today thinking about your letter. If you want to start writing it during your lunch break, do so but you'll have the opportunity to write it later on.

Read through the exercise you will be doing later today. Allow your-self to think about it during the day.

Exercise:

Write a letter from your ex to you.
In the letter, write:

1. Everything you ever wanted your ex to apologise for: ([Your name], I am so sorry I ever did xxxx or made you feel xxxx, or didn't love you like you deserved to be loved...) Make sure it is a long letter and do not leave anything out.

2. When done, read the letter out loud to yourself.

3. Journal how you feel.

4. When you are done, rewrite each point of the letter in your own words to yourself. (For example, I forgive myself for being with someone who I knew didn't love me in the way I deserved to be loved, xxxx.)

5. When done, read the letter out loud to yourself.

6. Journal how you feel.

KEEP THIS IN MIND FOR THE DAY: "I never regretted the relationships I had, they always made me better for the next one..." ~ David Beckham

Spend today thinking about what you learnt from your old relationship and how it has made you more aware and better prepared for your next one.

Theme: Framework for my future relationships

Date : Tuesday, _____

🕑 **Estimated time to complete the exercise: 90 minutes**

Remember to go through the daily checklist

Tick when done

Read through the thought for the day:

Now that you have written the letter from your ex to yourself, the next step is to forgive yourself for anything that you feel you did which contributed to the break-up as well as acknowledging your successes.

My Story

My divorce left me with a huge sense of failure. I had planned to spend the rest of my life with Bruce, so the relationship ending felt like an insult to myself and what I was meant to accomplish on every level. I worried about what other people thought about me and wanted to hide.

Today's exercise is about starting the process of getting those feelings of failure complete, so you can have a more balanced view of the relationship.

Read through the exercise you'll be doing later today. Allow yourself to think about it during the day.

Exercise:

Go through the letter you wrote from your ex to yourself.

1. Read the letter from your-ex-to-yourself out loud.
2. Read the letter from yourself-to-yourself out loud.
3. Write down what you are acknowledging yourself for in the relationship (in present tense; this is very important).
4. Write down what you are unwilling to tolerate in a relationship. Journal how you feel about it and write down what you notice.
5. What character traits does your ideal partner have?
6. What kind of due diligence will you do next time around?
7. Optional: When done, burn the letters.

Here is an example of what to write:

What I acknowledge myself for is...

- *I am supportive and caring*
- *I am a rock for the woman in my life*
- *I am courageous, adventurous and crazy*
- *I am responsible and aware*
- *I am sexy and fun to be with*

What I am unwilling to tolerate in a relationship is:

- *Cheating*
- *Stealing*
- *Lying or wimpish behaviour*
- *Hypocrisy*
- *Endlessly sitting with her phone texting people or taking drugs*
- *Uncommitted behaviour*
- *Unwillingness to grow or look at growing or developing*

day

13

METAMORPHOSIS

KEEP THIS IN MIND FOR THE DAY: There is a temptation to become obsessed with how your ex is doing, replaying the tape in your head of what was said and what it could have meant, and what should or shouldn't have happened in the relationship.

Instead of focusing on those thoughts, become fascinated with learning everything you can about the background dynamics of your relationship and the lessons you have learnt. Become keenly aware of yourself as a science project, where you use this event as a catalyst or experiment to learn everything you can about yourself and how you operate in a relationship. Learn those lessons now, so that you can put these to work successfully in your next relationship.

Theme: Learning from past patterns in your relationship

Date : Wednesday, _____

🕐 **Estimated time to complete the exercise: 90 minutes**

Remember to go through the daily checklist

Tick when done

Read through the thought for the day:

Today is all about learning some of the patterns that we commonly experience in a relationship. There are three in particular that I will cover today and they're truly fascinating. Put on your 'science experiment hat' and let's see whether you identify with any of these patterns in your old relationship!

Antony Robbin's five R's of romantic relationship communication

Far from running from the idea of relationships during my divorce, I found myself fascinated by the dynamics of successful relationships. I wanted to learn everything I could about relationships and what makes them successful. This model from world-renowned life coach and self-help author Antony Robbins made an enormous difference to my life. Essentially, he moves through the cycles of how we communicate with each other in a romantic relationship and how, if we're not vigilant, intimacy and love can break down. The five R's are:

- Resistance
- Resentment
- Rejection
- Resignation
- Repression

VIDEO: There is a video on my YouTube channel that talks about the 5 R's of relationships. Watch it here: **www.youtube.com/nakeddivorce**

Initially, you start out your married life with some kind of hope for a prosperous relationship. You're in love, your partner is amazing and everything is perfect. One day, something happens. They say something unkind or do something that elicits resistance in you. You get that, "Whoa! Hold on, that was not okay!" feeling. This initial resistance is a completely normal reaction to learning new things about your partner and also normal for any behaviour displayed that is not okay with you. Men generally don't like to make a big deal out of things. So you might wait and see if your partner noticed that they did something wrong and if not, you might withdraw into silence or unconsciously punish your partner in other ways.

Some people are very perceptive and will know something's up, others won't have a clue that their behaviour has made their partner unhappy. When we keep quiet about our resistance, the feeling can shift into resentment. Many people in unhealthy relationships simply avoid facing reality. Sometimes this can be because the people involved may be trying to make themselves appear superior. Or perhaps they don't want to face the fact that their partners really aren't who they say they are, or that they've fallen from the perfect mate perch.

> For example, Ben B covers up and makes excuses for his wife, Anne B, who is always late from work and almost always misses family functions. He might be trying to avoid the truth: that she's a workaholic, or having an affair. He does so because he doesn't want to destroy their perfect couple image in everyone's eyes – and perhaps even in his own eyes.

It's like ignoring that broken handle on a door in your home or not replacing that light bulb. If you don't address the resentment, other resistances and other resentments will begin to build up. Once there is some momentum with your resentment, then you or your partner may begin to experience rejection within the relationship.

Once rejection creeps into a relationship, it becomes overwhelming and makes it difficult to create or sustain an intimate sexual relationship. Those of us who have been married a long time know that once the relationship feels strained, the regularity of sex is affected, and things can spiral downhill very quickly. The bed becomes divided into zones and intimacy suffers. Even the smallest things are irritating and more resistance, resentment and rejection build up. If you don't discuss your feelings of rejection, then your relationship can shift into the place of resignation.

This is when you can so easily slip into co-habitation; operating as housemates or mere friends. Passion, love and chemistry, and all the elements needed to maintain the spark and fire within the relationship, exit through the window. You can end up with an amicable friendship.

This is dangerous! Contentment and harmony are wonderful hallmarks of a marriage, but be sure they're not camouflaging deep resignation in a relation-ship. When left too long, resignation can lead to repression. We've all been out to dinner and watched the married couple sitting in complete silence. They're courteous to one another and exchange pleasantries, but perhaps they have succumbed to resignation or repression and no longer actively engage in conversation or discuss their relationship.

Repression completely kills the passion and chemistry in a relationship. At this point you may begin to question your commitment to the relationship. You may wonder if your partner was ever right for you. You may begin to spend hours day-dreaming about escaping from the relationship. When we don't feel satisfied in our relationship, we can become obsessed with finding that special someone outside of it. This is when people start developing secret relationships, reconnecting with high school sweethearts or watching hours or porn to escape their reality.

When you're removed from the reality of your relationship and your life and escape into a fantasy world, then you're in real danger of seeking fulfilment outside your relationship and marriage. This is fertile ground for cheating. This is when midlife crisis happens and when we start eating for comfort.

Because we didn't communicate openly, vulnerably and humanly about all the little resentments, in the moment, they built up and killed the relationship.

Spend time today thinking about your communication in your previous relationships and what you can learn from the patterns established. In the exercise later today, you can look at your discoveries.

Karpman's Drama Triangle

The Drama Triangle is a psychological model of human interaction first described by world-renowned psychologist Stephen Karpman. According to various texts from Karpman, many of us fall into this triangle at some point in our romantic relationships. See if you can identify with this pattern in your previous relationship.

Think of a situation in your relationship where you were stuck in a rut or felt dis-empowered.

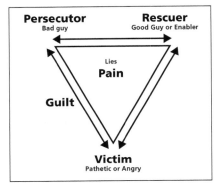

Typically, there will be three roles at play in those relationships:

- The person who is treated as, or accepts the role of Victim. This person needs to be rescued to feel validated as a person

- The person who pressurises, coerces or persecutes the victim (the Villain, Bully or 'Angry' victim). This person needs to feel power over others to feel validated as a person

- The Rescuer, Martyr or False Hero, who intervenes out of an ostensible wish to help the situation or the underdog. This person is not an honest rescuer in an emergency and needs to rescue to feel validated as a person

Whenever we operate within these roles, we act upon our own selfish needs, rather than acting in a genuinely responsible or altruistic manner.

The Victim

This person needs rescuing or feels victimised, somehow repressed or in need of help. Victims love drama and will sometimes unconsciously create situations high in drama where they are cast as the leading actor. Victims will always attract rescuers to rescue them from their situation but at the same time, by being rescued, it perpetuates their negative feelings. They will receive a great deal of attention and will simultaneously love being saved by the rescuer.

The trouble is, whenever you allow someone to rescue you, you hand over the reigns of your life and block yourself from solving your own problems and having the pleasure of being independent.

When dealing with Bruce's infidelities during my divorce, I was dying to play the victim. I wanted him to be the perpetrator and the bad guy, so I could feel absolved of all responsibility for the failure of my marriage. I got loads of attention from other people in being the victim.

I soon realised that being the victim sucked and I urgently looked for ways to move out of that dis-empowering space. If you're operating as a victim, you're going to get stuck there.

Common phrases the victim uses:

"Why don't you", "If it weren't for you", "Why does this always happen to me?" "I can't cope", "Please help me and tell me what to do. "

How to stop being a victim:

Start taking charge of your life and being responsible for your life. Stop telling everyone your sad story and leaning on others for support. It is very disempowering to yourself. Learn to set boundaries (see Day 19) and make your own decisions. Victims need to learn to stand on their own two feet without a rescuer. Stop being concerned about making the wrong decisions, just practice making your own decisions and being responsible for the outcomes, no matter what happens.

The Persecutor, Bully or Villain

This person blames, criticises and keeps the victim oppressed. Like the bad guy in the movie, they enjoy the feeling of authority and control.

Common phrases the villain uses:

"It's all your fault", "See what you made me do", "You got me into this."

How to stop being a villain:

Focus on your own problems. Realise that you get your kicks out of controlling others and that this makes you a bully. Give people the freedom to communicate and live their lives as they see fit.

The Rescuer, Martyr or False Hero

This person rescues even when they really don't want to. They have strong feelings of guilt if they don't rescue the victim. This person usually sighs a great deal and feels the burden of the world on their shoulders because there's so much rescuing to be done!

The relationship between the victim and the rescuer can be one of co-dependency. The rescuer keeps the victim dependent on them by playing into their victimhood. The victim has their needs met by having the rescuer take care of them.

Common phrases rescuers use include:

"Let me help you", "Look how hard I've tried", "I'm only trying to help you", "I will sort this out, you're not capable of doing it on your own".

How to stop being a rescuer:

By rescuing, you become an enabler of victim-like behaviour all around you. Realise that you have an unhealthy NEED to be NEEDED. Focus on your own life and your own problems. You may provide guidance, but your job is not to help the person, your job is to empower them to help themselves. Instead of giving them the fish, teach them to fish for themselves. Stop getting your kicks out of being a martyr - constantly needed by other people.

Harville Hendrix's Fuser-Isolator model

You end a relationship and a few months or years later, you meet a new partner. You fall in love again and everything feels rosy for the first few months. Then, before long you realise that you are basically in the same relationship as you were in before, just with a different person.

The same issues surface again. You have the same arguments and often, the relationship ends in the same way as your last one. Sound familiar?

Dr. Harville Hendrix has an interesting perspective on this phenomenon which he talks about in his book, 'Getting the Love You Want'.

In his years of research helping couples resolve their relationship challenges, Harville discovered that he could divide his clients into two broad categories, Isolators and Fusers.

Isolators seek independence and autonomy in life and unconsciously push others away. As such, they need a lot of space around them and the freedom to come and go as they please.

On the other hand, Fusers have an insatiable need for closeness and reassurance and often need to stay in constant verbal contact with their partners. Fusers are incredibly needy and struggle to spend time on their own. Fusers want to do things together and often are prone to feeling abandoned.

Here's the breakthrough phenomenon that Harville discovered...

Isolators and Fusers almost always end up in relationships together. They are attracted to each other like opposite side of a magnet, and so begins an infuriating game of push and pull that leaves neither partner satisfied. Isolators often report that their Fuser partners engulf them in their neediness and they just want to run away.

"I am feeling so trapped"

"I need to get away"

"I need some space"

Fusers in contrast often feel unloved or abandoned.

"Is my partner going to leave?"

"Is my partner unhappy?"

"Does my partner still love me?"

The more independence the Isolator craves, the more connection the Fuser craves.

When a Fuser-Isolator couple come together, they initially feel the magnetism of falling in love, but soon realise that they are not getting their need for connection or independence met. At this point, most couples end up in conflict and more often than not, either separate or only survive in the relationship (often for the sake of their children).

The reason these relationships fail is because the couple is totally unaware of the unconscious dynamics they are playing out.

Like most things in life, the solution is AWARENESS.

SO, if you can recognise that you are a Fuser, then your job is to give your Isolator partner space and independence. Slowly you will learn that your world does not come crashing down around you, and your partner does not leave. I do alot of coaching in this area in our couples programme where we save marriages. It's a critical lesson to learn!

Conversely, if you can recognise yourself as an Isolator, your job is to stretch yourself to reassure your partner and learn that your independence is not threatened and you can still be a separate self while being connected to another.

Read through the exercise you will be doing later today. Allow yourself to think about it during the day.

Exercise:

In examining the reading for today, journal about any patterns you can identify within your previous relationship. Look at which role you played and where you can be responsible for any negative patterns in your relationship.

1. Think about the five R's of relationships. Where didn't you communicate your resistances and resentments?

....

....

2. What can you be responsible for in not managing the five R's of your relationship?

....

....

3. What actions can you take to remedy this in the future?

....

....

4.Think about Karpman's Drama Triangle. Were you stuck in one of these roles?

....

....

5.What can you be responsible for being stuck in a disempowering role in your marriage?

....

....

6. What actions can you take to remedy this in the future?

....

....

7. Are you a **Fuser** or an **Isolator** in relationships?

....

....

8.In the next few weeks, practice the steps explained above. If you are a **Fuser**, grant **Isolators** around you space and independence. If you are an **Isolator**, Gift the **Fusers** around you closeness and reassurance.

....

....

day 14
METAMORPHOSIS

KEEP THIS IN MIND FOR THE DAY: It takes courage to find the root cause of your divorce, but if you can be responsible for what happened in your relationship, you will free yourself. Responsibility does not mean blame. It means acknowledging that you were part of what didn't work so that you learn from the situation.

You will carry this sense of empowerment within yourself and into any new relationship. Think of it as an investment in change. If you leave your marriage with nothing but blame and the feeling that you were a victim of a bad situation, you'll remain disempowered and stuck.

Theme: Finding the source of your divorce

Date: Thursday, _____

🕐 **Estimated time to complete the reading/ exercise: 120 minutes**

Remember to go through the daily checklist

Tick when done

Read through the thought for the day:

When things aren't working between couples, it's often because neither is taking responsibility for the relationship.

There is a misunderstanding in life that partnership means that each person is responsible for 50% of the relationship. It takes two people to be in the relationship so what is powerful is taking 100% responsibility in any of your relationships. In your failed marriage, owning your part of the demise of that partnership is courageous and freeing. Although you accept your ex did whatever they did, stepping up to own your part in the breakdown of your marriage leaves you free to be in your next relationship with ease and without blaming your ex. If you continue to blame your ex, it will impact your future prospects in relationships as it's not a very attractive quality.

Today I'd like you to spend some time thinking about the root cause of your divorce. Take a look at what you can be responsible for, irrespective of whatever your ex did or didn't do. What you learn from this exercise will be critical to the success of your next relationship. So this is about you and your new life and not about the final tally of the scoreboard of your previous relationship. Read through the list below and see how many of the root causes of the divorce you're big enough to own.

Finding the source of your divorce is about finding the origins of where the relationship stopped working so you can release the negative emotions from your body, shift your paradigm and make you think differently about your life. You may find that you identify with more than one source and if that is the case, learn everything there is to learn for your next relationship.

As I mentioned previously, finding the root of your divorce is absolutely essential to your next relationship. This exercise requires self-knowledge and honesty. You deserve that.

 NOTE: Ironically, if there is one you feel particularly strongly about, consider that this is probably the source of your divorce.

While this isn't an exhaustive list, it will give you some food for thought...

1. Not managing the five R's

Refer to Day 13. Not managing your daily resistances and resentments in your marriage or partnership can lead to its death. When one half of the partnership habitually shuns or ignores the other, it's a sure sign of an unhealthy relationship.

The reality

Confront the fact that you didn't communicate openly about resentments in each moment they arose during your marriage. What was the impact of not doing so?

What to do if this was the source of your divorce

Go back to the relationship story you wrote. Underline trigger points in your story so you can identify when things changed between you. If necessary, make amends with your ex and make a commitment to be aware of communication in your future relationship and to manage the five R's responsibly. Communicating vulnerably and openly in each moment takes commitment and courage. This is what a healthy relationship demands of you.

Question to ask yourself

Think about the five R's of relationships. Can you think of instances in the past when you didn't communicate your resistances and resentments?

2. You didn't let your partner win at loving you

Perhaps you never stopped testing your partner's commitment in the relationship. Nothing she ever said or did seemed good enough for you. You kept dishing out criticisms, comments and suggestions. Your partner felt invalidated and probably ended up thinking or even saying, "I just can't win."

NOTE:

A partner must feel they can win at loving you.

The reality:

To stay in love, your partner must feel that they can succeed in loving you. Your partner should feel that you need them in some way and that they make a difference to your life.

What to do if this was the source of your divorce:

If your life partner feels that they can never satisfy you, they will feel they have failed at loving you and will eventually withdraw their love and attention. Constant criticism of your partner says more about you than your partner. If you find yourself complaining a lot, then resolve the issues within you and practice being more accepting of others.

Follow the steps in the section entitled *Principles on Keeping Love Alive* in the final section of this book to keep the love fires burning. Ensure that in your next relationship, you stop being a know-it-all, dragging a sack-full of criticism around with you, and waiting to dish it out to the hapless person in your life. Relationships are fragile and if they're taken for granted and not nurtured, they will die.

Question to ask yourself:

Where did you not allow your partner to win at loving you in your relationship?

3. The checklist

No one is perfect but you handle your partners as if they should be. You have a checklist or scorecard against which you graded her and if she didn't make the grade, you punished her, criticised her, made her life hell, dumped her , become indifferent or discarded her. The sad thing is if you run your relationship according to a checklist of attributes, you'll never get to know your partner. You cannot be present to the person you are with because you are so busy comparing them to an unrealistic set of expectations that they cannot live up to. The fact remains that people don't like being with someone if you focus on their faults - you will drive your partner away.

The reality:

Those who can't respect their partner's right to their own space, opinions and ways of doing things can expect to see their future relationships nose-dive. Relationships fed on criticism and resentment soon become like wilted flowers.

What to do if this was the source of your divorce:

Consider letting go of the controls, and letting go of how things ought to be. If you drove your ex away with your checklist, you probably drive others away too.

Suspend your rules for how the house needs to be organised, what kind of work your partner should be doing, chores they should be performing or outfits they should not be wearing. Consider that if you have a checklist, you hold all the dominating energy within the relationship. There will be no space for anyone else to step up and live anywhere else but in your shadow. Count the costs of your checklist for partners. If you're not aware of the costs, complete the *Real Impact of my Divorce* Exercise earlier in the book. You're living in a dream world if you believe that anyone can measure up against your high expectations. You'll never be happy in a relationship. You'll move from partner to partner. Much like a dinosaur crashing through a forest with its tail swinging backwards and forwards, flattening everything in sight, you're oblivious to the destruction you leave in your wake. You'll also make your partner miserable because being with you will be hell.

This is your wake-up call. Bin the checklist and have a shot at an amazing relationship with someone who is not on tenterhooks all the time they are with you.

Question to ask yourself:

Think about your relationship. Did you hold your partner up against your checklist of perfection? This is probably why they are your ex today...

4. Living in a dream world

Many people in relationships simply avoid facing reality. There are many reasons for this. Perhaps they can't cope with the fact that their partners and lives aren't picture-perfect. Or perhaps they don't want to face the fact that their mates aren't who they say they are. Or perhaps they can't be bothered quitting a bad relationship. Facing reality is an important facet of maturity. Often we don't want to face reality because we are stuck in a child-like dream of what our lives are supposed to look like.

The reality:

Simulated relationships or those living under the illusion of a happy, healthy relationship are destined for failure. Wake up and smell the coffee. The disguise you've put in place won't last. If you can't see it as a façade, the people in your life probably can.

Often people who are resigned to living in a dream world are conflict-averse, pretending everything is perfect as a way to keep the peace.

What to do if this was the source of your divorce:

Realise that you were living in a dream world fairy-tale and this made you a little dead in your relationship. Whenever we are not truthful with ourselves and others, we kill our self expression and a piece of ourselves. Consider the impact of pretence on your life. Commit to growing up and moving past the child-like dream state. Part of being an adult in a relationship is about confronting reality in a relationship.

Start telling the truth to those around you. Start with a small group of people and then move onto your family. Tell the truth and blow the lid off the facade in your life.

Question to ask yourself:

Were you avoiding the truth about your relationship?

5. No perseverance or commitment, the propensity to be bored easily

A sign of a great relationship is not how you cope when things are going well, it's about the toolkit you've assembled and built up for when things go pear-shaped. Commitment is what keeps you in the relationship during bad times. If one person begins to feel disillusioned with the marriage, or trapped, tired, helpless, depressed or let down and turns to alternatives like drugs, elicit relationships, gambling, etc., the relationship will suffer. Caring only about having your own needs met and neglecting what's healthy for the relationship is a death-knell.

The reality:

The honeymoon period does end in every relationship. Those who are able to work at fuelling the love fires during their relationship, have a better chance of survival. Couples need to face issues together; add some new goals to the relationship, list some activities you both enjoy, talk more, etc. This can happen only when each person has both feet in the relationship, and is committed to ensuring the relationship is regularly spiced with fun, adventure, and romance. Selfishness is a prime cause of marriage breakdown. Growing couples need to put selfishness aside and develop maturity to work as a team as they face adult issues in life and marriage.

What to do if this was the source of your divorce:

Firstly, acknowledge that you weren't committed to the relationship. Ask yourself why. Do you run when things don't feel good or the relationship requires some adjustment or re-tuning? Wanting to run in the face of a test will impact all facets of your life. Nothing meaningful is ever accomplished without commitment. If you have a problem with commitment, set yourself a challenge and draw up some boundaries. What will it take to see the project through? What makes you lose commitment? Lack of a common end goal? Lack of success markers? Stick with it through to the end and make a note of what you learnt about yourself.

Secondly, acknowledge that you're a bit self-centred. List the things you did at the expense of your partner and your relationship. If you have lived your life thinking "it's my way or the highway", you'll probably accomplish a great deal, but it will be at the expense of your relationships. And if you're the kind who upsets the apple cart when you don't get your own way, you'll leave a trail of destruction in your wake. If you know that selfishness is your problem, commit yourself to finding that breakthrough. Practice being aware of your partner's needs.

Question to ask yourself:

Was your relationship characterised by a lack of commitment or selfishness on your part? Acknowledge the lessons you've learnt. Practise being selfless.

6. Stuck in the Drama Triangle/co-dependent relationship

See the reading on Day 13 for more on the Drama Triangle.

The reality:

If your relationship was modelled on the Drama Triangle, where neither party is willing to acknowledge the characteristic problems, or the need to shift to a healthier model of communication, then severing that relationship was possibly the best solution.

What to do if this was the source of your divorce:

Follow the recommendations listed in Day 13 in future relationships.

How to avoid victim mode:

Start taking charge of your life. Learn to set boundaries (see Day 19), make your own decisions (even if they're wrong) and accept responsibility for the outcome. Stop telling the world your sad story and leaning so heavily on others. Be aware of and avoid attracting rescuers into your life.

How to avoid being a persecutor/perpetrator:

Focus on your own life and your own problems. Leave other people to tend to their lives. Stop nit-picking and bullying people to do what you believe is right.

How to prevent being a rescuer:

Stop getting your kicks from being needed by other people. If you want to help someone, teach him/ her to take care of themselves. As they like to point fingers at others, it's very important that victims take responsibility for their own lives. Focus on your life and your problems. Provide guidance by all means, but remember, your job is not to help all the stray cats in your neighbourhood. Your job is to empower them. Read 'Codependent No More' written by Melodie Beattie.

Question to ask yourself:

Were you stuck in any one of these roles within your relationship? If so, what are you going to do moving forward?

7. Being a daddy vs. a husband...

You fathered your partner, took care of them, supported them, did everything for them, handled all the finances, told them what to wear, fed and clothed them and reminded them to take a jumper because it was cold. You took on the role of caretaker and being this needed was critical to your own sense of self. It's a very nurturing role but also very controlling and dominating. It's not the hallmark of an empowered relationship...

The reality:

Although you win top marks for taking care of your partner, they did not marry you for to then become their daddy. By doing everything for everyone, there's no room for anyone else to step up. This makes you an enabler of laziness and victim-type behaviour around you. This ensures that you never have anyone taking care of you because they have no opportunities to do so. You're communicating that you don't believe that others can be responsible. Do you struggle to delegate? Do you struggle to trust others to get on with things? If the answer is yes, your life will become exhausting and you will never be taken care of.

This happens at work, too. Someone indispensable leaves the company and for a few days' chaos reigns as people find their feet. And then someone steps up to take charge and things begin to run smoothly. But you need a gap for that to happen. Someone had to step down and someone had to step into the gap.

What to do if this was the source of your divorce:

Stop care-taking. Leave people to take care of themselves. Follow the steps in the section entitled *Principles on Keeping Love Alive* in the final section of this book to keep the love fires burning. If you're prone to being everyone's daddy, be aware of this in your next relationship. If you begin to feel responsible for your partner, stop and take a step back. Sometimes it's important to have the house a little messy, to eat frozen fish fingers for dinner or to forget to do the shopping. Sometimes it's important to take yourself out on an outing mid-week and leave your partner with no food in the refrigerator. All these little activities remind them in your life that they too need to step up and sort things out within the household and that all their caretaking needs are not your responsibility.

Note: To keep sexual chemistry alive in your relationship, remain masculine in your relationship.

Question to ask yourself:

Did you control your ex with too much caretaking?

8. Using the relationship as a dumping ground

An occasional outbreak during a stressful moment, such as swearing at your partner in moment of high tension, while not admirable, can be considered normal.

However, harmful, violent physical responses, actions or verbal abuse is not. The latter have no place in healthy relationships.

The reality:

Verbal abuse or a violation of your partner, their personal property, friends, etc., is a red flag for an unhealthy relationship.

What to do if this was the source of your divorce:

If you have problems expressing your anger in a healthy way, Day 9 has a recommended exercise for releasing anger in a way that doesn't affect anyone. You should also examine the way you deal with stress. If you're harming others when you express anger, you need help. Get in touch with the **Naked Divorce** team to discuss anger management issues.

Question to ask yourself:

Are you responsible for using your relationship as a dumping ground for your anger and issues?

9. Physical appearance

Disregarding your physical appearance is also a sign of an unhealthy relationship. It could signal substance abuse, depression or loss of interest in your partner.

The reality:

We all want to be with a partner we're attracted to. If you've let yourself go, either in the way you dress, your weight or physical attractiveness, it's time to do something about it.

What to do if this was the source of your divorce:

Consider the impact your physical appearance has on your life. If you put up with your partner's deteriorating physical appearance, practice the exercises listed on Day 19.

Questions to ask yourself:

Did you let yourself go during your relationship?

What will you do about that now?

10. Worrying that you love your partner more than they might love you

If you were always worried about your partner leaving you or doubting their commitment to you, you may just have gotten what you were most afraid of. Constantly fretting will only make you unhappy and precipitate all kinds of problems in your relationship as well as making you very needy.

The reality:

You're the one who's decided that you're not good enough, which means that you're the one who has to turn things around. Work on improving your self-image. Days 18-21 will help you.

What to do if this was the source of your divorce:

It's a matter of learning what creates attraction within a relationship. At the end of the book, there are some *Principles on Keeping Love Alive* which cover some core concepts on how to keep your partner in love with you. Maintaining separateness, moving to your own rhythm, understanding that longing is often equated with love and focusing on making yourself happy whenever your partner disappears on you are some of the lessons from that section. Ultimately, love is a risk. Love cannot be controlled and nor can relationships. Sometimes they end. Control is an illusion and when we live our lives completely focused on controlling everyone and everything around us, we kill the joy and spontaneity. Living without loving is not living at all.

> **" Worrying is praying for what you don't want. "**

Follow the steps on beating worry in the Worry Buster exercise on Day 17 and practice your Daily Declarations to improve your self-image as well as combating worry in the moment whenever it arises.

Question to ask yourself:

Did you suffocate your partner with your neediness and love and did you worry constantly that something would go wrong?

11. Being a control-freak

Did you boss your partner around? Did you attempt to control them to the point where they lost their identity or even their true essence? Did they become someone less than they are with you?

The reality:

If you were Mr. Control-freak in your relationship then I can tell you for sure, your partner was suppressed and depressed being with you. No one likes being controlled or told what to do every minute of the day. The reality is when you boss your partner around, your partner will withdraw and disappear from the relationship. This can develop into you becoming more suspicious of your partner unnecessarily. Ask yourself:

1) Did you make all the decisions?

2) Were you the more forceful one?

3) How does your partner handle you exploding? Did your partner withdraw?

4) Who dealt with all the finances?

5) Who took the sexual initiative? Did you have an active sex life?

6) Did your marriage end with your partner having an affair?

What to do if this was the source of your divorce:

Follow the steps in the section entitled *Principles on Keeping Love Alive* in the final section of this book to keep the love fires burning. Empower your partner and listen to their point of view. If you are constantly telling your partner they are doing something wrong, or controlling or bossing them around, pretty soon your partner will not enjoy how they feel about them self when around you. Your partner may seek to feel different about them self by having an affair SO focus on your partner feeling like the best version of herself with you.

Forgive yourself for being Mr. Control – you didn't have the insights about life back then that you have today.

Questions to ask yourself:

Are you willing to step back from how you think things must get done in life?

12. Being a doormat

A doormat is usually at the receiving end of a control freak. Perhaps you can recognise that you spent most of your marriage jumping through hoops for your partner and being willing to do anything for them. Perhaps you were always rushing in to take responsibility for everything. Perhaps you take care of everything and clean up after everyone so that you can be at peace. But by the end of the day you're exhausted and resentful. You probably do this elsewhere in your life.

The reality:

You're the one who decided to be a doormat. It's time to work on your self-image.

What to do if this was the source of your divorce:

Follow the steps in the section entitled *Principles on Keeping Love Alive* in the final section of this book to keep the love fires burning. Follow the tips on Day 19 and practice the Daily Declarations to improve your self-image.

Question to ask yourself:

Were you a doormat in your relationship?

13. Incompatibility

This can be an easy one to hide behind. Everyone can cite instances of incompatibility in their marriage. But in this instance we're talking about the odd couple; the super manager and the super sloth; the ugly guy and the beauty queen, or the couple who have a 40 year age gap.

The reality:

The old adage tells us that opposites attract. But do they? You knew your ex wasn't your type, but somehow you fell into a relationship anyway. There was that strange attraction... Opposites may attract, but ensuring you have some basic things in common is important for a lasting relationship. Some of these odd relationships do work, but it's not commonplace.

What to do if this was the source of your divorce:

Examine how you got into the relationship. Did you fall into it? Next time, be clear about what you're looking for in a mate and be more conscious about your compatibilities. Having common pursuits, activities and interests will feed your relationship and keep the fun alive.

Question to ask yourself:

Were you in an incompatible relationship? If so, what actions can you take now to prevent a repetition of this in the future?

14. Not making the relationship #1

You, your partner and your relationship must be ring-fenced. This triangle is paramount. Other obligations and commitments come second. Not being able to draw boundaries or sustain limits is a death knell to many marriages. And while it is fine for your marriage to take a back seat once in a while, in healthy relationships both parties need to feel and share the value of being number one in their partner's eyes.

The reality:

Relationships have a life and they need to be fed and nurtured.

What to do if this was the source of your divorce:

Make your relationship the centrepiece of your life. Spiritual considerations aside, in marriage there is nothing and no one else that should take precedence.

Questions to ask yourself:

Am I responsible for not making my relationship number 1? Am I hiding behind other activities? Have other people become my confidants?

15. The end of an exchange of benefits

Every relationship is based on an exchange of benefits, such as companionship, love, caring, friendship, and so on. When the exchange of benefits ends and neither of you is gaining anything from the relationship, it will naturally fizzle out.

The reality:

You must identify the source of the problem that got you to this point. When did you stop being friends, companions, lovers? This is usually not the root cause of divorce but a flag alerting you to the fact that your relationship is in danger.

What to do if this was the source of your divorce:

Look for the true source of your divorce that led to the exchange of benefits ending.

Questions to ask yourself:

Why do you think you stopped exchanging benefits in your relationship? What can you do to ensure this doesn't happen in the future?

Read through the exercise you'll be doing later today. Allow yourself to think about what you read during the day.

Exercise:

After examining the reading for today, find the source(s) of your divorce. If the source is not on this list, describe it in your own words.

The primary objective of this exercise is to take responsibility for what the source of the divorce is.

Note: The more honest you are with yourself now, the better chance you have at a successful relationship in the future.

Release

You are now on the home stretch.

Statistically, most road accidents happen just outside cities. When people begin their journeys, they are alert, focused and have a high level of concentration. They take breaks and drive cautiously. They stop for lunch and let their co-driver take the wheel.

But close to the destination, they begin to relax and become complacent. They let their mind wander with arbitrary questions like, "How is the dog doing?" "Has the garden been watered?" OR they may think it's a good idea to take a detour.

Be vigilant in the final five days – they are very important to your healing. Don't allow your mind to wander. Stay focused on your healing as you are not done yet and the next 5 days are the most fun because they are all about you, your life and what is next for you!

day
15
RELEASE

KEEP THIS IN MIND FOR THE DAY: Forgiveness doesn't mean you're condoning what the other person did, but holding a grudge is like drinking poison, hoping the other person will die. Forgiveness is about setting yourself free...

Theme: Stepping into forgiveness

Date: Friday, _____

🕐 **Estimated time to complete the exercise: 120 minutes**

Date: Thursday, _____

🕐 **Estimated time to complete the reading/ exercise: 120 minutes**

Remember to go through the daily checklist

Tick when done

☐

Read through the thought for the day:

> **❝** *The pathway to love is forgiveness and forgiveness is the tablet that dissolves resentment and resignation* **❞**

When someone you care about causes hurt, you can hold on to anger, resentment and thoughts of revenge and remain stuck, or you can embrace forgiveness and move forward.

How you forgive is very important. There are two distinctive types of forgiveness:

1. Shallow or 'cheap' forgiveness

Shallow or cheap forgiveness is when we forgive quickly and without thought, perhaps to look good, avoid conflict, or convince ourselves that we're fine and aren't holding a grudge. This type of forgiveness is a quick and easy pardon that doesn't get to grips with your emotions or how you come to terms with the injury to yourself.

When you forgive cheaply, you simply let your anger go but without truly feeling 'ready' to do so. Often, when people have moved through the **Naked Divorce** *grieving cycle*, they mistake the stage of Acceptance for Forgiveness. Acceptance means that you have come to terms with the reality of the situation and you accept the situation for what it is and for what it isn't. Authentic forgiveness goes hand-in-hand with responsibility. When you're ready to be responsible for your part in the relationship not working out, when you reach a point of being grateful for everything that has happened and for everything you've learnt from your marriage and subsequent divorce, then you're ready to authentically forgive your ex.

The **Naked Divorce** *grieving cycle*

1. Denial
2. Anger and betrayal
3. Panic and negotiation
4. Humiliation, fear of failure or looking bad
5. Despair
6. Loss, grief and depression
7. Space and nothingness
8. Acceptance   **◄ Acceptance ≠ Forgiveness**
9. Responsibility and forgiveness
10. Gratitude

2. Authentic forgiveness

To get to a place of authentic forgiveness, you need to wrestle with it. Often we refuse to forgive because it feels like we are surrendering control or pride. We feel entitled to our hurt and not forgiving our ex is like us punishing them. When you hold on to pain, old grudges, bitterness and even hatred, many areas of your life suffer. Your health suffers. When you're unforgiving, it's YOU who pays the price, over and over. You can bring your anger and bitterness into every relationship and new experience. Your life can become so wrapped up in the wrongs of the past that you can't enjoy the good things in the present.

Sometimes you need to wrestle with it until you have had enough of all the suffering. You need to realise that your need to hold onto not forgiving ONLY hurts you and those you love, like your children.

Forgiveness is a choice to let go of resentments, hurt, anger and thoughts of revenge. Forgiveness is the act of untying yourself from thoughts and feelings that bind you to the offence committed against you. This can reduce the power these feelings exert over you, so that you can live a freer and happier life in the present. Forgiveness can even lead to feelings of understanding, empathy and compassion towards the person who hurt you. It is easier to get to this place if you're willing to look at what you can be responsible for in the breakdown of your marriage. Forgiving isn't the same as forgetting or condoning what happened to you. Forgiveness doesn't mean that you deny the other person's responsibility for hurting you, and it doesn't minimise or justify the wrong. Forgiveness, however, can lessen its grip on you and help you focus on other more positive parts of your life.

You can forgive the person without excusing their actions.

My story:

> I forgave Bruce when I completely accepted him, both for what he was and what he couldn't be, combined with taking personal responsibility for the role I played in the failure of our marriage. This was the key. I acknowledged that he is who he is and me suffering because of it was pointless. He just wasn't that into me and wasn't that into monogamy either and there was nothing else to say about that. For most of our marriage I'd tried to change him into someone who embraced monogamy and traditional family values or into someone who would truly desire me. I secretly hoped that once we signed the marriage certificate he would change his ways and no longer need to be a wild child, or need to be around beautiful women. This was the lie I lived.

> The day I accepted him completely and took responsibility for my inability to acknowledge the truth in our relationship, I sat on the couch and laughed. I laughed at the absurdity of how I suffered in anger over someone I could not control. Once I let go that he is who he is and I am who I am, I forgave him completely.

Forgiveness is a function of acceptance. What makes acceptance easier is that you're not condoning the behaviour, you're simply accepting the person for who they are to release yourself from unnecessary suffering. If the person you need to forgive is yourself, then this is no different. Accept that who you are today is different from the person who made mistakes in the past. Learn what you need to learn from the past and record those lessons in the exercise below. You don't need to continue suffering or punishing yourself. Just choose to let go. Forgiveness is also a commitment to let go of your own suffering.

What if I'm the one who needs forgiveness?

My story:

> When I found out about Bruce's betrayal, I began to feel guilty about cheating on an ex-boyfriend when I was at university. The thought went around and around in my head that because of my own betrayals, Bruce had betrayed me in our marriage and I'd deserved it. Not only did I need to forgive Bruce, I needed to forgive myself, too. I also felt angry with myself for all the times I confronted Bruce and whenever he denied any wrongdoing, I believed I was paranoid and stopped trusting my judgment. I was also angry with myself for cheating and for ignoring all the signs that my marriage was doomed.
>
> It took two hours but when I completed the exercise for Day 15 and focused on my healing, I realised that harbouring resentment against myself could be just as toxic as holding on to resentment against someone else. I recognised that poor behaviour or mistakes didn't make me worthless or bad. I came to a place of acceptance that I, like everyone else, am not perfect. I accepted myself, warts and all. I admitted my mistakes and chose to contact my ex-boyfriend from university to apologise for being a jerk all those years ago. It was great doing that. He was gracious and I released myself from guilt. I felt compassion for my imperfect self and I also felt compassion for imperfect Bruce. I committed myself to treating others with compassion, empathy and respect.

Forgiving yourself or someone else, though not easy, can transform your life. Instead of dwelling on the injustice and revenge, instead of being angry and bitter, you can move toward a living in peace, and with compassion, mercy, joy and kindness.

I want you to wrestle with forgiveness today. Do not stop until you have got there. If it takes you 12 days to do Day 15, so be it. Wallow in the experience of not forgiving for as long as it takes until you are sick of it. Always ask yourself: is this really worth it?

Steps to forgiveness:

➡ Recognise the value of forgiveness and its importance in your life

➡ Reflect on the facts of the situation: how you've reacted, and how this combination has affected your life, your health and your well being

➡ Work out a list of actions you can take to take steps closer to forgiveness

➡ Choose to forgive. Move away from the role of a victim and free yourself from the control and power the person or situation has exerted on your life

➡ If you are the person who needs forgiveness, take responsibility and make amends with anyone you have hurt in the process. You will feel so much better

➡ Read through the exercise you will be doing later today. Allow yourself to think about it during the day

Exercise:

Forgiving my ex:

1. What do you not accept about your ex that you are still holding on to?

2. What expectations of your ex and your marriage were not fulfilled and how did this make you angry?

3. What impact does holding this grudge have on your life?

4. Does holding onto this resentment change the situation in any way?

5. Make a list of the things you'd like to forgive your ex for being or doing. Write each point like this...

I forgive [your ex's name] for XXX because YYY

For example: I forgive Sarah for being with other men. Taking the poison of resentment, hoping she will die, is only hurting me. I release myself from this pain, knowing I cannot change what is and what isn't true about the past.

6. Read the list out loud to yourself in the mirror until you genuinely 'feel' different about the situation and your ex

7. Work out what you need to hear from your ex to move on. Say those words to yourself over and over again

8. When you genuinely feel differently about the situation and your ex: Make a list of everything you are grateful for from having been married

9. When you genuinely feel differently about the situation and your ex: Make a list of everything you are grateful for in getting divorced

Forgiving myself

1. What don't you accept about yourself that you are holding onto?

2. What expectations of yourself didn't you fulfil on? Why does this make you angry?

3. Does holding onto this resentment change the situation in any way?

4. What commitments do I need to make to myself or what actions can I take to move on?

5. Make a list of what you would like to forgive yourself for. Write each point like this...

I forgive myself for XXX because YYY

For example: I forgive myself for cheating on my ex-girlfriend at university because it happened so many years ago and the person I was then is not the person I am today. I learnt many lessons from that betrayal. I learnt about the pain and impact my actions had on her and on my own life. I learnt how important it is to apologise for the wrongs I committed. I learnt the valuable lesson of trusting myself and my fidelity in relationships

6. Read the list out loud to yourself in the mirror until you genuinely 'feel' different about the situation and your ex

7. When you genuinely feel differently about the situation and about yourself: Make a list of everything you have learnt about yourself from the marriage

8. When you genuinely feel differently about the situation and about yourself: Make a list of anything you are grateful for from your marriage

9. When you genuinely feel differently about the situation and about yourself: Make a list of anything you are grateful for following your divorce

Note: If you're still holding on and struggling with this exercise, book a coaching call with the team at Naked Divorce

day
16
RELEASE

TIP FOR THE DAY: This is the final stage of washing the bitterness, resentment and anger of your divorce out of your hair. Today is about the Vow Break.

Theme: The Vow Break

Date: Saturday, _____

🕐 **Estimated time to complete the exercise: 2-3 hours**

Remember to go through the daily checklist

Tick when done

Read through the thought for the day:

When two people get married, there is usually a beautiful ceremony and celebration in the company of friends, family and community.

Everyone is willing you on to succeed. Sadly, when two people get divorced there's is no ceremonial breaking of the sacred vow you made. You're on your own.

Today is about completing the Vow Break, an exercise to help sever the ties with your ex in a healthy, ethical and supportive way.

VIDEO: I created a YouTube video on the topic of the *Vow Break*. To watch me explaining the steps in more detail, go to **www.youtube.com/nakeddivorce**

Complete your daily homework – start this in the morning.

Exercise:

The *Vow Break*

Begin by journalling the following about your ex (do this as if you were talking to them):

• What can I acknowledge you for in our relationship?

• What was awesome about our relationship?

• What hurt me and what did I need to hear from you while we were married?

• What parts of you did I not acknowledge or accept while we were married?

• What are all the things I learnt from our marriage?

• What are all the things I learnt from our divorce?

• What do I need to hear from you now? (Do this after your letter from her to you)

• What I wish for you now?

• What promises and commitments do I make to you for the future (if applicable)?

• What promises and commitments do I make with regards to our children and your relationship with them (if applicable)?

Separately:

• Review your marriage vows and look at the promises you made. Acknowledge which promises you did and didn't keep

• Forgive yourself for any promises you broke and acknowledge yourself for all the promises you kept

When complete, here is a bonus opportunity for you

Bonus opportunity:

Write a completion letter to your ex saying everything you want to say from the *Vow Break* above.

If you feel really brave, approach your ex to do the Vow Break together or send her your letter. What I can say is that doing the exercise WITH your ex is a truly remarkable experience full of forgiveness and completion.

NOTE: Do not approach your ex if you were in a toxic relationship where contact is unhealthy

day
17
RELEASE

THINK ABOUT THIS FOR TODAY: "Our lives improve only when we take chances and the first and most difficult risk we can take is to be honest with ourselves." ~ Walter Anderson

Everyone has some form of baggage from a relationship, a nasty break-up or divorce. Without being insensitive, if you're really committed to making your next relationship work, you need to purge that baggage, or manage it. Many people I have worked with have unresolved baggage spanning more than a decade. This baggage ruined any chance of happiness in their lives. Dealing with your baggage today could add years to your life. It could even save your life.

Theme: Unpacking your relationship baggage

Date: Sunday, _____

🕐 **Estimated time to complete the exercise: 3-4 hours**

Remember to go through the daily checklist

Tick when done

Read through the thought for the day:

☐

Relationship baggage is something everyone who has ever been in a relationship has to manage in every moment. We have baggage whenever our negative chatter in our head is trying to warn us of the perceived dangers of a new relationship. If you have been burnt before, your warning system will trick you into thinking things are happening when they are not. Your overactive warning system needs awareness and soothing to calm down.

Don't expect to be healed by the end of the day. The goal is to become aware of what your baggage is and to focus on releasing it completely over the coming weeks. Some baggage takes a few minutes to be released whereas some baggage may take some practice over a few days or weeks because you need to catch it and manage it within each passing moment.

Let's start by looking into the different types of relationship baggage and then look into what to do about it.

The 'waiting to be hurt' baggage

What is it?

You desperately WANT to be in a relationship but you have incredible fear inside of you. One minute you are happy, but the next minute you are overwhelmed by anxiety. You have a belief that you are bound to get hurt and unconsciously, you may even attract partners who will hurt you to reinforce this pattern in your life.

What are the facts?

It was Henry Ford who said, "Whether you think you can or whether you think you can't, you're right"

So, if you feel you don't deserve to win, achieve success or to be happy in your new relationship, you'll tend to manifest your worst fears. If this baggage is running the show, when things finally go right and happen the way you want them to, it will feel too good to be true and will somehow disappear.

Love is a risk. Love demands courage because it makes you vulnerable. Relationships end. If you constantly think about the end of your relationship, you may unwittingly be working to that end. Love can't be controlled and neither can relationships. Control is an illusion and when you live life completely focused on controlling everyone and everything, you smother the sense of joy and spontaneity in your life. You can avoid love, hoping you'll never be hurt again, or you can surrender to the experience of love, with all its benefits. So, let go. You may get hurt; you're human after all. But you'll be living life and not avoiding it.

No longer succumbing to worry is easier said than done. I was a prize-winning worrier, so let me go through what I did to put worry in its place.

What can you do to put this baggage in its place?

Here is the technique I use to put my worry in its place. If you are a prize-winning worrier, too, then let me tell you it's something you will always need to manage.

However, the better you get at managing it when it arises, the less worry you'll experience over time. You can train your mind to stop seeing worrying as a viable option. This works very well for people who can visualise well. If you struggle with visualisation, then contact our team for some other suggestions to reduce worry in your life.

This Neuro-linguistic programming-based technique may seem like a game at first but let me assure you: visual imagination has a very powerful effect on feelings.

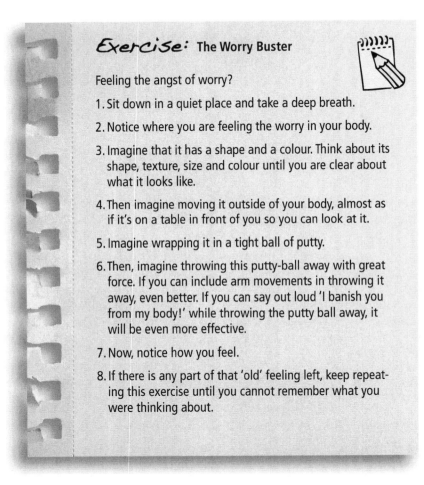

Exercise: **The Worry Buster**

Feeling the angst of worry?

1. Sit down in a quiet place and take a deep breath.

2. Notice where you are feeling the worry in your body.

3. Imagine that it has a shape and a colour. Think about its shape, texture, size and colour until you are clear about what it looks like.

4. Then imagine moving it outside of your body, almost as if it's on a table in front of you so you can look at it.

5. Imagine wrapping it in a tight ball of putty.

6. Then, imagine throwing this putty-ball away with great force. If you can include arm movements in throwing it away, even better. If you can say out loud 'I banish you from my body!' while throwing the putty ball away, it will be even more effective.

7. Now, notice how you feel.

8. If there is any part of that 'old' feeling left, keep repeating this exercise until you cannot remember what you were thinking about.

The 'ex' baggage
What is it?

This is the type of baggage whereby you just can't get over your ex and you nurse the idea that your ex may come back into your life or you compare everyone new to your ex. This will be horrible for your new partner who will hate feeling compared and may even leave you if you don't resolve your feelings.

What are the facts?

Your relationship ended and you need to confront that perhaps the relationship was not so great to begin with. Maybe you were living in a dream world, fantasising about the relationship, rather than being real about what it was truly like. The fact that you're no longer together with your ex should be sufficient indication that you were not meant to be together forever.

What can you do to put this baggage in its place?

Having completed days 7 and 8, you should be feeling much better about your ex and you should be able to see both sides of the relationship. If you're still struggling, repeat the exercises from days 7 and 8 until you can see the relationship in its true light.

The 'angry' baggage
What is it?

This is the most damaging kind of relationship baggage because you're just extremely angry at anyone who reminds you in any way of your ex. I have seen this happen when men label all women as cold bitches because of what one woman did or if someone decides all red-haired women are to be hated because their ex-wife was a red-head.

What are the facts?

One bad situation from your past does not mean that all similar looking, similar cultured people or people with long hair or big noses etc. deserve your anger. Anger makes us tired. You have a choice:

- ✓ either you waste your life by being angry at life and remaining a bitter, twisted angry person, or
- ✓ you let go of the anger in a healthy way

What can you do to put this baggage in its place?

Day 9 has a great exercise for dealing with extreme anger. If you still feel angry then it may be necessary for you to repeat the anger releasing exercise three to six times until you feel no more animosity. There is also the *Real Impact of my Divorce* Exercise. Substitute the problem statement with, "I refuse to let go of the anger I feel towards my old relationship" to realise the impact holding onto this anger will have on your life.

The 'I'm not attractive enough' baggage
What is it?

You just never feel good enough. Perhaps this issue came about because your ex cheated on you. Perhaps you have some issues from childhood.

What are the facts?

If you are constantly dependent on the affirmation of those around you to feel attractive then those around you have a great deal of control of you.

This is not a particularly powerful way to live.

What can you do to put this baggage in its place?

Simply act like you are good looking man. Imagine yourself as desirable and act accordingly. There are so many examples of men who are not stereotypically handsome but because of the way they see themselves and because of their own confidence in themselves, they are totally gorgeous. There is a strong connection between the body and the mind, so fake it, until it feels real.

The Daily Declarations are also very useful here. Repeat them daily, the repetition will be healing in a few days or weeks.

The 'I am just going to get cheated on' baggage
What is it?

If you have previously been cheated on or cheated on a partner before, you may be suspicious of people cheating on you. If you've been cheated on in the past, you might not be able to trust your instincts.

What are the facts?

This baggage creates extreme paranoia. You may become that man who checks your partner's phone, email, computer and anything else for evidence of affairs. If you assume your partner will cheat on you and you are always looking for problems; you'll eventually manifest it.

Case study: John

John always worried that his wife would cheat on him. He had a history of women who had cheated on him and this made him hyper vigilant in his marriage. He persistently asked where she was going and who she was going with. Whenever she assured him that nothing was going on, he'd apologise for mistrusting her. But the next day he continued asking. Eventually she got fed up of all his questioning. She realised she was no longer happy in the relationship and confided in someone from work. One thing led to another and she had an affair. Now, I am not going to condone what she chose to do but she did admit to John that she'd felt pushed into the arms of another man. She was happy in their marriage but John's suspicions had sowed the seed in her mind. They divorced a year later. During the 21 Day Programme, John realised that he'd contributed to her unfaithfulness by believing she would cheat on him. He is now engaged to be married to someone new and makes a concerted effort to trust her at her word in everything she says and does. Why? John says, "Because if she is going to cheat, she will cheat. I cannot control what my partner does anyway so might as well relax. It's a more stress free way to live"

Note:
Whatever you believe to be true, you will make true – so be careful about what you believe.

What can you do to put this baggage in its place?

Ask questions but a tip is to tell your new partner that you trust her completely and then make a total effort to trust her. Walking around wondering if you will get hurt again is bound to cause pain and anguish. Love is a risk, so surrender to your new relationship and practice chilling.

The 'I am terrible in bed' baggage

What is it?

This baggage is usually linked to previous relationship history. This baggage can make you very insecure during sex and can turn you off trying anything new and exciting.

What are the facts?

Great sex has absolutely nothing to do with how many acrobatic antics you can perform. It also has nothing to do with how in shape you are, your stamina or what your body looks like. Great sex is about feeling sexy, enjoying yourself and losing yourself in having fun, experiencing the pleasure and moment of it. Sex is also a form of self-expression and an opportunity to express to your partner how you feel about her.

What can you do to put this baggage in its place?

I'm going to suggest something controversial... Have sex for you and not only to make your partner happy. Have a go at losing yourself during sex. If you struggle with this, pretend you're someone else.

Start a little project focused on having sex for the sake of simply having sex. Go on.

Complete your daily homework – start this in the morning.

Exercise:

Spend some time today diagnosing your baggage type and complete the remedial work. You may have more than one baggage type running the show. If this is the case, do the remedial work indicated for all these baggage types.

There is some work you will need to do consciously whenever this baggage comes up over the next few weeks or months. It may come up from time to time but whenever it does, knock it on the head immediately. Focus on what you want to have happen in your life rather than indulging in the negative thoughts of your baggage.

But make a choice today to dump the relationship baggage.

My story:

The biggest compliment I received after my divorce came from my partner Simon. A few days into our relationship he said to me, "You know, Adèle, you have never felt like a divorced woman to me. You just don't have that brittle wounded thing that so many divorced women have. You are strong, confident and clear about who you are and what you want."

I burst into tears. I was determined to truly heal from my divorce, take responsibility and come out fresh, clean and pure. This statement was testament that I had achieved that goal. I felt immense pride in myself over what he said that day.

day
18
RELEASE

KEEP THIS IN MIND FOR THE DAY: 'Our deepest fear is not that we are inadequate. Our deepest fear is that we are powerful beyond measure. It is our light not our darkness that frightens us. Actually, who are you not to be? You are a child of God. Your playing small doesn't serve the world. There's nothing enlightened about shrinking so that other people won't feel insecure around you. We were born to make manifest the glory of God that is within us.' ~ Nelson Mandela, inaugural address, written by Marianne Williamson

Theme: Your values and what you want out of your next relationship

Date: Monday, _____

🕑 **Estimated time to complete the exercise: 90–120 minutes**

Remember to go through the daily checklist

Tick when done

Read through the thought for the day:

One of the common phrases I hear after people experience a divorce is, "I don't know who I am now that I'm not in my relationship anymore…"

There is a great deal of fear associated with being suddenly single when your identity has been bound up with someone else for several years or decades.

It's vitally important that you distinguish where the centre of your life is after your divorce. And if you don't know, this is a great opportunity to do so!

If the centre of your life is no longer healthy or supportive to you, make a choice to change it to something you feel will be worthy.

WARNING:

Be careful that you don't centre your life around your children. As a role model, you want to ensure your children see you having a life beyond them. They shouldn't be suffocated by your neediness and control. Develop interests outside your family. Think about the dreams you had as a child and make some choices about living some of those dreams today.

1. What do you value in your life?

It's great to re-evaluate your values now that you have a new life ahead of you. You may notice that in the past, your values were intimately tied to whatever your ex valued. Now it's your opportunity to choose your values for yourself.

2. What do you want in a relationship?

Begin to think about what is important to you in a relationship. Even if you don't want to have one for the foreseeable future, it's key to think about what you want so when that lucky person comes bounding into your life, they are someone you have chosen rather than just someone who chose you.

Once you have articulated what you want, be responsible for getting it. Many people fall into a trap of believing that it's up to their partner to make them happy and give them what they want and deserve. This is not a very powerful way to approach a new relationship. Your job in a relationship is to make **yourself** happy and ensure you are fulfilled first and foremost.

Your partner's job is simply to top up or add that extra *sweetener or sugar* to your life. The exercise today shows you how to be responsible for giving yourself what you deserve in a relationship.

Tip-

A single man who feels happy in his own skin has great charisma. This charisma acts like a magnetic force and is very attractive to a new partner.

3. What is at the centre of your life?

Take a minute and list the people or things that your life revolves around. It may be one thing or a combination.

Here are some examples:

- *Romantic relationship*
- *Job*
- *Children*
- *Hobbies*
- *Financial resources*
- *Favourite activities*
- *House, car and possessions*
- *Friends*
- *Health*

What would you like the centre of your life to be?

Now, rewrite the list above in the order you'd love your life to reflect.

4. When done, look at what are the things you value in your life?

Look at the list below and put these values in the order of what you value most in your life.

1. Acknowledgement
2. Security and stability
3. Family
4. Wealth/abundance/excess
5. Relationships
6. Having fun
7. Travel
8. Material things
9. Looking good
10. Relaxing (reading/ watching movies/massage)
11. Confidence
12. Learning new things
13. Mastering something
14. Having children

5. Being responsible for getting what you want out of a relationship

Complete this table below in your journal. Give at least 3 examples. The first example is from my own relationship journal:

What I need to feel honoured and secure in a relationship?	At least 3 actions I can take to provide this for myself
To know that I look good and am desirable as I am and that I have a healthy self-esteem about my body and looks.	• To look in the mirror every day and tell myself how good looking I am • Go to the gym 4 to 5 times a week and train for and complete a triathlon • Eat healthily (lots of healthy salads, no snacking in -between meals, no junk food, drink 10 glasses of water daily).

You need to know how to achieve each of those objectives yourself or you will be no help in educating your new partner in how to fulfil on those objectives for you. How else will you tell your partner HOW to help you feel good looking and desirable if you do not even know yourself?

day
19
RELEASE

KEEP THIS IN MIND FOR THE DAY: Today is also an opportunity to learn about and define your boundaries in life. A strong sense of self-esteem is a function of your boundaries. A person with weak boundaries will have low self-esteem.

Theme: Loving yourself is often a function of setting boundaries in your life

Date: Tuesday, _____

🕐 **Estimated time to complete the reading/ exercise: 90 minutes**

Remember to go through the daily checklist

Tick when done

☐

Read through the thought for the day:

Today is about learning to set boundaries with others. If you struggle to love and honour yourself, this is a wonderful exercise. People who have healthy boundaries naturally have a healthy self-esteem and love themselves compared to those who do not.

Go back to Day 12 and reacquaint yourself with what you said you wouldn't be prepared to tolerate in a relationship. Have this with you as you complete this exercise. In terms of this section on boundaries, I want to provide some background context and explore the concept of archetypes which is essentially a model of a type of behaviour.

Psychologist Carl Gustav Jung described several archetypes in his many bodies of work. Certain energies, personalities and behaviours are encapsulated within those archetypes and are very useful in exploring different ways of being.

Many of us experience some difficulty in setting boundaries in our lives. This is largely because we are unconsciously stuck in a particular paradigm or archetype which is undistinguished for us. We set boundaries using those paradigms without even being aware of them.

I am describing these archetypes in a way that is only relevant in exploring boundaries in a particular way.

Archetype	Boundary Personality	How I set Boundaries	Energy
King	You are a careful and respected leader in your life. You are confident, powerful and knowledge-able. You have no problem setting boundaries with people in your life and you do so with no dramas and with ease. You know who you are, know what you want and do not allow anyone to take unfair advantage of you.	Powerful, regal and centered	Spiritual and Integrative
Magician	You are the performer and will come up with an elaborate clever excuse rather than admit the truth as to why you are setting the boundary. You don't enjoy conflict, so think of wily ways to set boundaries so that you achieve your objective without causing any discomfort.	Manipulative, sly, strategic and can be slimy	Cunning and Intellectual
Lover	You are a hopeless romantic. You have no boundaries and everyone is allowed to come into your space. You allow anyone close to you, allow people to walk over you and are often unable to say the word 'No'.	Doormat, poodle, dependant, coward, easily manipulated or cajoled	Emotional with no boundaries - everyone is let in
Warrior	You are full of action and direction, you know what you are doing. You have no problem with conflict or in setting boundaries but sometimes your approach in setting boundaries leaves a trail of destruction in your wake.	Curt, abrasive, bully, can cause offence	Physical with too many boundaries - no one is let in

It's important to acknowledge what your default is in setting boundaries in the past. Perhaps you struggled to say no or perhaps you developed an elaborate story to squirm out of unpleasant situations. Study the table above and identify which archetype you generally stepped into when it came time to set a boundary.

Learning to set boundaries is a vital part of learning to communicate in a direct and honest manner. It's impossible to have a healthy relationship with someone who has no boundaries or with someone who cannot communicate directly, and honestly.

Learning how to set boundaries is also a necessary step in learning to be a friend to yourself. It is your responsibility to take care of yourself and protect yourself when necessary. It is impossible to learn to love yourself without owning yourself and owning your rights and responsibilities as co-creators of your life.

The most effective archetypal approach in setting boundaries is that of the King. The King can say no, but with power, composure and peace with no side agenda or abrasiveness. The King is taken seriously and has a healthy personal relationship. Setting personal boundaries is key to truly loving, respecting and honouring yourself. Boundaries let other people know that you deserve and command respect.

Setting boundaries

Any person who has become powerful, went through the journey of learning to assert them self. Setting a boundary is not making a threat or behaving in a warrior-way, it is communicating clearly what the consequences will be if the other person continues to treat you in an unacceptable manner.

Setting a boundary is also not an attempt to control the other person in a magician-way by adopting a sophisticated way of manipulation.

The difference between setting a boundary in a healthy way and manipulating is that when you set a boundary you let go of the outcome.

Whenever you set a boundary, adopt the approach of HIGH INTENTION of what you want and LOW ATTACHMENT to the outcome. When we are attached to outcomes, we can become manipulative and strategic...

> **“ With boundaries, as in every area of the healing process, change starts with awareness. ”**

Codependency Therapist, Robert Burney, defines the formula for emotionally honest communication as follows:

Your sentences begin with phrases such as:

> **"When you..."**

> **"I feel..."**

> **"I want..."**

The key to Robert's formula is in being incredibly specific and questioning the assumptions you have made before accusing the person you are talking to.

An example of this is below:

"When you…"

The 'When you… ' statement describes their exact behaviour in detail so that it's not subject to personal interpretation or assumptions.

Examples include:

"When your face gets red and your voice gets louder and your hands clench into fists"

"I feel…"

This is the part where you express your emotions.

Examples include:

"When your voice gets louder and your face gets red and you clench your fists, I feel like withdrawing and watching TV. I don't feel I can talk to you when I am not sure it is you I am talking to."

"I want… "

"I want" is a clear description of what you are looking for from this person to alter the situation. Again, be completely specific. Saying, "you want to feel more love" is too general.

Examples include:

"I want you to tell me directly and clearly what you are angry about, so if you are angry about me bringing the kids home late, tell me, rather than me wondering if you are angry with me"

I have found that in setting boundaries that what works is finding your own self expression in it. I often use humour. I am direct and straight but not overly heavy or significant about it.

I say things very firmly and loudly but with a broad smile on my face. Examples include:-

- *"I am not very happy about that. If you continue that, I am outta here!"*

- *"Look, this happened, but if it happens again, I won't be as understanding. I deserve more than that so please don't do it again."*

I wrote a blog on the BUCKET exercise which is a method you can use for each party to get rid of their frustrations in an emotionally honest way. It's very effective in getting rid of frustrations, communicating honestly with your partner without putting blame on anyone else.

Go to
www.nakeddivorce.com/blog

Dealing with your children's strong emotional outbursts

You may become an expert in dealing with your own emotions but there may be situations whereby you need to handle someone else's strong emotions and setting boundaries at these points is very useful. Whether this be your ex's outbursts or your children, having an effective way of handling other people's outbursts will be helpful in life. But first, let me share an example. It's of a client Rosie. Now even though she is a woman, this case study is excellent learning.

Case study: Rosie

I had a client Rosie, whose daughter Sophie was very angry that her parents were going through a divorce. She would have angry outbursts at her mother on regular occasions. This left her mother completely distraught and at the effect of her daughter's mood swings. She kept asking me, "How could Sophie be so insensitive to my feelings? It's not my fault that her father left but she keeps saying it is."

After some coaching, Rosie realised that even though Sophie was 18, the divorce was hitting her much harder than her younger sister who was revelling in all the attention she was suddenly receiving from her father now that her parents had split up. Sophie felt incredible rage that there were no custody battles over her and felt that her sister who was 9 was being favourited.

Sophie would say the vilest things to her mother. It included statements like, "It's your fault dad left, you are the worst wife in the world and you pushed him away with all your nagging." "I hope you die, because you are worthless now that dad has left us" and my personal favourite, "You are a worthless horrible mother, I hate you and wish my sister was never born because I hate her too."

These outbursts upset Rosie incredibly and all outbursts would descend into an argument, followed by slamming of doors and many tears. When things had calmed down, the guilt would set in and Sophie would apologise but Rosie was beginning to feel like she was walking around on eggshells in her house.

Additionally, whenever she had an open mediation session with her soon-to-be ex-husband, he would shout, scream and perform, telling her it was her fault he left and that she was a horrible woman.

Rosie needed a mechanism to not get riled by her ex or Sophie's outbursts. She followed a particular process I taught her and within a few days, her relationship with Sophie improved so remarkably that she received a card from her saying that she was the best mummy in the world. Sophie also felt validated and heard, so consequently became calmer and more pleasant to be around. Rosie realised that whereas her younger daughter was coping quite well, her elder daughter's model of relationship and family was shattered. Most children believe in the fairy tale aspect of marriage, i.e. that you get married and live happily ever after, forever. Sophie's model of marriage and paradigm for relationships was broken so she was trying to reconcile if marriages ever worked and trying to work out why this fairy tale did not have a happy ending. It HAD to be someone's fault and unfortunately she decided it had to be her mother so she focused all her anger on her. Once Sophie had calmed down, she and Rosie were able to have long discussions about marriage and through counselling sessions, Sophie healed. She still had the occasional outburst but Rosie knew how to handle it and the anger would die down quite quickly.

Rosie also noticed that her mediation sessions and contact with her soon-to-be ex-husband became much more relaxed as she became more powerful. She stopped resisting and fighting against him, which diffused his anger. She is now well on her way to achieving a settlement.

This is the process she learnt:

Being powerful in the face of your children's strong emotional outbursts

STEP 1: Understand that the angry or emotional outburst is not personal to you. It's about the wounded little boy or wounded little girl inside your child who is shouting or screaming.

Stand tall and BE THE PARENT. In other words, this is the time to step up and be powerful, stable and reassuring. Getting angry and upset will not help the situation.

STEP 2: Look intently at your children, to assure them that you are listening. Crouch down to their level and look them straight in the eye. Stop doing what you are doing. Do not fidget and switch off the distractions. Often what riles people the most is the feeling that they are not being listened to. Eliminate this possibility by giving them the assurance that you are listening to them.

STEP 3: Do not react. Allow whatever they are saying to wash over you, like it is simply words that have no meaning. Even if they say that they wish you were dead or that they hate you. Often, these words are not meant when things have calmed down. When they are done ranting or having their say, simply do the following:

Take a deep breath and say, "I understand that you are feeling angry *[or upset, or disappointed, etc.]* and I understand that because of this situation, you feel this emotion very strongly."

Be calm and speak with an even tone. Visualise a positive outcome. Apologise that this divorce has had this impact on their life. Say you are sorry that they feel this strong emotion and simply continue to reassure him or her that no matter what they say, you still love them and are here for them. When your child has calmed down, ask him or her how they are doing and how they are feeling. Talk about the divorce and talk about it from their perspective. There is no need to react. This is the moment to be stable and reassuring. Sometimes children will test you to see if you will stop loving them. It's therefore important to be loving and BE the parent.

STEP 4: Once done with the discussion, give a reassuring hug and ensure you let them know that they are loved as they are and that they have a right to their anger or emotions. This ensures that they know they can always come to you with any discussion they wish to have and that you will listen to them and respect their emotions. Try to do something together, like going for a walk. Often these kinds of outbursts are cries for attention.

STEP 5: Write regular reassuring letters to your children so that they always know that this divorce is not their fault and that they are precious and perfect as they are. Invite them to discuss with you how they feel at any time.

Dealing with your ex's strong emotional outbursts

The vast majority of boundaries are in fact a negotiation rather than a rigid line in the sand. Adults need to negotiate boundaries between themselves. This is the standard for all relationships and is particularly true for romantic relationships.

If you don't risk sharing how you feel and don't speak up, you'll blow up and/or become passive aggressive and damage the relationship.

Being powerful in the face of your ex's strong emotional outbursts

STEP 1: Understand that the angry or emotional outburst is not personal to you. It's about the wounded little boy or wounded little girl inside the person who is shouting or screaming.

If seated, stand up and stand tall with your shoulders back and hands at your sides. As the person is saying whatever they are saying, tell yourself that whatever they are saying is about them feeling hurt and wanting to hurt someone else. It has nothing to do with you.

STEP 2: Look intently at your ex, to assure them that you are listening. Stop doing what you are doing. Do not fidget and switch off the television. Often what riles people the most is the feeling that they are not being listened to. Eliminate this possibility by giving them the assurance that you are listening to them.

STEP 3: Do not react. Allow whatever they are saying to wash over you, like it is simply words that have no meaning.

When they are done ranting or having their say, simply do the following:

Take a deep breath and say, "I understand that you are feeling angry (or upset, or disappointed, etc.) and I understand that because of this situation, you feel this emotion very strongly." Do not respond to the specific points of what they said. Simply say that you are, "willing to talk when things are calmer."

STEP 4: Simply walk out of the room and leave. Have a cup of tea and be still. Try not to raise your voice to match them, just refuse to play the game.

STEP 5: If you feel that discussions are impossible, write a letter adopting a very factual matter-of-fact tone.

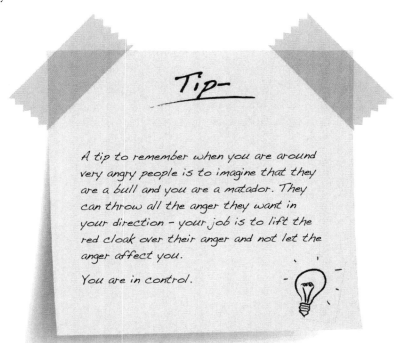

Tip-

A tip to remember when you are around very angry people is to imagine that they are a bull and you are a matador. They can throw all the anger they want in your direction - your job is to lift the red cloak over their anger and not let the anger affect you.

You are in control.

You always have a choice

You always have a choice. The choices may seem to be awful, but in reality, allowing yourself to buy into the illusion that you are trapped will have worse consequences in the long run.

Owning your choices, no matter how outrageous, is a step in owning responsibility for your life. If you are blaming and being the victim, you will never be happy. Personal boundaries exist to teach us to be discerning in our choices, to teach us to ask for what we need, and to teach us to be assertive and loving in meeting our needs.

Read through the exercise you will be doing later today. Allow yourself to think about it during the day.

Exercise:

Make a list of all the relationships in your life in which you experience a loss of power. Plan the emotionally honest conversations you want to have with these people, or the boundaries you will set with them. Schedule times over the next few weeks to have those conversations. If possible, have one of those conversations in the next 48 hours.

Getting really good at emotionally honest conversations and setting boundaries, needs practice. The good news is that the more you practice, the better you will become, so your job for the next thirty days is to practice, practice, and practice!

day 20

RELEASE

KEEP THIS IN MIND FOR THE DAY: *"Life is too short to wake up in the morning with regrets. So love the people who treat you right, forget about the ones who don't and believe that everything happens for a reason. If you get a chance, take it. If it changes your life, let it. Nobody said that it'd be easy, they just promised it would be worth it."* ~ *Author unknown*

Theme: What is your new life going to look like?

Date: Wednesday, _____

🕐 **Estimated time to complete the exercise: 90–120 minutes**

Remember to go through the daily checklist

Tick when done

Read through the thought for the day:

Today is all about your future and what you want to do with your life.

1. Firstly, today you will have an opportunity to assess how you feel about the various areas of your life using the Wheel of Life

2. Next, you will sit back and think of all you dreamed for your life when you were a child. You will have the opportunity to create a list of things you'd like to do before you die

3. You'll be asking yourself: 'What do I want to change about my life?', and 'How can I use this divorce as a catalyst to live my dream life?'

4. You will also develop a *Personal Manifesto* whereby you will define who you are from today onwards. What will your life be about?

5. You will choose a *Personal Anthem*. This is a song that lifts you up and is the theme tune for your new life. You may already have your

song in mind but if you don't, there are some suggestions in the exercise list below

Today is the day you reconnect with the dreams you had for your life. You have one life, so live it!

Read through the exercise you'll be doing later today. Allow yourself to think about it during the day.

Exercise:

1. Below is an image called the Wheel of Life. Firstly, assess the various areas of your life by putting a score between 0 and 10 in each area, 0 being the score that requires the most work and 10 requiring no additional work at all.

2. Next, decide on three actions you can take in each area to bring the scores in all areas of your life up to 10.

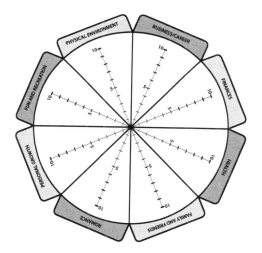

Ask yourself: What do I want to change about my life? How can I use this divorce as a catalyst to live my dream life?

3. Take a moment to think of the dreams you had as a child for your life. Create a comprehensive list of things you'd like to do before you die. Here are some examples from my list. I've crossed off quite a few off since articulating my list, so you never know where your life will take you! Whether you have five or 200 things on your list, allow yourself to dream big!

1. *Fly into space*

2. *Climb Mount Kilimanjaro*

3. *Scuba dive the Great Barrier Reef in Australia*

4. *Raft the Colorado river*

5. *Ride the 10 biggest, baddest rollercoasters*

6. *Dog sled in Norway*

7. *Boat trip through the fjords in Finland / Norway*

8. *Fly a MIG jet to the edge of space*

9. *Go on safari in north Africa*

10. *Ride a motorcycle from Cape Town to Cairo*

11. *Ride a motorcycle from LA to Buenos Aires*

4. Develop a Personal Manifesto where you define who you are from today onwards. What will your life be about?

5. Choose your own Personal Anthem or Theme song. This is a song that lifts you up and is the theme tune for your new life. You can listen to it whenever you want to feel pumped up, moved or excited about your life. If you don't have something in mind, here are a few suggestions:

- *It's My Prerogative - Bobby Brown*
- *We Will Rock You - Queen*
- *Welcome to the Jungle - Guns n' Roses*
- *Lose Yourself - Eminem*
- *Gonna Fly Now - Bill Conti / The Rocky Orchestra*

Think of your anthem now…

day 21
RELEASE

KEEP THIS IN MIND FOR THE DAY: *Today is your chance to celebrate your enormous achievements over the past 21 days. You are a hero!*

Theme: Celebration!

Date: Thursday, _____

🕐 **Estimated time to complete the exercise: 30 minutes**

Remember to go through the daily checklist

Tick when done

Read through the thought for the day:

☐

This is it, the final day! I acknowledge your courage and your immense achievement. I don't take it lightly that you've accomplished what you have as I've walked this path myself. I know how tough it is and, you did it!

Spend today getting reacquainted with who you are, how extraordinary you are and how damn fantastic your life will be from today onwards.

I'd like you to walk around with your head held high wearing your invisible crown. You did it. You are a hero and you are free. Make a list of everything you acknowledge yourself for today. Today there is no homework, only celebration.

Jump around in your shower, put on your new theme song and celebrate. Throw yourself a *Divorce Party* and invite your closest and dearest friends, or go out on a mission to have fun or buy yourself a motorcycle or Playstation. You have completed the 21 Day Programme and that is a great effort.

I'd love to hear your story so you can inspire other men around the world, so please email us on info@nakeddivorce.com, also send us your postal address and we will send you a special T-shirt to acknowledge your achievement.

Checklist for the programme

DAYS 15–21: RELEASE

DAY 15   THEME: STEPPING INTO FORGIVENESS

DAY 16   THEME: THE VOW BREAK

DAY 17   THEME: UNPACKING YOUR RELATIONSHIP BAGGAGE

DAY 18   THEME: YOUR VALUES AND WHAT YOU WANT OUT OF YOUR NEXT RELATIONSHIP

DAY 19   THEME: LOVING YOURSELF AND SETTING BOUNDARIES IN YOUR LIFE

DAY 20   THEME: WHAT IS YOUR NEW LIFE GOING TO LOOK LIKE?

DAY 21   THEME: CELEBRATION!

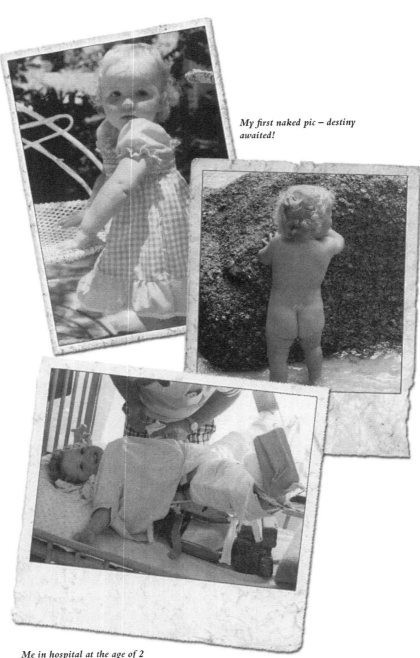

My first naked pic – destiny awaited!

Me in hospital at the age of 2 getting my hip sockets built

Happier times with Bruce

My many cousins and beloved Ouma

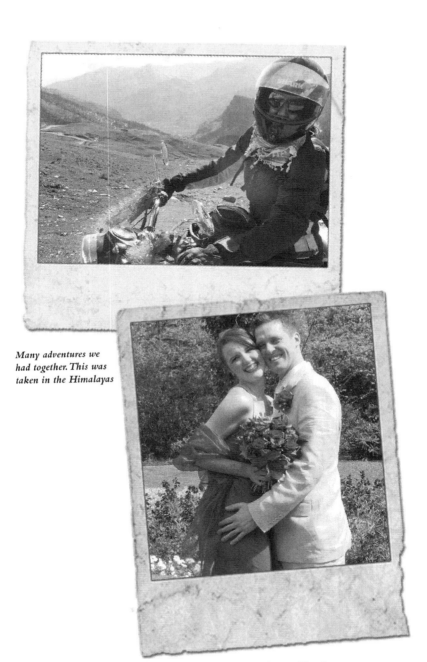

Many adventures we had together. This was taken in the Himalayas

Our wedding day

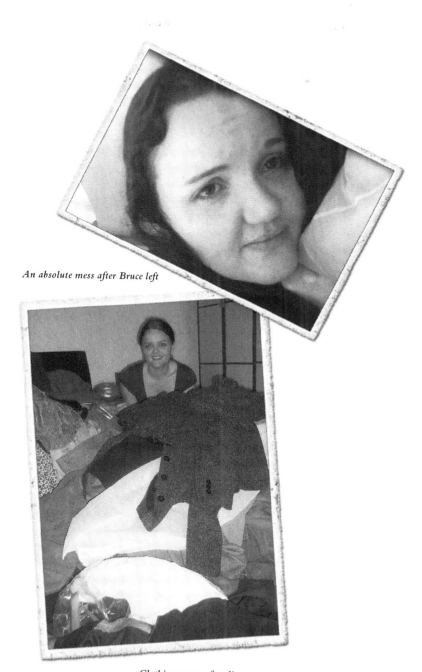

An absolute mess after Bruce left

Clothing purge after divorce

My amazing parents

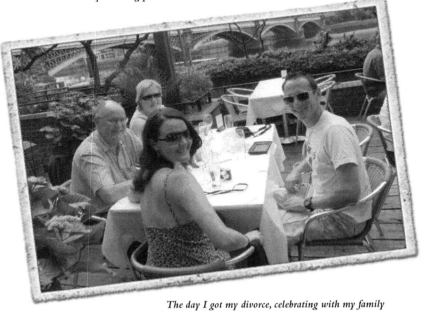

The day I got my divorce, celebrating with my family

My amazingly supportive friends

With my ex-stepmother in law post-divorce. I was a bridesmaid at Bruce's cousin Roz's wedding.

Getting back on track, I had a little makeover!

*With my wonderful
husband Simon*

My corporate self

My 2nd triathlon

Some participants from a change management workshop I led in Zurich, Switzerland

Speaking about Naked Divorce

part five

Your Future

What's next?

Well done! You've completed the 21 Day Programme. Well done! You've completed the 21 Day Programme. Not only did you conquer this divorce, you can categorically say that you are not shit at it!

Does this mean your transformation is complete? To put it briefly, no.

But don't be discouraged. This is good news. You are only just beginning your new life and learning how to handle challenges along the way is part of living a full life, the life you've been working towards realising by completing the **Naked Divorce**.

Imagine how mundane your existence would be without challenge, upsets or emotions to deal with?

Here are some tips to deal with some of the longer-term challenges that are certain to come your way...

The first year after your divorce

➡ Keep working with the ETHICS and 7 Foundations of Transformation for a minimum of three weeks after completing the programme. Whenever I have a tough time of anything, I go back to those elements and make them part of my life so that I'm contained. In those low moments, I feel strong no matter what comes my way

➡ Review your fitness regime and audit how you feel physically

➡ Review your finances and ensure you have finalised things with your ex

➡ Put into action some of the activities you came up with from Day 20 Get sucked into creative endeavours that inspire you

➡ Plan activities throughout the year so that you have events to look forward to, especially on anniversary dates and special holidays

➡ Take up some new hobbies. Have you always wanted to run a marathon, take up motorcycling or do karate? Now's the time to do it and find some new avenues to make new friends

Dealing with down days

Whatever comes up in the next twelve months, be kind to yourself. Accept that there will be reminders and times when you feel sad, or have a flash back to the past. When negative emotions surface, feel them and BE with them. If you surrender to them, they will pass. There's no reason you can't keep practicing many of the exercises you've done over the 21 days of the **Naked Divorce** for years to come. Here are some suggestions:

- ✓ What to do when you feel you've lost the 'love of your life': Repeat the Pedestal Shift exercise from Day 8. You can never do this exercise too many times

- ✓ What to do if you put your ex back on a pedestal: Repeat the homework exercises for Days 7 and 8 (Different Points of View, and Perception is Projection)

- ✓ When you're feeling overly emotional: Re-read the sections on emotions, ensuring you follow the tips to understand your emotions and where they're coming from

- ✓ When you're angry or upset: Repeat the exercise from Day 9. Many of my male clients make a point of doing this exercise every few months. It's very cathartic

- ✓ When things are a bit haphazard in a new relationship: Re-read and practice all the tips from Days 13 and 17

- ✓ When you're worried or stressed: Repeat the Worry Buster exercise from Day 17. It really works, particularly if you are a visual based person

- ✓ When you are feeling like a victim or need to set some boundaries: Re-read Days 13 and 19 and practice the suggested exercises

- ✓ When feeling extreme emotions at work: Practice the Awareness exercise for handling emotions whilst at work

Anniversaries

Certain times of the year are loaded with memories and if you can anticipate these occasions and prepare for them, they'll be easier to get through. Those old important dates will gradually lose their significance as you fill your life with new memories, events and people.

Tip-

Buy a new calendar and mark only those dates that are meaningful to your new life. Plan ahead for days marking old anniversaries, etc. so that you're busy doing something special when that date rolls around. Plan an activity or an outing with family or friends. Make sure you have a great day.

➡ **Your divorce day**: If your divorce has finally come through, it's natural to have a bit of a strange day. You could swing between extreme happiness at it being all over or sadness at the loss. Prepare yourself, as you could be feeling anything on that day. Better to have a plan of action for the day than just seeing what might come up, so do plan something you enjoy doing on that day

➡ **Your wedding anniversary:** The first wedding anniversary after a divorce can be difficult if you were in a long-term partnership. I always take myself out on a date or purchase something special to commemorate my achievement. So find a game to watch or throw a party with key friends so you have a plan in place rather than drifting

➡ **Your birthday:** Do something you have always wanted to do, but never gave yourself permission to do when you were married

➡ **Your ex's birthday:** It's up to you how you handle this one, but plan ahead so that you're not caught out. If you have a good relationship with your ex, you might want to call them or send them a gift or a card. Do whatever feels comfortable for you. Be careful to respect her space. You don't want to be a stalker!

➡ **Your children's birthdays:** Prepare for the day well ahead of time. Ensure that the day is about your child. Agree with your ex ahead of time on who does what, particularly when it comes to a party.

KEEP THIS IN MIND FOR THE DAY: Discuss presents in advance so that you and your ex don't duplicate gifts or try to outdo each other or compete against each other

Managing finances in the future

➡ Have you finalised all financial dealings with your ex and are there any further loose ends to be tied up?

➡ Even if the split was amicable, you need to agree on what will happen to joint accounts, the house and shared assets

➡ Consider that if you haven't drawn up a financial clean-break order to resolve your finances legally, your ex could lay claim to any money you inherit. If you need to, get things in writing and seek financial advice

➡ Have you discussed what happens if you re-marry or your ex re-marries?

➡ Are you entitled to any benefits that you aren't claiming?

➡ Do you have a long-term financial plan? Do you have savings, investments, a pension plan and a Last Will and Testament in place?

➡ Review your finances every three months and take independent advice if you're unsure of anything

Ex-Factor Etiquette when there are no children involved

Being friends with your ex

Good for you if you can make the transition from married to divorced to friends, especially if you don't have children and have no real reason to stay in touch. I recommend ensuring that you've established your new, separate life before you make this transition. If you become best buddies too soon, your relationship with your ex could become a social crutch, or something you hide behind in place of creating a life for yourself.

The important point about being friends with your ex is that the relationship should evolve naturally. Don't force it.

Also, it will not happen immediately – it cannot. You will need some time to ensure the relationship evolves into something clear where you can be friends.

In the beginning I recommend going cold turkey and not seeing your ex at all. Break all contact, delete contact on all social media networks and stop stalking your ex at the supermarket or on Facebook - it will drive you crazy. Use the exercise on setting boundaries to set crucial boundaries with your ex.

When you have a new relationship you must honour your divorce. That means putting your new partner first. Any new relationship takes time to develop and you don't want an ex hanging about in the wings to jeopardise things. The same goes for if your ex has a new partner: don't get in the way and give them their privacy.

You judge whether a natural friendship with your ex is healthy or not. If it interferes in your new life or theirs, cool it down.

Sex with your ex

Sometimes partners continue their sexual relationship after a break-up. It may be that you're less familiar with each other after your divorce so the sex can feel more passionate.

Some couples will 'use' each other for sex although this prolongs the hurt. I know of many men who continue to sleep with their ex-partners long after they've remarried and had children. One such man was Brad.

Case study: Brad

Brad continued to have sex with his ex-wife for six years after their divorce. Neither of them saw any harm in pursuing their 'Friends with Benefits' arrangement and felt that they got on better now that they were divorced than when they were married. After six years, Brad met someone at work and began a relationship with her which eventually became sexual. He found himself feeling very confused as he was cheating on his new girlfriend with his ex-wife. He eventually decided to break it off with his ex-wife and she was incredibly distraught and upset. She hadn't acknowledged that the relationship had become a social crutch for her and was completely devastated by it coming to an end. Brad realised that although he could keep his feelings at bay with his ex-wife, she could not and by continuing to sleep with her they both delayed moving on with their lives.

Having sex with your ex is not moving on. There was a reason your relationship didn't work out and a clean break is better for closure. Don't waste your life clinging to old relationships whilst you wait in a departure lounge going nowhere.

Some people find it very difficult to separate sex and intimacy and if your ex is sleeping with you, it is inevitable that things will get very complicated in time. For some people, sex might mean intimacy but to others, sex simply means sex. It's important to be responsible for how your actions impact others so be clear on your competing agendas before embarking on a sexual relationship.

The next time you feel compelled to contact your ex, ask yourself:

➡ Do I miss being with my ex or do I simply miss being in a couple?

➡ What if my ex says, "Let's give it another go." Will you be able to change what didn't work the first time in your relationship?

➡ If you're leaving the outcome of your relationship in your ex's hands, ask yourself, "What do I want? Is my ex the person I want to be with for the rest of my life, even if nothing changed?"

If you are still harbouring resentment and anger towards your ex

If you have completed the 21 Day Programme, and still feel strong anger or bitterness, then it is possible you skipped steps during your programme so contact the **Naked Divorce** team immediately, as this is not a common response.

If you can't be friends

Be civil and friendly. When you bump into your ex, greet them, shake hands or hug but ONLY do what you feel comfortable with. Keep your interactions brief and then move on.

Ex-Factor Etiquette when there are children involved

Don't expose your children to marital conflict

When children are involved in divorce it's very important for parents to behave civilly. I accept that this can be hard. It might always be hard. But there will be times you have to see your ex, particularly at school events or if you need to discuss something related to their parenting. In these cases, the rules are easy:

➡ **Don't speak badly of your ex in front of your children**

   Respect your children have a right to have a relationship with both their parents and do not use them as a go-between or carrier of nasty messages. KEEP your children out of any marital conflicts

➡ **Do not volunteer unsavoury information about your ex in front of your children**

➡ **Do not argue in front of your children.** Be polite and set a good example

➡ **Prioritise having an amicable relationship with your ex.** It is important that your children feel you are still presenting a united front

➡ **Make sure your marital settlement or divorce agreement is clear on ALL the details.** This ensures that there are no misunderstandings in the future

➡ **Don't give your children false hopes of reuniting.** It's important that they do not receive confusing messages

➡ **If your ex does push your buttons, think ahead before you see them and ask yourself:**

• What are the triggers?

• How will you keep the peace and stay calm?

• What do you want to achieve in your interactions?

Get yourself a great coach

Everyone who wants to achieve success in whatever they do in life needs to treat himself like an athlete and always have a great coach, if not several. Now that you have seen what is possible when you have someone rooting for you and standing next to you as you move through the programme, find someone that you can set goals with and check in with on a weekly/bi-weekly/monthly or quarterly basis.

If you like the way we work within the **Naked Divorce** team, we have a team of angels within our sister website called **Naked Recovery Online** and we support many people in follow-up programmes long after the programmes have completed in our **Momentum** and **Propulsion** courses. We help people to recover from other traumas and breakdowns too.

We also have lifeline calls so you can just book an hour when you need to talk through a particular challenge you are dealing with.

For more information:

      Web: www.nakedrecoveryonline.com

      Email: info@nakedrecoveryonline.com

Momentum and Propulsion

      Quote discount code: M&P-GOB-10%

Helping your children through your divorce

I'm not an expert and can't speak from experience about children and divorce, but I have successfully coached many men and women with children. I have also helped many children and teens accept and process their parents' divorce and run Tantrum Clubs to help them handle the emotions.

Using my experience with my clients who are parents, and having consulted the best parenting-after-divorce experts in the field, I have included this section to help you support your children through the trauma of divorce and its aftermath. What you read below is a distillation of what these experts' advice and recommend and what I have learnt from coaching people, children and teens. All books, interviews and recommended reading is listed in the bibliography at the back of this book.

In my reading, one of the most useful resources (I highly recommend it) I came across is from 'Don't Divorce Your Children', written by paediatricians Jennifer Lewis and William Sammons, the website www.helpguide.org as well as in my interview with Sherlyn Luedtke, founder of Present Parent Training.

What do children believe during divorce?

Many children believe that they had something to do with the divorce. They may remember times when they argued with their parents, got poor grades, or got into trouble. They may associate that conflict with their parents' conflict and blame themselves. Also, some children may worry that their parents will stop loving them, or that they will never see the estranged parent again. Sometimes young children don't understand the meaning and permanence of divorce. Sometimes they believe that it's one parent's fault or that someone else is to blame.

Reassurance and consistency is important in the early days of divorce.

Sherlyn Luedtke says, "Tell your children that although the love between mom and dad has changed, that this kind of love is different than love between parent and child. This love is forever and special." Sherlyn also believes in telling your children the same things over and over again to prove that there is consistency.

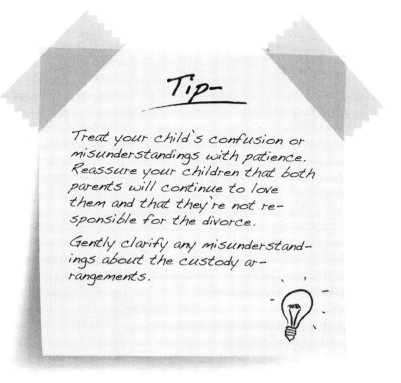

Tip-

Treat your child's confusion or misunderstandings with patience. Reassure your children that both parents will continue to love them and that they're not responsible for the divorce.

Gently clarify any misunderstandings about the custody arrangements.

What do children want from their parents?

This list is taken from a study done at the University of Missouri where children of divorce were asked what they needed from their mum and dad. The list is written by children themselves:

➡ "I need both of you to stay involved in my life. Please write letters, make phone calls, and ask me lots of questions. When you don't stay involved, I feel like I'm not important and that you don't really love me"

➡ "Please stop fighting and work hard to get along with each other. Try to agree on matters related to me. When you fight about me, I think that I did something wrong and I feel guilty"

➡ "I want to love you both and enjoy the time that I spend with each of you. Please support me and the time that I spend with each of you. If you act jealous or upset, I feel like I need to take sides and love one parent more than the other"

➡ "Please communicate directly with my other parent so that I don't have to send messages back and forth"

➡ "When talking about my other parent, please say only nice things, or don't say anything at all. When you say mean, unkind things about my other parent, I feel like you are expecting me to take your side"

➡ "Please remember that I want both of you to be a part of my life. I count on you both to raise me, to teach me what is important, and to help me when I have problems"

How you communicate with your children is key

Difficult as it may be to do, try to strike an empathetic tone and address the most important points, right up front. Give your children the benefit of an honest, but child-friendly, explanation.

If you go to www.helpguide.org and read the texts I have recommended, they indicate there is a specific way to speak to your children so that you have told them enough but not too much. A summary of all the texts say:

➡ **Provide continuity.** Children need the sense of continuity provided by a certain amount of structure such as dependable meal and bed times, leisure and work times

➡ **Be consistent in routines and explanations of what happened.** Children have very keen attention to detail when stressed. Repeat the same reason for your divorce several times if necessary. Sometimes they need to hear the same message 100 times. Try to have a plan with your ex that they do the same thing

➡ **Explain that there are different types of love.** One of the sad things that children believe during divorce is that if love could end for mum and dad, then their love for me could end too. It's your job to reassure them that whilst romantic love is fragile and sometimes does end (like in a marriage), other types of love are forever loves like friendship love and the love we have for our children. If you can achieve a co-parenting friendship with your ex then you can explain to your children that your love for their mom has morphed into a forever-friendship love. Your kids knowing that mum and dad are good with each other helps their healing by a massive factor

➡ **Stable parent.** A parent being all emotional and all over the place is very destabilising to a child. You need to get yourself together so you are in a position to actually support them vs. use them as your crutch or purpose for living

➡ **80% of communication is related to tone and body language.** Ensure you are calm and grounded before engaging in communication

Normal reactions to separation and divorce

The resources www.childrenanddivorce.com, www.parentcoordinationcentral.com and www.helpguide.org state that although strong feelings can be tough on children, it is normal for them to experience some anger, anxiety and mild depression BUT if things get worse rather than better after several months, it may be a sign that your child is stuck in depression, anxiety or anger and could use some additional support. www.helpguide.org states you must watch for these warning signs of divorce-related depression or anxiety:

➡ Sleep problems, nightmares or bed-wetting

➡ Poor concentration

➡ Trouble at school

➡ Drug or alcohol abuse

➡ Self injury or cutting

➡ Frequent angry or violent outbursts

➡ Withdrawal from loved ones

➡ Avoiding favourite activities

Steps to reduce traumatic effects of a divorce on your children

There are several steps to follow to reduce the traumatic effects of divorce on children and now that you have taken care of yourself, study the resources, books and texts I have provided in this chapter to ensure you provide stability, structure and continuity for your children. Support them by helping them express emotions, and commit to truly listening to these feelings, without getting defensive. Listen and help them find words for their feelings, acknowledging their right to their feelings.

Also let your children know that even though the physical circumstances of the family unit will change, they can continue to have healthy, loving relationships with both of their parents. Help them make a hand-drawn picture of the family to help express how they feel. If they draw angrily, allow it to happen and discuss their feelings with them.

I run Parenting and Mediation sessions within **Naked Divorce**, so check out our website if you want help with specific situations. If ever in doubt, get support.

Develop a Parenting Plan

Paediatricians and authors Jennifer Lewis and William Sammons recommend that divorced parents develop a parenting plan for their children.

Most divorcing parents are understandably concerned about the custody status of their children because it defines how the major decision-making responsibilities will be allocated, and may influence where the children live. However, what primarily impacts the children's lives is not their custody status but the schedule of time that they spend with each parent and the nuts and bolts of how that schedule is implemented.

This blueprint for the children's care, Lewis and Samons call the parenting plan, should be a much more comprehensive document than the typical visitation agreement. A successful parenting plan needs to incorporate sufficient details to ensure children will not experience ongoing arguments and conflicts between their parents about the arrangements they are putting in place. A parenting plan could contain the amount of time that the children will spend with each parent, the time(s) and place(s) of handover, guidelines to holidays and vacations, calendar of joint schedule, joint-parenting rules and guidelines so that there is consistency in parenting (including bed times, diet, watching television, homework etc.) It has also been advised to include details such as what to do in the event of last minute delays or cancellations.

Letters to your children

In my weekly newsletter, you will find LOADS of tips, techniques and letter templates for helping your children comes to terms with the divorce. The templates include letters to young children, older children and letters to the school. Sign up at www.nakeddivorce.com today.

Falling in love again

Ensure you feel completely fulfilled

Relax. Focus first on getting over everything and being happy with yourself before you start focusing on finding a new partner. If you focus on being fulfilled as a person whilst your are single, then you are immediately more attractive to a potential partner. If you limp along like a broken butterfly needing another 'half' who will complete you, you will attract the wrong type of person into your life.

Take that trip you always wanted to take. Start a new hobby or hire a style consultant to freshen up your wardrobe or hairstyle. Develop your own interests and pursuits. Become happy on your own. You have just spent the past however many years focused on being in a relationship. This is now YOUR time to live your life and savour it.

NOTE: It's often when you stop worrying about finding a new partner that serendipity steps in and things start falling into place. If you're enjoying life again and looking after yourself - mind, body and soul - you're bound to make an impact and attract attention. But remember, no one wants to be around someone who has lost their sense of humour or who is depressed and uncommunicative.

Be aware of attracting rescuers while you're healing

As you discovered in Day 13 with the Drama Triangle, be wary of attracting rescuers during your time of healing. The potential partners you meet while you're in a compromised state may well be attracted to your vulnerability and that part of you that is needy and wanting to be comforted and cared for.

Don't attach yourself to any new acquaintances or friends who see you as less than you are.

Create your Dream Relationship blueprint

Answer these questions below in your journal:

➡ Do you have a certain type of partner you attract and where did this come from? Is this type healthy for you? What type of partner do you believe is the type who will be the best for you in your life?

➡ How was your life before you met your ex? Were you happy and confident or feeling needy and desperate?

➡ What were your ex's positive traits that attracted you and what good aspects or attributes of that relationship would you like to create in your next relationship?

➡ What are your expectations now? What are you looking for in a "dream relationship"?

➡ Close your eyes and create a little movie scene in your mind of you with your dream partner. How do you know it's your dream partner? What's happening in this scene? Write down everything you see, feel, hear, touch and experience. Ensure it's a vivid scene

Attract your dream relationship in 12 weeks

When it comes to attracting the partner of your dreams, your unconscious beliefs are more powerful than your everyday thoughts. You cannot re-programme your conscious mind. Your subconscious mind, however, is like a giant computer hard drive that can be programmed with mental software (i.e. thought patterns and belief systems) to control your thinking.

For example, if you currently have a mental programme installed in your subconscious mind that says, "I am too old, will never get what I want and I'm not good enough", your subconscious mind will make sure that you don't have any opportunities to attract that amazing person into your life. And even if you consciously want nothing more than to be in an amazing relationship, your subconscious mind can ensure that you sabotage your success.

Until you re-programme your mind to support you attracting your dream partner, your limiting belief systems (or programmes) in your subconscious mind will make you think thoughts that limit what you can attract into your life.

The **Dare2Date** programme is an effective way to attract your dream partner into your life. It's a similar programme to the **Naked Divorce** but with a twist: it's all about finding the one and creating yourself as someone who effortlessly attracts the one. This really worked for me and for several of my clients and it can work for you too. 72% of our participants are married or engaged today.

For more information:

Web: www.nakedrecoveryonline.com

Email: support@nakedrecoveryonline.com

Dare2Date

Quote discount code: D2D-GOB-10%

Principles of keeping love alive

I am sometimes really frustrated that the education system today does not prepare us for what it TRULY takes to make a romantic relationship work in the long-term. Many of my male clients have told me that they wish that they had known some of these principles before they got married.

Unfortunately many of us had to make mistakes before we learnt these lessons for the future.

Develop some compassion for yourself because you didn't have the insights you have today back when you might have needed them. Read the section below and focus on mastering the principles of keeping love alive, not only to ensure that you find your dream partner but more importantly, that your relationship will last. Some of these principles apply to both heterosexual and same-sex relationships. My top tip would be to read all of them and take the learnings that work for you.

Keeping Love Alive Principle #1: Let your partner win at loving you

This is a lesson I learnt the hard way. I had to own up to the fact that I never let my ex-husband win at loving me. I spent most of the time playing hard to get, being difficult, dramatic or testing my ex. Now, as a man, it's important for your wife or partner to feel she can succeed in making you happy.

Your partner needs to feel that by simply being around you, they can make you happy and that you're at peace and fully satisfied in their company. If not, then your partner might feel like a failure and might even say things like "I just can't win."

NOTE:

For someone to feel love, they must feel they can win or be successful at loving you

Think back on your marriage. Were you overly critical or condescending with your ex? Did your partner seem like the best version of herself with you? Consider that if you held your partner up against a checklist of perfection where they could never match your ideal and never make you happy, it could precipitate their infidelity. So, if you're resisting this one, I get it! Ask yourself, "Have I let my partner feel they can always win at loving me?" This is a crucial lesson for keeping love alive.

When you come home and you're feeling grumpy, ensure your partner knows they are amazing and that they make you very happy and that your moods have nothing to do with their amazingness.

Keeping Love Alive Principle #2: Maintain the polarity of your relationship

In heterosexual relationships, this is a critical component to maintaining sexual chemistry. In same-sex relationships, one partner will be more masculine than the other and it's critical to maintain that polarity or difference to keep the chemistry alive. The masculine essence seeks a relationship with the feminine essence to provide freedom, fun and lightness in life. The feminine essence seeks a relationship with the masculine essence to feel protected, loved and claimed. Understanding the masculine vs. feminine essence is really important to keeping the polarity and sexiness of your relationship alive.

The masculine essence is: Manly, clear, powerful, straight, strong, bossy, stakes a claim on the feminine essence, takes control, has a plan, is rational, logical, practical, makes plans, is deliberate, peaceful, wise and protective.

The masculine essence is not: extremely chatty, nice, sweet, emotional, weepy, needy, shouty, fussy, throwing tantrums, being hysterical, wanting to talk about emotions all the time.

The feminine essence is: Loving, caring, spontaneous, crazy, unpredictable, free, fun, mental, dramatic, turbulent, shrieking at the sight of a mouse/spider/creature with too many legs, outspoken, honest, vulnerable, raw, carefree, real, weepy, emotional, a hurricane, self-expressed, creative, chatty, babbling and making no sense, making things, painting things, cooking, being loud, noisy, peaceful, sexy, mysterious, dancing, wanting to be comforted, nurtured, supported and loved.

The feminine essence is not: controlling, overly organised, bossy, nagging, mothering, changing light bulbs (even if she is perfectly capable of doing so), killing snakes, doing manly chores that require power tools, silent, talking about her emotions instead of feeling them, too intellectual, so damn independent that her partner will feel unvalued and not needed (sadly, her partner will be right).

If you are in a relationship with a woman and she is beginning to be bossy or controlling then it's time for you to step up in your masculine energy and become more commanding. I can be very masculine at times and my husband Simon is very good at shoving me straight back into my feminine essence by using humour. He will say things like, "hmm, you are so gorgeous when you are fierce and angry. Come here and show me how angry you are!" He will then pull me close and kiss me and I will melt and giggle like a schoolgirl. To ensure a woman remains in her feminine self, the man needs to exert his masculine power over her. Another reason a woman can become bossy or controlling is when she is worried or anxious. This usually happens when she feels burdened and like she needs to take responsibility or take charge of something. If you want to ensure your lady is chilled, ask yourself, "where am I being irresponsible or lazy which is making my lady stressed and anxious?" If there is something you can think of, take swift action to help her relax.

Relationships are always more harmonious, passionate and sexually charged when the polarity is maintained. If both parties are in their feminine energy, then the polarity could reverse where the woman adopts the masculine role and the man feels harassed.

If both parties are in their masculine energy, then the relationship will become competitive and argumentative.

In same-sex relationships, one partner will always gravitate more towards a masculine energy and another towards feminine. Try to maintain this balance if possible.

 NOTE: To keep sexual chemistry alive in your relationship, remain masculine in your relationship and true to your masculine essence.

Focus on remembering these points whenever you feel your partner slipping away from you.

Step back into your masculine essence and your partner will come straight back to you.

Keeping Love Alive Principle #3: Maintain separateness and move to your own rhythm

It was Sherry Argov who said that 'people equate longing with love.' If you do everything together, there will be no opportunity for your partner to experience any longing for you. So, don't jump through hoops, don't suffocate your partner by always wanting to be where they are or checking up on them. If your partner texts you, don't respond immediately if you are busy with something else. Wait a little while until you have completed what you were doing before texting back. If you get home and see there is a message from your partner, wait until you've settled in, are sitting in front of the television or anything else you need to do before checking the message. This is not a game – it's just running life by your own schedule vs. jumping to attention whenever your partner gets in touch.

Keeping Love Alive Principle #4: When your partner disappears on you, focus on making yourself happy

This principle applies whether you are in a heterosexual relationship or same-sex relationship. Sometimes people disappear from time to time and go into their proverbial 'caves'. As we saw in Day 13, it is not necessarily the man that disappears but the 'Isolator' partner that needs to regenerate themselves. In some cases, that is the masculine partner in the relationship but in some cases, it is the feminine partner.

The important thing is when your Isolator partner disappears, they are usually still physically present, but emotionally distant and distracted. At these times, dig deep, practice the Worry Buster exercise on Day 17 and reassure yourself that this has nothing to do with you. This is just someone regenerating.

Our natural instinct is to want to know why. We'll want to know if there's something wrong.

No! No! No! This will drive your Isolator partner further into the cave. So, if you are in a relationship with an Isolator and you are not this way inclined, you need to learn to chill in the moments that they need to be by themselves to regenerate. You have to focus on making yourself happy. Go play a computer game or go to the gym and have a beer with a friend. Whistle while you're cooking dinner. Leave your partner be. Don't question or enquire. Smile, give their hand a squeeze, then walk away and go and be happy.

This will surprise your partner enormously because most Isolators are used to their partners acting very clingy whenever they retreat into their caves. By you being happy and having your own life, they will suddenly realise that your life does not revolve around them and that you seem happy without them. This is a very attractive quality to an Isolator. After some time, they will be curious as to where you are and will come looking for you. So, when your Isolator partner retreats into a cave, throw them a torch and go chill with your friends. When they realise that you are unaffected by their moods, they will come back.

Keeping Love Alive Principle #5: Communication strategies

You have learnt some valuable communication strategies in this book like the five R's from Day 13 and Setting boundaries on Day 19.

If you want your partner to do something for you, avoid giving a command. Try this communication approach:

➡ Acknowledgement… "Thank you darling for doing xxx…"

➡ I really need yyy to get done…

➡ Can you possibly help me with [solution]?

VIDEO: Watch me explain this communication method on the Naked Divorce YouTube channel on **www.youtube.com/nakeddivorce**

NOTE:

Help your partner by providing a clear roadmap of what you would like provided.

Here's an example of asking your partner to help you with something:

> "Hun, thanks so much for breakfast today, loved the way you cooked the eggs just the way I like them. You always remember that and I appreciate that about you. As you know, I gotta take Brian to the game this afternoon but I am not sure what to put into his bag. Can you help me out by packing his bag for me? I will watch so I can learn to do this next time."

Keeping Love Alive Principle #6: Don't lecture your partner...

Sometimes people can be real bad-tempered grumplestiltskins. Perhaps they had an argument with someone or maybe they had a bad day at work or someone cut in front of them in traffic. They come home and are grumpy or angry with you or they know they have done something wrong.

What is important is your partner is not dating their father, so this is not an opportunity to lecture them when you can see they are upset. People generally do not respond well to being lectured or bossed about. They respond much better to action.

So if your partner came home and started shouting or screaming at you for no reason, the best way to handle this bad behaviour is to get up and go out. Your silence or absence will tell them that you will not tolerate being around them under these conditions. If you show your partner that you are not affected by their bad behaviour, you are just busy, by the time you arrive home, they will have had time to reflect on their behaviour and you can have a civilised conversation.

Keeping Love Alive Principle #7: Maintain the mystery

One of the biggest mistakes men and women make when they get married or settle down is they become boring. They tell their partners every mundane detail of their day. I have listened to conversations where the man was going on and on about how he found a carwash which does a wash and dry on their car for 9.99 or each detail of what Brian at work said. Additionally, I don't understand couples who go to the toilet in front of each other, or who wear their sweats or tracksuits all the time, or get fat or stop making a special effort to look great.

It's important to remember that it was back when you were an awesome swaggering guy that your partner fell in love with you. This was the time you had an allure of mystery about you and put in the work with your appearance. Maybe you went to the gym or played regular squash. You also didn't tell your partner everything. You left details out because you wanted to appear sexy or cool.

This is a secret I have learnt from my mother (who has been married for more than four decades), namely: Maintain some mystery. There is no need to over-communicate. Here is what this looks like:

➡️ Get a haircut or buy a new aftershave but don't tell your partner. Let them notice. You looking amazing must appear effortless, like it simply happens with ease. No one needs to know how excruciating your last back wax was or how long it took to find trousers that fit

➡ Plan some fun days out with the boys. Play golf or go fishing. It will give you time-out to reflect and time to miss your partner. Women particularly like it when their man disappears for the day and is able to miss them until they come home.

➡ If you have found the secret to unlocking your partner's desire for you – don't give your game away. Never tell them so they are like a pawn in your game

➡ Wherever possible, don't go to the toilet in front of your partner, don't let them clean up your vomit or see you with body unwashed. You immediately go from being sexy to someone entirely ordinary. Your partner might conclude that you do not respect yourself and don't care what you look like around them and something dies in that moment.

➡ The bottom line is we can all be feminists and fight for equality, OR we can have great sexy relationships with great sex. All I know is that equality sometimes creates an environment for women to emasculate men. My male clients swear that mystery maintains the passion and chemistry in their relationships

Keeping Love Alive Principle #8: Let your partner help

It's important for your partner to feel like they can contribute to you and make a difference to your life.

Let them advise you from time to time and listen intently to their advice. It doesn't mean you need to follow what they say but strongly considering their advice will help them feel valued.

Keeping Love Alive Principle #9: The five love languages

Gary Chapman is a genius for writing this book 'The Five Love Languages'. I recommend you go and get yourself a copy immediately. I believe that every couple committed to having a happy long-term relationship, needs to read this book and do his Love Language test.

Gary's premise is that there are five love languages that are ways that human beings give and express love. The overarching idea is that you give love in the language that you need it expressed to you. If you don't receive love in your love language, you will feel unloved and unfulfilled in your relationship. The five love languages as Gary describes them are:

→ Words of affirmation (feeling more connected through talking and telling someone you love them)

→ Physical touch (feeling more connected through physical touch and sexual intimacy)

→ Gift giving (feeling more connected through the giving and receiving of gifts)

→ Acts of service (feeling more connected through doing things for your loved one)

→ Quality time (feeling more connected by spending undivided time together)

The idea is that each of has one of these as our primary love language and we will naturally express love in this language. To feel loved, we need to have love expressed in this language. Most often, couples are not matched in their love languages so there will be conflict for the one who wants to spend quality time to connect whereas the other partner doesn't understand this need because they had just given their partner a nice necklace this morning thinking, "surely that's enough."

What is so great about his book is that it explains why a person may struggle with their partner's sexual advances unless they have spent some quality time together. In this particular instance, that person's primary love language may be quality time, whilst their partner's primary love language is physical touch.

By each partner understanding their love languages better, they can ensure that they spend some time together before the other makes any advances. It also explains why someone may say the words ,"I love you" 100 times but the words mean nothing to someone who values act of services higher than words of affirmation.

Keeping love alive principle #10: Handle with care

It's important to remember that relationships are vulnerable. You may relax into your new relationship and then think you can get away with some bad behaviour from time to time. In reality, there is a limit on how much bad behaviour a relationship can handle.

Be cautious of how much you shout, criticise, or humiliate your partner in public before you will find the love and intimacy between you has died.

Keeping Love Alive principle #11: Women need to feel...

I surveyed 68 women over a period of six years and found there to be certain feelings they need to feel when they are in a relationship with you. These feelings are:

➡ Honesty - women cannot stand men who lie. Ensure you tell the truth in all matters (unless she asks you if she looks fat in a dress, in which case just run up to her and hug her and tell her she looks gorgeous)

➡ Acceptance – she needs to feel that you completely accept her just the way she is and that her worst qualities are endearing and adorable

➡ Appreciation – she needs to feel that you appreciate her and notice the little things she does for you

➡ Treasured - women desire to be claimed more than anything. They want to belong to someone and you claiming her and treasuring her as your goddess will ensure she thrives in your relationship and becomes the best version of herself with you

➡ Approval – she needs to feel that you approve of her decisions

➡ Encouragement – she needs to feel encouraged, even when you are both terrified of something. She looks to you as her rock in life and when she doubts herself, your belief in her can help her blossom

➡ Inspiration - she needs to feel like your muse. That she inspires you and captivates you. That you only have eyes for her

So whenever you feel like you want to draw her closer to you, focus on how you can make her feel these feelings when she is with you.

Join the Naked Divorce community

Share your story with the world

I would love to hear your story so you can share it to inspire other men around the world, so email us on info@nakeddivorce.com

Community

Go to www.nakeddivorce.com and join the Naked Divorce community, receive loads of free newsletters, information, free tips, insights and friendship by signing up to the weekly messages in a bottle from the Naked Divorce: www.nakeddivorce.com.

Blog

Subscribe to www.nakeddivorce.com/blog to receive information, insights and updates.

Youtube

Naked Divorce: www.youtube.com/nakeddivorce
Naked Recovery: www.youtube.com/nakedrecovery

Twitter

@naked_recovery

A final word

Hey you,

I honour you for coming on this journey with me. I honour your strength, courage and wisdom.

I know what it took for you to take the road less travelled. Your courage of spirit and bravery you displayed as you walked through the flames of your divorce.

As you look back, do you recognise yourself?

Are you aware of how you have grown in the past few weeks?

You experienced pain and discovered that you are stronger than you ever imagined. You experience purification and this massive change and pain triggered a rebirth within you. I pray that this rebirth freed you from any suffering, from any upset and from focusing on your ex.

I pray that you discovered and remembered who you are. Your dreams, your life and your purpose. Thank you for tumbling down the rabbit hole with me. Thank you for trusting me with your heart and with your healing. It was a privilege to walk this path with you. If you ever need any support again, you know where to find us.

Now Go. Go and have the most wonderful life.

LIVE and suck the marrow from every moment.

Do everything you have ever wanted to do. Do it now and waste not another moment.

I wish you the brightest, most powerful and amazing life!

With love

Pages to Print

Pages to print: x1

The Healing Formula:

Healing Formula = Focused Intensity +

3 Key Breakthroughs + 7 Foundations of Transformation

The Naked Divorce Foundations of Transformation

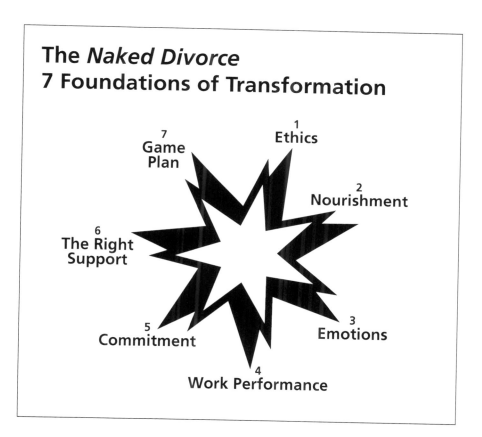

The *Naked Divorce*
7 Foundations of Transformation

1 Ethics

2 Nourishment

3 Emotions

4 Work Performance

5 Commitment

6 The Right Support

7 Game Plan

Pages to print: x21

The Naked Divorce Checklist

Day: ....

Date: ....

MORNING

Drink a glass of hot water with a squeeze of lemon, take your supplements.

Read through the Thought for the Day

Read through the exercise you'll be doing later today.

Allow yourself to think about it during the day.

I feel...

(Circle the emotions that are most appropriate. At the end of the day update the chart to see what other emotions you experienced.)

Angry Confident Confused Content Elated Flirty Frustrated Gloomy

Happy Insecure Irritable Relaxed Spacey Stressed Tired Weepy

Do your Daily Declarations while in the shower. ☐

Shower and get dressed ☐

Make an effort to look good, even if you're not going to work.

GOING TO WORK

Drink at least six glasses of water during the day.

Emotional times make us thirsty.

Practice the four A's.

When you're feeling overly emotional at work and you feel you need to put your emotions aside to focus on your day, practice the four A's taken from the **Naked Divorce** exercise for handling your emotions whilst at work. Practice being Aware of your emotions as they arise. Accept them. Acknowledge your right to have them. And then simply Act Normal. The moment you get home, you can let loose!

NOT GOING TO WORK

If a weekend, start on the exercise for the day as soon as you can.

HOME

Prepare dinner. ☐

Try to get some exercise today, even if it's a 10 minute walk or boxing some pillows on the bed

Check in with your Divorce Angel ☐

and let them know very briefly how you're doing.

List at least five successes you enjoyed today: ☐

1 ....

2 ....

3 ....

4 ....

5 ....

Did you notice anything you did to sabotage your healing ☐ or detract from your goal of healing today? If so, list what happened below:

ETHICS of the Programme (Rate yourself on a scale of 1 to 10, with 1 being 'needs work' and 10 being 'I feel absolutely balanced here'):

Ethics	Rate yourself on a scale of 1-10	Actions I will take to move this ETHIC to a level 10 in my life
Full self-expression		• • • •
Avoid STEATs		• • • •
Establish a Grounded Routine		• • • •
Sleep on any drastic changes you wish to make in your life		• • • •
Say no		• • • •
Cause vs. effect		• • • •
Focus on yourself vs. your ex		• • • •

Check in with your kids.

If you have children, remember to check in with them and ask the they're doing. Ensure that you give them the space to communica vulnerability, knowing that you will have the time to experience your emotions later.

Complete your daily homework.

When in bed, listen to the **Naked Divorce** break-up Reboot and allow yourself to drift off to sleep. It will help you relax. Visualise your HEALING GOAL whilst you are listening to it and if you fall asleep while listening, that's fine. It also works on your subconscious while you sleep.

Pages to print: x1

The Daily Declarations

I AM A POWERFUL FORCE TO BE RECKONED WITH WHO DESERVES ALL THAT IS GREAT IN THIS WORLD.

I FORGIVE MYSELF COMPLETELY FOR ANYTHING I HAVE SAID OR DONE TO MYSELF OR OTHERS IN MY LIFE.

I HAVE ENORMOUS VALUE TO ADD TO THE LIVES OF THOSE I LOVE, AND PARTICULARLY TO THE PERSON I CHOOSE TO SHARE MY LIFE WITH.

I KNOW WHO I AM AND WILL NEVER COMPROMISE MYSELF FOR ANYONE OR ANYTHING.

I AM DESERVING OF LOVE AND HAPPINESS AND THERE ARE MANY PEOPLE IN MY LIFE WHO LOVE AND ADORE ME.

I AM ENOUGH. I AM ATTRACTIVE ENOUGH, GOOD ENOUGH AND ACCOMPLISHED ENOUGH. I AM MORE THAN ENOUGH.

I LOVE WHO I AM AND WILL FOCUS ON DEVELOPING MYSELF AND FULFILLING MY DESTINY.

I AM HONEST, HAVE HIGH INTEGRITY AND HAVE A LOUD CLEAR VOICE DESERVING TO BE HEARD.

I TAKE CARE OF MY PARTNER AND AM SUPPORTIVE IN SPECIAL WAYS. I AM ALWAYS THERE.

BUT NOW IS THE TIME IN MY LIFE TO CARE FOR MYSELF AND TO PUT MY NEEDS FIRST.

I SET HEALTHY BOUNDARIES WITH OTHERS IN MY LIFE, GAINING POWER AND RESPECT.

I AM SEXY, FANTASTIC IN BED AND GREAT FUN TO BE WITH.

I AM THE AUTHOR OF MY LIFE. I ALONE CAN MAKE THE CHANGES I NEED TO BE FULFILLED.

TODAY I WEAR MY POWER CLOAK BECAUSE IT IS MY DAY, THIS IS MY WORLD AND I LOVE IT.

I AM THE MAN AND YOU CAN ALL KISS MY ASS!

Acknowledgements

There are so many people to thank for helping bring this book together. Firstly I wish to thank Mike Harris for that day that he looked me straight in the eye and told me to write this book and take the **Naked Divorce** concept out to the world. Without that conversation, I am not sure I would have written this book or developed this programme as well as my other trauma recovery programmes. I would also like to thank Daniel Priestley for his support and for believing in my process and what my message is. His KPI programme helped this book to come about. I would also like to thank S.N. Goenke for developing Vipassana, the 10-day silent retreat that provided such clarity and inner power - without this clarity, I would never have had the foresight to develop all my work. Werner Erhardt for being an important mentor throughout my life and for giving me the understanding of how to transform anything in my life and for understanding the importance of full self expression and emotions like anger.

I would like to thank Ilya Prigogine for his work on dissipative structures and Perturbation and to Marilyn Ferguson for suggesting that this concept could be used in human transformation too. I wish to thank my publishers, editors and proof readers. I wish to thank Dickie Bielenberg for all his support and guidance throughout the early stages of the **Naked Divorce** development, many of our conversations resulted in breakthroughs within this book. To my amazing family for their love and support - my mum for being an early 'victim' in reading the book cover-to-cover and to my dad for being the original change management guru. I also wish to thank my ex-husband Bruce for our story that gave rise to all of this happening. Thank you for all the good times and for all the learnings we both experienced in the bad times. I wish to thank the thousands of people who have done this programme and for the early adopters who ensured that the concepts were tested and for proving that the **Healing Formula** worked. I would like to thank those four ladies in the coffee shop in Los Angeles. That was my sliding doors moment in my life.

Last, but by no means least, my amazing husband, Simon Williams for being the most empowering person I have ever been with. He is my beacon and my home.

Bibliography

- Abraham, R. (1994). Chaos, Gaia, Ero: A chaos pioneer uncovers the three great streams of history. New York. Harper San Francisco.
- Abrahams Spring, J. (2004). How can I forgive you? Perennial Currents.
- Angrist, S. W. and Hepler, L. G. (1967). Order and chaos: Laws of energy and entropy. New York. Basic Books.
- Argov, S. (2011). Why men marry bitches. Argov and Adams Media.
- Assagiolo, R. (1974). The act of will. NY. Penguin.
- Atkins, P. W. (1984). The second law. New York. Scientific American.
- Aziz, R. (1990). C. G. Jung's psychology of religion and synchronicity. New York. State University of New York Press.
- Bailey, Kenneth D. (1990). Social Entropy Theory (term: "Prigogine entropy", pg. 72). New York. State University of New York Press.
- Bailey, Kenneth D. (1994). Sociology and the New Systems Theory: Toward a Theoretical Synthesis (term: "Prigogine entropy equation", pg. 123). SUNY Press.
- Balfour, M. (2004). Smart Dating – how to find your man. Mary Balfour Publishing.
- Bandler, R. (2009).Conversations: Freedom Is Everything & Love Is All the Rest. Health Communications.
- Bandler, R. (2008).Get the Life You Want: the secrets to quick and lasting life change with neuro-linguistic programming. Health Communications.
- Baynes, J., Dominiczak, M., Medical Biochemistry. Elsevier Limited; Third Edition (2009). ISBN 978-0-323-05371-6.
- Beattie, M. (1989).Codependent No More: How to Stop Controlling Others and Start Caring for Yourself. Hazelden Information & Educational Services.
- Beattie, M. (1990). Beyond Codependency: And Getting Better All the Time. Hazelden Information & Educational Services.
- Behrendt, G; Tuccillo, L. (2004). He's just not that into you. Harper Element.
- Blackerby, R. F. (1993). Applications of chaos theory to psychological models. Austin, TX. Performance Strategies.
- Bolen, J. S. (1979). The Tao of psychology: Synchronicity and the self. New York. HarperSanFrancisco.
- Briggs, J. and Peat, F. D. (1989). The turbulent mirror: An illustrated guide to chaos theory and the science of wholeness. New York. Harper & Row.
- Brown, S. (1999) Do you Regret your divorce? Daily Mail
- Burney, R. (1995). Codependence: The Dance of the Wounded Souls. Joy to you and Me.
- Butz, M. R. (1997). Chaos and complexity: Implications for psychological theory and practice. Washington, DC. Taylor & Francis.
- Capek, M; Whitrow, J.G. (1974). Time/Time & Measurement: Two essays (18 pages) in the 'Dictionary of the History of Ideas'. Studies of selected pivotal ideas, Volume IV. Scribner's Sons
- Çambel, A. B. (1993). Applied chaos theory: A paradigm for complexity. Boston. Academic Press.
- The Canadian National Statistics Agency. (2000-2011). Divorces across Canada. Each year between 2000-2011. <http://www.statcan.gc.ca>
- Carnegie, D. (1944). How to Stop worrying and start living. Pocket Books.
- The Census Bureau of the United States of America. (2000-2011). Divorces across the United States of America. Each year between 2000-2011. < http://www.census.gov/compendia/statab/brief.html>

- Clark, N. (23 June 2011). Email Interview into Therapy vs. Naked Divorce 21 Day Programme.
- Chapman, G. (1992). The Five Love Languages. Northfield Publishing.
- Chopra, Dr. D. (1992). Quantum Healing. Bantam Books.
- Choquette, S. (2000). Balancing your chakras. Piatkus.
- Christ, C. (1979). Womanspirit Rising: A Feminist Reader in Religion. Harper & Row.
- Moore, R. and Gillette, D. (1990). King Warrior Magician Lover: Rediscovering the Archetypes of the Mature Masculine. Harper Collins.
- Cullington, D. (1988). Breaking up Blues. Routledge.
- Dakin, R. (2009). The Girlfriend Experience. John Blake.
- Davies, (1980). Other worlds: Space, superspace and the quantum universe. NY. Touchstone.
- Deida, D. (1997). It's a Guy Thing. HCI.
- Deida, D. (1995). Intimate Communion. HCI.
- Deida, D. (1996). Dear Lover. HCI.
- Deida, D. (1995). The way of the superior man. HCI.
- Demartini, J. F. (2002). The Breakthrough Experience. Hay house.
- Dickens, C. (1992). Great Expectations. Wordsworth.
- Doherty, William J. (1999) Australian poll conducted asked people if they wished they could have made more effort to make their marriage work: 40%
- Easton, D; Hardy, J. (1997). The Ethical Slut. Celestial Arts.
- Eckel, S. (2002). Unpack your Relationship Baggage. Ladies Home Journal.
- EHOW. (2010). How to create your last will and testament. <www.ehow.com>
- Eleoff, S. (2003). An Exploration of the Ramifications of Divorce on Children and Adolescents. The Pennsylvania State University College of Medicine.
- Ferguson, M. (2005). Aquarius Now. Weiser.
- Ferguson, M. (2003). The Aquarian Conspiracy. Weiser.
- Forest, Lynn. (2004). The Three Faces of Victim. http://lynneforrest.com/articles/fov.html
- Fitzgerald, M. (2009). 6 Signs You're Dating A Woman With Baggage. <Ask Men.com and Marie Claire Magazine>
- Furstenberg FF. Morgan SP. Allison PD. (1987). Paternal Participation and Children's Well-Being After Marital Dissolution. American Sociological Review. 52: 695-701.
- Gallagher, M and Waite, L. The Case for Marriage they Don't want you to hear. (Doubleday)
- Gawain, S. (1978). Creative Visualisation. New World Library.
- Gibran, K. (1991). The Prophet. Pan Books; New edition.
- Gilbert, E. (2006). Eat pray love. Bloomsbury.
- Gladwell, M. (2000). The Tipping Point. Abacus.
- Gladwell, M. (2008). Outliers. Penguin.
- Gleick, J. (1987). Chaos: Making a new science. New York. Penguin Books.
- Glenmullen, J. (2006) Coming Off Antidepressants: Successful Use and Safe Withdrawal. Robinson Publishing.
- Godwin, C. and 14 others (2005-2011). How to understand your emotions. Wikihow.com
- Goleman, D. (1995). Emotional Intelligence. Bantam Books.
- Gottman, J.M. (1993). A theory of marital dissolution and stability. Journal of Family Psychology 7 57-75.
- Gottman, John & DeClaire, Joan. (2001). The Relationship Cure: A 5 Step Guide for Building Better Connections with Family, Friends, and Lovers. Crown Publishers.
- Gottman, John & Gottman, Julie. (2002). Why Marriages Succeed or Fail. Simon & Shuster.

- Gould, S. J. (1987). Time's arrow, time's cycle: Myth and metaphor in the discovery of geological time. Cambridge, MA. Harvard University Press.
- Gray, J. (2010). Venus on Fire. Mars on Ice. Mind Publishing.
- Gray, J. (2008). When Mars and Venus Collide. Harper Collins Element.
- Gray, J. (1992). Men are from Mars, Women are from Venus. Harper Collins Element.
- Gray, J. (1996). Men are from Mars, Women are from Venus in the Bedroom. Vermillion.
- Gribbon, J. (2012).In Search Of Schrodinger's Cat. Black Swan; New edition.
- Groenendijk, C. (2000). My Prozac (Sarafem, Fluctin, fluoxetine) Experience. A Prozac-induced "Brain/Body-Crash" at the age of 29. < www.antidepressantsfacts.com>
- Groenendijk, C. (2001). The Serotonergic System, the Pineal Gland & Side-Effects of Serotonin Acting Anti-Depressants. < www.antidepressantsfacts.com>
- Grof. S. (1985). Beyond the brain: Birth, death and transcendence in psychology. Albany, NY. State University of New York Press.
- Gschwendt, K. (2009). Creative Financial and Creative planning. <http://www.divorceandfinance.org>
- Guagenti-Tax, E. (2003). Integrating Imago Therapy and educational techniques for court ordered men who batter: A preliminary investigation. The Journal of Imago Relationship Therapy, 5 (2), 45-54.
- Haken, H. (1983). Synergetics: An introduction: Nonequilibrium phase transitions and self-organization in physics, chemistry and biology. Belin. Springer-Verlag. First published in 1977.
- Haken, H. (1987). Synergetics. In F. E. Yates (Ed.), Self-organising systems: The emergence of order. New York. Plenum Press.
- Hall, P. (2007). Help your children cope with your divorce. Relate.
- Hall, P. (2007). How to have a healthy divorce. Relate.
- Hannah, M.T., Case, B.A., Fennell, B.A., Argesta, V., Lisi,K., Zebrowski, L.,Berkery, K. (1996). Dyadic Adjust-ment and the practice of Imago skills by Imago therapists in their current romantic relationships. The Journal of Imago Relationship Therapy, 1(1). 55-65.
- Hannah, M.T., Luquet, W. & McCormick, J. (1997). COMPASS as a measure of efficacy of couples therapy. American Journal of Family Therapy, 25 (1), 76-90.
- Hannah, Mt., Luquet, W., McCormick, J. Galvin, K., Ketterer, K.,May, K., Hayes, R.,& Kott, L.A. (1997). Brief report: Short-term Imago therapy and changes in personal distress. The Journal of Imago Relationship Therapy 2 (2), 55-67.
- Hannah, M.T., Marrone, J.B., Luquet, W., Gondek, D., Long, J., Squadrito, S.J., Bause, M., Clay, M. (1998). The development and psychometric properties of two measures of Imago theoretical constructs. The Journal of Imago Relationship Therapy 3 (1), 49-62.
- Harvey, S. (2009). Act like a lady, Think like a man. Amistad.
- Hay, L. (1987). You can heal your life. Hay House.
- Hayman, S. (2001). Moving on. Breaking up without breaking down. Relate.
- Heath, S. (2008). The Essence of Womanhood – reawakening the authentic feminine. Ecademy Press.
- Hendrix, H. (1988). Getting the love you want: A guide for couples. New York. Pocket Books.
- Hetherington EM. Furstenberg FF. (1989). Sounding the Alarm. Readings: A Journal of Review and Commentary in Mental Health. 6: 4-8.
- Hogan, T., Hunt, R., Emerson, D., Hayes, R., Ketterer, K. (1996) An evaluation of client Satisfaction with the "Getting the Love You want" weekend workshop. The Journal of Imago Relationship Therapy 1 (2), 57-66.
- Horne, F. (2001). 7 days to a magickal new you. Thorson.
- Houck JC, Sharma VK, Patel YM, Gladner JA. Induction of collagenolytic and proteolytic activities by anti-inflammatoes this by inhibiting collagen formation, decreasing amino acid uptake by muscle, and inhibiting protein synthesis.

- Husband AJ, Brandon MR, Lascelles AK (October 1973). The effect of corticosteroid on absorption and endogenous production of immunoglobulins in calves. Aust J Exp Biol Med Sci 51 (5): 707–10. doi:10.1038/icb.1973.67. PMID 4207041.
- James, T; Woodsmall, W. (1988). Time Line Therapy and the basis of personality. Meta Publications.
- James, J; Friedman, R. (2009). The Grief Recovery Handbook. Harper Collins.
- Jens C. Pruessner, Frances Champagne,Michael J. Meaney,and Alain Dagher. (2000). Dopamine Release in Response to a Psychological Stress in Humans and Its Relationship to Early Life Maternal Care: A Positron Emission Tomography Study Using [11C]Raclopride
- Johnson, R. A. (1991). Owning your own shadow: Understanding the dark side of the psyche. United Kingdom: HarperCollins.
- Jung, C. G. (1965). Memories, dreams, reflections. Jaffé, A. (Ed.). Winston, R. and Winston, C. (Trans.). New York. Vintage. First published in 1961.
- Jung, C.G. (1954). The practice of psychotherapy: Essays on the psychology of the transference and other subjects. CW 16. Princeton, NJ. Princeton University Press.
- Jung, C.G. (1968). Analytical psychology: Its theory and practice, the Tavistock lectures. New York. Vintage Books.
- Jung, C.G. (1968). The Aion: Researches into the Phenomenology of the Self, in the Collected Works of C.G. Jung, Volume IX part II, Carrie Lee Rothgeb (Ed.), Princeton University Press,
- Jung, C.G. (1981). The Archetypes and The Collective Unconscious. Princeton University Press
- Karpman, S. (1968). Fairy tales and script drama analysis. Transactional Analysis Bulletin, 7(26), 39-43.
  Karpman, S. (1971). Options. Transactional Analysis Journal, 1(1), 79-87. * *
  Karpman, S. (1975). The Loser's Loop. Transactional Analysis Journal. 5(1), 74-75.
  Karpman, S. (1976). Feeling rackets: Notes from State of the Art Winter Congress, January 1976. Transactional Analysis Journal, 6(3), 339-346
  Karpman, S. (1979). Five trust contracts for couples. Bulletin of the Eric Berne Seminar. 1(3), 26-27.
- Kast, V. (1992). The dynamics of symbols: Fundamentals of Jungian psychotherapy. Schwarz, S. A. (Trans.). New York. Fromm International.
- Katie, B. (1988.) Loving what is. Rider Books.
- Korem, D. (1997). The Art of Profiling. International Focus Press.
- Kubler-Ross, E; Kessler, D. (2005). On Grief and Grieving. Simon and Schuster.
- Kelso, Scott J. A. (1999). Dynamic patterns: The self-organization of brain and behaviour. Cambridge, MA. MIT Press.
- Erhardt, W. (1990). Landmark Education Cost/ Payoff exercise from The Landmark Forum. <www.landmarkeducation.com>
- Lewis, J; Sammons, J. (1999). Don't Divorce Your Children. Contemporary Books.
- Lewis, J; Sammons, J. (2000). Children and divorce. Contemporary Books.
- Lickerman. (2010). How to Forgive Others. Psychology Today.
- Luquet, W., & Hannah, M.T. (1996). The efficacy of short-term Imago therapy: Preliminary findings. The Journal of Imago Relationship Therapy, 1 (1), 67-75.
- Mainzer, K. (1994). Thinking in complexity: The complex dynamics of matter, mind, and mankind. Berlin. Springer-Verlag.
- Maltz, M. (1960). Pycho-Cybernetics. Pocket Books, Simon and Schuster.
- Manchester, K.L., Sites of Hormonal Regulation of Protein Metabolism. p. 229, Mammalian Protein [Munro, H.N., Ed.]. Academic Press, New York. On p273.
- Manfield, E. (3 January 2011) Secret Regrets about divorce. Huffington Post
- Markman, H.J., & Hahleweg, K. (1993). The Prediction and prevention of marital distress: An international perspective. Clinical Psychology Review 13 29-43.

- Maslow, A.H. (1968). Toward a psychology of being (2nd ed.). New York. Van Nostrand Reinhold.
- Maslow, A.H. (1971). The farther reaches of human nature. New York. Penguin.
- Mellody, P. (1989.) Facing Codependency. HarperOne.
- McCarthy, B, E. (2003). Rekindling desire. Brunner-Routledge.
- McMillen, A. (2006). When I loved myself enough. Sidgwick and Jackson.
- McKenna, P; Wilbourn, H. (2003). I can mend your broken heart. Bantam press.
- Mintel Consumer Research Reports(2000-2011). Divorces in England and Wales. Each year between 2000-2011. The British Library.
- Moore, T. (1994). Soul Mates. Harper Perennial.
- Mountain-Dreamer, O. (1999). The Invitation. Harper Collins Element.
- Muzik, B. (2007). Mind-Mastery-101. <www.designer-life.com/mindmastery101>
- Namka, Lynne. (2003). Goodbye Ouchies and Grouchies, Hello Happy Feelings. EFT for Kids of All Ages. Talk, Trust & Feel Therapeutics.
- Namka, Lynne. (2001). The Doormat Syndrome. Talk, Trust and Feel Therapeutics.
- Namka, Lynne. (2001). Violence in Families. www.AngriesOut.com.
- Namka, Lynne. (2001). The Right Man and Right Woman Theory. www.AngriesOut.com.
- Naschie, El M. S., Rossler, O. E. & Prigogine, I. (Eds.) (1995). Quantum mechanics, diffusion and chaotic fractals. Great Britain. BPC Wheatons (Pergamon).
- Neumann, E. (1995). The origins and history of consciousness. Bollingen Series XLII. Princeton, NJ. Princeton University Press. First published in 1954.
- Nicolis G. and Prigogine, I. (1989). Exploring complexity: An introduction. New York. W.H. Freeman.
- O'Connor, J; Lages, A. (2004). Coaching with NLP. Harper Collins Element.
- Office of National Statistics. (2000-2011). Divorces in England and Wales. Each year between 2000-2011. < http://www.statistics.gov.uk>
- Officer, C; Page, J. (1993). Tales of the Earth – Paroxysms and Perturbations of the Blue Planet. Oxford.
- Olfsen, Dr. M. (2010). Antidepressant Use Rising as Psychotherapy Rates Fall. Columbia University/ New York State Psychiatric Institute.
- Pang, S. (2011). Interview about helping children through divorce. <www.presentparenttraining.com>
- Parkin, J; Pollini, G. (2009). The way of F**k it. Hay house.
- Peck, Scott, M. (1979). Blame and Forgiveness: 009 [Audio Cassette]. Simon and Schuster.
- Peele, S. (1991). The Truth about addition and recovery. Fireside Simon and Schuster.
- Pert, Candace B. Ph.D. (1997). Molecules of Emotion. Simon & Schuster.
- Pinkola-Estes, C. (2001). Women who run with wolves. Ryder Books.
- Piroli, G. G.; Grillo, C. A.; Reznikov, L. R.; Adams, S.; McEwen, B. S.; Charron, M. J.; Reagan, L. P. (2007). Corticosterone Impairs Insulin-Stimulated Translocation of GLUT4 in the Rat Hippocampus. Neuroendocrinology 85 (2): 71. doi:10.1159/000101694. PMID 17426391.
- Posey WC, Nelson HS, Branch B, Pearlman DS (December 1978). The effects of acute corticosteroid therapy for asthma on serum immunoglobulin levels. J. Allergy Clin. Immunol. 62 (6): 340–8. doi:10.1016/0091-6749(78)90134-3. PMID 712020.
- Prigogine, Ilya. (1945). Etude Thermodynamics des Phenomenes Irreversibles (Study of the Thermodynamics of Irreversible Phenomenon). Presented to the science faculty at the Free University of Brussels (1945); Paris. Dunod, 1947.
- Prigogine, Ilya. (1955). Introduction to Thermodynamics of Irreversible Processes, (pg. 16). New York. Interscience Publishers.
- Prigogine, I. (1980). From being to becoming: Time and complexity in the physical sciences. San Francisco. W. H. Freeman.

- Prigogine, I. and Stengers, I. (1984). Order out of chaos: Man's new dialogue with nature. Toronto. Bantam.
- Prigogine, I. (1997). The end of certainty: Time, chaos, and the new laws of physics. NY. The Free Press.
- Rand, A. (1957). Atlas Shrugged. Penguin Modern Classics.
- Robertson, R. & Combs, A. (Eds.) (1995). Chaos theory in psychology and the life sciences. Mahwah, NJ. Lawrence Erlbaum.
- Robbins, A. (1996). The power of successful relationships audio CD.
- Robbins, A. (2000). A 7-day programme to transform your life audio CD.
- Santos, R. (2009). Should you keep the house in a divorce? <http://articles.moneycentral.msn.com/College-AndFamily/SuddenlySingle/ShouldYouKeepTheHouseInADivorce.aspx?page=2>
- Scott Peck, M. (1987). The Different Drum. Simon and Schuster.
- Seligman, Martin. (1990). Learned Optimism. Pocket Books, 1990.
- Soffer, L.J.; Dorfman, R.I.; Gabrilove, J.L,. The Human Adrenal Gland. Febiger, Phil.
- Spurr, Dr. P. (2001). The Break-up Survival Kit. Robson Books.
- Surhone, L. (20). Target Fixation. Betascript Publishing.
- Talbot, N. (2007). Get over your break-up. Hodder Arnold.
- Tolle, E. (2005). The power of now. Hodger Mobius.
- Underwood, Y. (2010). MA, NCC, LPC. Citation: Setting Boundaries. Red Rock Counselling Services <http://www.redrockcounseling.com>.
- United States: Poll statistics conducted in 1999 in State of Minnesota - 66% of those currently divorced answered "yes" to the question "Do you wish you and your ex-spouse had tried harder to work through your differences?". In 2003 in the State of California, 83% of those currently divorced answered "yes" to the question "Do you wish you and your ex-spouse had tried harder to work through your differences?". In 2004 in State of New Jersey - 46% of those currently divorced answered "yes" to the question "Do you wish you and your ex-spouse had tried harder to work through your differences?"
- Ury, W. (2007). Getting past no. Random House.
- Utain, M & Oliver, B. (Eds.) (1998). Scream Louder. Through Hell and Healing with an Incest Survivor and her Therapist. Columbia University Press. http://www.abebooks.com.
- Vaughn, P. (1989). The Monogamy Myth. Newmarket Press.
- Wallerstein, JS. Corbin SB. (1989). The Child and the Vicissitudes of Divorce.
- Wallerstein, JS. (1989) Children After Divorce: Wounds That Don't Heal. The Psychiatric Times. Medicine and Behaviour. 8: 8-11
- Wang, Yingxu. (2008). Novel Approaches in Cognitive Informatics and Natural Intelligence (section: Prigogine entropy, pg. 45). Idea Group Inc.
- Whitfield, Charles L. (1993) Boundaries and Relationships: Knowing, Protecting and Enjoying the Self. Health Communications; illustrated edition.
- Williams, L. (1991). Moving On. Pure Praise Publishing.
- Wolcott, I and Hughes, J Australian Institute of Family Studies (1999). Post-divorce regret versus satisfaction. WOMEN http://www.aifs.org.au/institute/pubs/WP20tables.html#table8 MEN http://www.aifs.org.au/institute/pubs/WP20tables.html#table9

About the author

Adèle Théron has spent over twenty years working with individuals within some of the world's largest corporations as a change management specialist, helping people adapt to new situations and experiences created by mergers, acquisitions and large software implementations. The techniques and processes she created have helped companies and individuals adapt to change and have successfully aided thousands of individuals within 47 separate global organisations.

Having separated from her husband in March 2009, Adèle researched to find that there was no structured process or programme to heal from divorce and that many professional women and men wound up in years of counselling or experience long-term illness and depression as a result of divorce. Adèle was also astounded at the high second and third-marriage divorce rates worldwide and decided that healing from divorce was critical to successful relationships in the future.

She tried therapy and counseling but found the lack of structure and goal-oriented healing didn't work for her. She realised that as a process-expert, she could use her change management techniques to develop a systemised process and programme for healing from divorce within 21 days. She was her own case study and experienced a life-altering transformation resulting in a new life for herself but also a healed relationship with her ex-husband. The process she used has since evolved into the **Naked Divorce**, capable of dealing with the most dramatic of divorce situations.

Adèle has worked with professional men, women and couples as a family counsellor and divorce negotiator and completed a PostGrad in PTSD and Trauma healing and has expanded the **Naked Divorce** concepts to deal with other traumas in similar programme design and style with her team of Trauma Angels.

Today Adèle spends her time consulting with companies as a change agent, writing and piloting new trauma programmes with her network of worldwide partners at www.nakedrecoveryonline.com, running Tantrum Clubs or coaching and supporting professional career people through traumas as a Trauma Angel.

She lives between London in the United Kingdom and Chiang Mai in Thailand with *Mogwai* her most beloved Beagle.